The Alley Cat And The Buffoon In The Suit

By Christopher McConnell

Table of Contents

PREFACE

There's a battle being waged every day in offices, schools, and streets across the world an invisible war between conformity and authenticity, between those who follow the predetermined path and those who forge their own. I've spent my life on the frontlines of this conflict, watching the casualties stack up as creative minds are suffocated by conventional thinking, as brilliant potential is squandered in pursuit of societal approval, and as real prosperity is sacrificed at the altar of appearances.

This book isn't for everyone. It's not for those comfortable in their cages, content to run the hamster wheel while the lights above them power someone else's dreams. It's not for those who believe that dignity comes from a suit or that respect flows from titles. It's not for those seeking permission to succeed or validation for their vision.

This book is for the Alley Cats those who know in their bones that there's a different way to live, to succeed, to create prosperity that doesn't require surrendering your soul to systems designed to extract your value while leaving you with just enough to keep running.

I grew up in North Tulsa, in neighborhoods where opportunity was as scarce as quiet nights. As a straight-A student who became a target for violence, I learned early that society's prescribed paths weren't built for everyone. I was given a set of circumstances that demanded adaptation where conventional wisdom failed and innovation became the only path to survival.

From selling crack cocaine at 12 years old to transforming failing manufacturing plants, from sleeping in subway stations to driving luxury vehicles while delivering food, my journey has been anything but conventional. I've lived in the shadows of society's margins and in the spotlight of business transformation. I've failed spectacularly and succeeded against overwhelming odds. I've been indicted by grand juries and celebrated by corporate executives in the same year.

What I've learned through it all is that the most dangerous limitation isn't your environment, your education, or your starting point it's your mindset. The difference between the Alley Cat and the Buffoon in the Suit isn't resources, connections, or luck. It's the willingness to think beyond what you've been told is possible and the courage to act on that vision, even when it contradicts everything society has trained you to believe.

This book won't teach you how to fit in. It won't show you how to climb conventional ladders or how to win approval from those who guard the gates of traditional success. What it will do is challenge you to question every assumption you've been fed about what it takes to create extraordinary prosperity, to experience remarkable freedom, and to build a life on your own terms.

1

These pages contain hard-earned wisdom from streets you've never walked and boardrooms you've never entered. They contain strategies that work not despite breaking conventions but precisely because they do. They contain the mindset that has allowed me to transform from a kid with nothing to an adult with everything that matters. You are about to read about mental freedom through mental clarity, and the ability to create prosperity regardless of circumstances.

In a world that rewards conformity with mediocrity, the Alley Cat thrives by seeing opportunities where others see only obstacles. While the Buffoon adjusts his tie and waits for permission to succeed, the Alley Cat is already three steps ahead, creating possibilities that weren't visible from inside the box.

My name is Christopher McConnell. I'm from Tulsa, Oklahoma. I've never lived in a home larger than 1,000 square feet with fewer than four people in it. I grew up poor, facing adversity, and I've defeated all odds while still wielding my shield and sword of confidence, faith, and charisma to achieve substantial prosperity. This book is not my story it's your guide to transformation.

Welcome to the Alley Cat mentality.

CHAPTER 1: INTRODUCTION TO ALLEY CAT THINKING

The difference between extraordinary success and mediocrity isn't talent. It isn't opportunity. It sure as hell isn't luck, It's mindset.

Look around at the people in your life. The ones stuck in the same situations year after year. The ones complaining about the same problems today that they complained about five years ago. The ones who talk about what they're going to do "someday" but never seem to make progress.

Now look at the rare individuals who consistently transform their circumstances. The ones who build something from nothing. The ones who face the same obstacles as everyone else but somehow find a way through, around, or over them.

What separates these two groups isn't what most people think.

The difference is what I call "Alley Cat thinking" versus "Buffoon in the Suit thinking." And understanding this distinction will change everything about how you approach your life.

The Alley Cat doesn't play by conventional rules. The Alley Cat finds ways to survive and thrive regardless of circumstances. The Alley Cat doesn't waste energy trying to impress others or fit into systems designed to limit them. Instead, the Alley Cat creates their own systems, their own opportunities, their own reality.

Meanwhile, the Buffoon in the Suit follows all the prescribed steps. Goes to the right schools. Gets the right credentials. Wears the right clothes. Says the right things. The Buffoon in the Suit looks the part of success without achieving the substance of it. They mistake the trappings of achievement for achievement itself.

The world is full of Buffoons in Suits making six figures while living paycheck to paycheck, trapped in debt, dependent on employers for their survival, one setback away from disaster. They look successful to those who don't know better, but they've merely built more elaborate cages for themselves.

I've lived both sides of this equation. Growing up in North Tulsa, I wasn't afforded the luxury of conventional paths. My schools weren't preparing me for success they were barely providing physical safety. My neighborhood wasn't offering positive role models it was offering daily lessons in survival.

By age twelve, I was dealing crack cocaine. Not because I wanted to, but because in my environment, this seemed like the only path to something better. I wanted respect. I wanted to stop being mocked for my clothes, for my circumstances, for things beyond my control. I wanted to create some measure of stability in a chaotic world.

What I didn't realize then was that I was developing the very mindset that would eventually allow me to build legitimate businesses, to travel the country making deals, to create prosperity on my own terms. I was learning to see opportunities where others saw only obstacles. I was learning to create resources rather than simply consuming them. I was learning to think like an Alley Cat.

This isn't about glorifying illegal activities. It's about recognizing that the same hustle, the same strategic thinking, the same resilience that helps people survive in difficult environments can be channeled into extraordinary legitimate success. The skills are transferable. The mindset is invaluable.

When I eventually entered the conventional business world, I watched as people with degrees from prestigious universities floundered in situations that required real-world adaptability. I watched as they followed rulebooks that no longer applied to rapidly changing markets. I watched as they waited for permission to innovate while their companies lost ground to more agile competitors.

These were the Buffoons in Suits. They had the credentials. They had the appearances. They had the titles. They lacked the substance. They lacked the ability to create value outside of rigid structures. They lacked the mental flexibility to adapt when rules changed. They lacked the courage to challenge conventions that no longer served their purposes.

Alley Cat thinking isn't about breaking rules for the sake of breaking them. It's about understanding which rules actually matter and which ones exist only to keep you confined to someone else's system. It's about maintaining your authenticity in a world that rewards conformity with mediocrity. It's about having the courage to be judged by results rather than appearances.

This distinction transcends race, class, gender, and background. I've met Alley Cats who grew up in mansions and Buffoons who grew up in projects. I've met female Alley Cats breaking barriers in male-dominated industries and male Buffoons following paths laid out by their fathers without questioning whether those paths still lead anywhere worth going.

The external trappings don't define the mindset. The mindset defines everything else.

When I show up delivering food in a luxury convertible, people are confused. They've been conditioned to believe that certain jobs correspond to certain lifestyles, certain appearances, certain possessions. They can't reconcile seeing someone performing what they consider a lower-status job while driving a higher-status vehicle.

Their confusion reveals the limitations of their thinking. They don't understand that true Alley Cats aren't concerned with how things appear they're concerned with where things lead. They don't understand that delivering food can fund the launch of businesses that generate passive income. They don't understand that breaking free from conventional thinking means breaking free from conventional limitations.

Most people will never understand this. They'll continue judging books by covers, continue following paths that lead nowhere, continue trading authenticity for approval. They'll continue being Buffoons in Suits, looking the part while missing the point.

You don't have to be most people.

Throughout this book, I'll share specific strategies for developing Alley Cat thinking. I'll show you how to identify and challenge the invisible constraints that limit your potential. I'll show you how to create opportunity regardless of your starting point. I'll show you how to build prosperity that doesn't depend on permissions, credentials, or conventional validation.

This isn't theory. This is the actual blueprint I've used to transform my life from sleeping in truck yards to building businesses that support my family and create opportunities for others. This is the mindset that's allowed me to operate in environments designed for my failure and find success where others find only obstacles.

The first step is making a fundamental decision: Would you rather be comfortable or free? Would you rather conform and remain confined, or would you rather think differently and create possibilities beyond conventional imagination?

The Buffoon chooses comfort every time. The Alley Cat chooses freedom, even when that freedom initially comes with discomfort.

Everything else flows from this choice.

As we continue, remember that developing Alley Cat thinking doesn't happen overnight. It requires consistent effort to identify and challenge limiting beliefs. It requires the courage to make decisions based on where you want to go rather than where others expect you to stay. It requires the discipline to pursue results rather than appearances.

With each step in this direction, your world expands. Possibilities multiply. Resources appear where previously you saw only scarcity. Opportunities emerge where previously you saw only obstacles.

This is the power of Alley Cat thinking. This is the mindset that separates those who merely survive from those who truly thrive.

The choice is yours.

CHAPTER 2: THE ALLEY CAT IN THE ROOM

You can put an Alley Cat in a boardroom, but you can't take the Alley Cat out of their soul. You can dress them in expensive suits, put them behind mahogany desks, surround them with credentials and symbols of conventional success but the unmistakable energy of the Alley Cat remains. It radiates through every interaction, every decision, every approach to problems and opportunities.

This is what terrifies the Buffoons. They sense the difference, even if they can't articulate it. They feel threatened by an energy they can't replicate through external appearances alone.

Because true Alley Cat energy comes from something deeper than circumstances. It's forged through adversity, honed through adaptation, and maintained through deliberate choice. It's not something you wear; it's something you become. Let me illustrate this principle through experience rather than abstraction.

I've been in rooms with corporate executives making seven figures who revealed themselves as Buffoons within minutes. Despite their titles, their educations, their expensive wardrobes, and their carefully cultivated appearances, their Buffoon energy was unmistakable. They repeated corporate jargon instead of expressing original thoughts. They prioritized appearance over substance. They valued compliance over competence.

I've also been in rooms with individuals wearing simple clothes, lacking formal credentials, possessing none of the traditional markers of success yet their Alley Cat energy was immediately apparent. They spoke with authentic conviction rather than borrowed phrases. They focused on solving real problems rather than maintaining appearances. They valued results over recognition. The difference isn't superficial. It's fundamental, and it's visible to anyone paying attention.

When I walk into upscale coffee shops wearing my casual clothes, baseball cap, and unique socks while others are dressed in business attire, I sometimes get dismissive looks. The Buffoons assume that appearance directly correlates with substance. They judge books exclusively by covers because they themselves are all cover and no content.

Then they watch as I leave in a luxury convertible while they return to entry-level sedans purchased to project success they haven't actually achieved. The confusion on their faces reveals the disconnect in their understanding they can't reconcile someone rejecting superficial markers of success while simultaneously possessing genuine prosperity.

This confusion stems from a fundamental misunderstanding. They believe that success is something you display rather than something you create. They think prosperity comes from appearing prosperous rather than from making decisions that generate actual wealth.

The Alley Cat knows better. The Alley Cat understands that true success has nothing to do with appearances and everything to do with results. The Alley Cat recognizes that energy, mindset, and approach matter infinitely more than external trappings.

Take the Buffoon out of the suit, and what remains? Often, nothing of substance. Remove the props, the titles, the borrowed phrases, the carefully constructed persona and you're left with someone who hasn't developed authentic capabilities beyond performance.

Take the Alley Cat out of their environment, strip away their possessions, remove every external advantage and what remains? The exact same energy, mindset, and capability that would allow them to rebuild from nothing. Again.

This isn't theoretical for me. I've lost everything multiple times and rebuilt from scratch. When my business collapsed and I found myself homeless in Seattle, the suits were gone. The appearances were stripped away. The external trappings of success had vanished, but the Alley Cat remained.

That's why I could sleep in a truck yard at night and still approach each day with strategic purpose. That's why I could deliver food on foot while simultaneously laying groundwork for larger opportunities. That's why I could transform $200 into the foundation for rebuilding while others in similar circumstances remained paralyzed by their changed status.

The Alley Cat in me wasn't dependent on external circumstances. It was the core identity that circumstances couldn't touch.

This distinction explains why some people crumble when facing setbacks while others transform obstacles into opportunities. The former have built identities dependent on external validation; the latter have developed identities anchored in internal conviction. Consider how this principle manifests in various settings.

In business meetings, the Buffoon focuses on impressing others with their knowledge, connections, and status markers. They name-drop, use industry jargon, and emphasize their credentials. They're more concerned with being perceived as valuable than with creating actual value.

The Alley Cat focuses on solving real problems, identifying genuine opportunities, and creating tangible outcomes. They prioritize substance over appearance, results over recognition, impact over impression. They're concerned with being effective rather than with being perceived as important.

In social settings, the Buffoon carefully curates their image, associations, and topics of conversation to project a specific persona. They're performing rather than participating, constantly aware of how they're being perceived rather than genuinely engaging with those around them.

The Alley Cat shows up authentically, engages sincerely, and connects genuinely. They're not performing a role; they're expressing their actual identity. They're focused on the quality of interactions rather than the impression those interactions create.

In challenging circumstances, the Buffoon becomes disoriented when separated from the props and settings that support their persona. Without the external trappings that define their projected identity, they struggle to maintain coherence and direction.

The Alley Cat maintains consistent identity regardless of changing circumstances. Their core remains stable even when everything around them is in flux. Their self-concept doesn't depend on external validation, so external changes don't create internal crisis.

This difference explains why some outwardly successful people live in constant fear of being "exposed" as frauds. Their success is a performance rather than an expression. They haven't developed the internal substance that would make their external position secure.

Meanwhile, true Alley Cats rarely experience impostor syndrome despite often operating in environments very different from their origins. They're not pretending to be something they're not; they're expressing something they genuinely are, regardless of setting or circumstance.

I've experienced this contrast directly. When I transformed that manufacturing plant from dysfunction to efficiency, I didn't have the formal qualifications traditionally associated with such roles. I didn't have the degrees, certifications, or conventional background that would typically "justify" my position.

I had something more valuable: the actual capability to solve real problems.

I wasn't performing competence; I was demonstrating it through tangible results.

I wasn't pretending to be effective; I was actually being effective.

That's the Alley Cat approach. It's about developing genuine substance rather than projecting the appearance of substance. It's about becoming valuable rather than trying to appear valuable.

The Buffoon spends enormous energy maintaining appearances. They carefully manage impressions, curate their image, and perform the role they think others expect.

8

This performance consumes resources that could otherwise be directed toward creating actual results.

The Alley Cat invests that same energy in developing genuine capability. They focus on building real skills, solving actual problems, and creating tangible value. They direct resources toward substance rather than appearance, toward results rather than impressions.

Over time, this difference in allocation creates a widening gap. The Buffoon becomes increasingly dependent on external validation while producing diminishing actual value. The Alley Cat becomes increasingly independent of external validation while producing expanding actual value.

This is why you'll often find true Alley Cats in unexpected places, doing unexpected things, in unexpected ways. They're not confined by conventional expectations about who should be where, doing what, how. They go where opportunity leads, do what circumstances require, in whatever way produces optimal results.

That's why I can be delivering food one day and consulting with business owners the next. It's why I can sleep in my car when necessary and stay in luxury accommodations when appropriate. It's why I can work manual labor in manufacturing plants and develop sophisticated inventory management systems.

The Alley Cat isn't defined by specific activities, environments, or appearances. The Alley Cat is defined by approaching every situation with authentic capability, strategic purpose, and genuine value creation.

And this is precisely what cannot be faked, imitated, or performed. You can dress someone in an Alley Cat's typical clothes, put them in an Alley Cat's typical environments, and instruct them to say Alley Cat-typical things. But without the core identity the fundamental approach to challenges and opportunities they'll still reveal themselves as Buffoons through their actions, decisions, and priorities.

Similarly, you can put an Alley Cat in conventional business settings, traditional professional roles, and standard corporate environments. But the Alley Cat energy remains unmistakable to those paying attention. It manifests in problem-solving approaches, decision-making processes, and fundamental priorities.

The Alley Cat in the room isn't trying to be noticed. They're focused on creating results that make noticing inevitable. They're not performing importance; they're demonstrating value. They're not projecting capability; they're applying it. That's a difference the Buffoon can never understand, much less replicate.

They're too busy pretending to be what the Alley Cat actually is.

CHAPTER 3: THE HAMSTER WHEEL THEORY

Most people aren't living, they're just spinning.

Round and round on a hamster wheel of activity that creates the illusion of forward motion while actually keeping them in exactly the same place. They run faster and faster, exhausting themselves without changing their position. They mistake movement for progress, activity for achievement, effort for results.

This is what I call the Hamster Wheel Theory. A perspective I developed watching generations before me work themselves to exhaustion without substantively changing their circumstances. It applies to far more people than most would care to admit, regardless of income level or professional status.

Let me break down how this works.

The hamster inside the wheel runs frantically, generating just enough energy to power a small light. This light creates the illusion of significance with enough visibility to convince the hamster that its efforts matter. The moment the hamster stops running, the light dims and reality becomes apparent: nothing meaningful has changed despite all that effort.

Meanwhile, the providers of the wheel those who designed this system of perpetual motion without progress enjoy lights four times brighter, powered by the collective energy of countless hamsters running nowhere together.

This isn't just some poetic metaphor. This is the literal structure of modern economic reality for the vast majority of people, including many who appear successful by conventional standards.

Consider the typical life path promoted as "successful" in contemporary society:

1. Spend your formative years in educational institutions that prepare you primarily to follow directions and meet external expectations.
2. Graduate with significant debt that necessitates immediate income, limiting your ability to take risks or pursue opportunities without guaranteed short-term returns.
3. Accept employment that exchanges your most valuable asset your time and energy for just enough compensation to maintain your participation in the system, but rarely enough to escape it.
4. Work for decades, creating substantially more value for your employers than you receive in compensation.
5. Gradually increase your expenses to match or exceed income increases, ensuring continued dependence on the wheel regardless of salary level.

6. Retire when your productive capacity diminishes, living on whatever resources you managed to retain despite a system designed to extract maximum value while returning minimum compensation.

This is the hamster wheel. And it's not limited to those with low incomes or minimal education. I've met physicians, attorneys, executives, and entrepreneurs who earn substantial incomes while remaining trapped in essentially the same system, just with more expensive wheels and slightly brighter lights.

They make $500,000 a year but spend $490,000 maintaining their lifestyle. They build businesses that require their constant presence and energy. They create careers that extract their vitality while providing material comfort but minimal freedom. They mistake better cages for actual liberation.

What makes this particularly insidious is how thoroughly we've been conditioned to view the wheel as natural, inevitable, and even desirable. We celebrate getting "better" wheels rather than questioning why we're running on wheels at all. We measure success by how their wheels compare to others' wheels rather than by whether we're actually making meaningful progress.

This conditioning begins early and runs deep. Think about the messages most children receive from the earliest ages:

- Work hard in school so you can get into a good college.
- Get into a good college so you can get a good job.
- Get a good job so you can make good money.
- Make good money so you can buy nice things.
- Buy nice things so you can appear successful.
- Appear successful so your life seems worthwhile.

Notice what's missing from this progression? Actual fulfillment. Genuine freedom. Meaningful impact. Substantive progress. The entire framework is designed to keep you running without questioning whether running is actually getting you anywhere worth going. The Buffoon accepts this framework without examination. They measure success by how fast they can run on slightly better wheels than those around them. They mistake higher positions within fundamentally limiting systems for actual freedom from those systems.

The Alley Cat recognizes the wheel for what it is: modern slavery disguised as opportunity. Not slavery enforced by physical chains, but by mental conditioning that prevents us from even recognizing our confinement, much less challenging it. I call it mental slavery because the primary restraints aren't physical they're psychological. The barriers preventing escape aren't external forces but internal limitations. We stay on the wheel not because we can't physically leave, but because we've been conditioned to believe there are no viable alternatives.

I learned this firsthand growing up in North Tulsa. I watched my parents work themselves to exhaustion my father as a hard-of-hearing mechanic and welder, my mother eventually transitioning from retail to the medical field after their divorce when I was twelve. They worked and worked and worked, because that's what they were taught: work hard, go to school, work hard again, go home, and repeat until death.

The result? Survival, but barely. Just enough to keep running, but never enough to actually break free. Just enough light to see the wheel, but never enough to illuminate pathways beyond it.

What struck me most as a child wasn't their struggle it was their acceptance. They didn't question the framework that kept them running in place. They didn't challenge the system that extracted their energy while providing minimal return. They accepted limitation as natural, confinement as inevitable, and running as the only option. I decided early that this wouldn't be my fate. I couldn't articulate it clearly then, but I was rejecting the hamster wheel before I even had language to describe it. I was looking for exits while others were seeking slightly better positions within the same confining structure.

Here's what I didn't understand until much later: Recognizing the wheel doesn't automatically free you from it. Many people see the limitations of conventional paths but remain trapped by fear, conditioning, and lack of viable alternatives. They intellectually reject the wheel while emotionally remaining dependent on it.

Breaking free requires more than recognition it requires reconstruction. You must build new mental frameworks that allow you to envision possibilities beyond conventional limitations. You must develop capabilities that generate value outside traditional systems. You must create resources that provide freedom rather than just maintaining participation.

This doesn't necessarily mean rejecting employment entirely or living off the grid. Some of the freest people I know still participate in conventional economic systems but do so on their own terms, with clear awareness of the difference between leveraging these systems and being controlled by them.

The key distinction is this: Are you running the wheel, or is the wheel running you?

When I was at that manufacturing plant, working those grueling hours for minimum wage, my coworkers thought I was just another hamster running faster than them. They couldn't understand why I would exert so much effort without immediate proportional compensation.

What they didn't see was that I wasn't running their wheel I was building my own. I wasn't working for the company; I was working for myself, using their environment to develop skills, experience, and relationships that would eventually allow me to create systems rather than just participate in them.

The external appearance was the same a person working hard in a conventional setting. But the internal reality was entirely different one person running someone else's wheel faster, another person using the wheel to build capacity for eventual liberation.

That's the first step toward breaking free: changing your relationship with existing systems while you develop capacity to create your own. Using conventional structures as development platforms rather than permanent habitats. Participating strategically rather than dependently.

But this is just the beginning. True liberation comes when you create systems that generate resources without requiring your constant energy. When you build assets that produce value while you sleep. When you develop skills that can't be commoditized or outsourced. When you establish relationships based on mutual value creation rather than transactional exchange.

In other words, when you stop being the hamster and start being the one who owns the wheel or better yet, designs entirely new systems beyond wheels altogether. This transition isn't easy or quick. It requires deliberate intention, strategic action, and consistent reinforcement. It often involves temporary sacrifices of immediate comfort for long-term liberation. It demands courage to challenge deeply ingrained programming about what success means and how it's achieved.

But the alternative is spending your entire life running nowhere, mistaking exhaustion for accomplishment, confusing better wheels for actual freedom. The choice between these paths often becomes clear during times of crisis or transition. When my business collapsed and I found myself sleeping in a truck yard in Seattle, I had two options: try to get back on a slightly better wheel, or use this reset to build something fundamentally different.

I chose the latter. I used that challenge as an opportunity to redesign my approach from first principles. I examined which activities actually generated meaningful progress versus which ones just created the illusion of advancement. I focused on building assets and capabilities that couldn't be easily taken away rather than just securing better positions within fundamentally limiting systems.

That's the Alley Cat approach to the hamster wheel. Not running faster on the same wheel. Not seeking slightly better wheels. But recognizing the entire framework for what it is a system designed to extract your energy while providing just enough return to maintain your participation and methodically building alternatives that actually move you forward instead of just making you tired.

The Buffoon never questions the wheel. The Alley Cat refuses to be defined by it.

Which will you choose?

CHAPTER 4: DISCIPLINE AS CURRENCY

The most valuable currency in the world isn't money. It isn't time. It isn't even knowledge.

It's discipline.

Money can be lost in an instant. Time is constantly depleting. Knowledge without application is just trivia. But discipline true self-discipline creates a compounding return that transforms everything it touches.

When I was working at that manufacturing plant for minimum wage, living in a hotel room with my family, most of my coworkers couldn't understand why I was working so hard. They'd ask me: "Why are you killing yourself for this company? They don't pay you enough for this."

What they didn't understand was that I wasn't working for the company. I was working for myself. I was investing in my future through present discipline. I knew something they didn't: discipline is a form of currency that can be exchanged for opportunities that money alone can't buy.

While others were taking extended breaks, smoking outside, doing the minimum required, I was showing up at 2:00 AM, counting inventory, creating systems, solving problems nobody had asked me to solve. I was demonstrating a level of discipline that made me impossible to ignore.

Did the company initially compensate me financially for this extra effort? No. But that didn't matter, because I understood something fundamental: you don't get paid for your worth until you've first demonstrated your worth. You can't demand higher compensation for discipline you haven't yet shown.

The Buffoon mindset says: "Pay me more, and then I'll work harder."

The Alley Cat mindset says: "I'll demonstrate extraordinary discipline first, and the compensation will follow."

Within months, my discipline currency was exchanged for a promotion, an office, and a substantial pay increase. But more importantly, I gained knowledge, skills, and experiences that no one could ever take away from me. Meaning that I gained assets that continue generating returns long after that company closed its doors.

Discipline as currency works in every aspect of life. Financial discipline creates wealth that far exceeds what your income alone would suggest. Physical discipline builds a body that serves you rather than limits you. Mental discipline develops a mind that can solve problems others can't even comprehend.

But here's what separates true Alley Cats from everyone else: they understand that discipline isn't just about doing hard things. It's about building systems that make the right decisions automatic.

When I was rebuilding after business failures, sleeping in my car, delivering food on foot in downtown Seattle, I wasn't relying on motivation to keep going. Motivation is fickle. It comes and goes. I was relying on discipline systems I had built over years habits and routines that kept me moving forward regardless of circumstances.

I would wake up in a truck just before 4:30 AM before the truck yard owner arrived, clean myself up at a public bathroom, plan my delivery routes for maximum efficiency, and work until I physically couldn't continue. Not because I felt like it, but because my discipline systems didn't give me the option of doing anything else.

This wasn't punishment. It was power. True discipline doesn't restrict freedom it creates freedom by removing the internal negotiation that wastes energy and prevents progress.

The Buffoon sees discipline as a burden. Something they have to force themselves to do. Something that makes life less enjoyable. They're constantly fighting against themselves, exhausting their willpower on internal conflicts that produce minimal external results.

The Alley Cat sees discipline as liberation. Something that simplifies decisions. Something that makes life more meaningful. They align their desires with their actions through consistent practice, creating internal harmony that allows all their energy to flow toward external results.

This difference in perspective explains why Alley Cats can maintain discipline for decades while Buffoons struggle to maintain it for days. One is constantly fighting against themselves; the other has made peace with themselves.

Consider how this applies to wealth building. The Buffoon earns money and then decides what to do with it, constantly negotiating between immediate gratification and future security. This internal conflict ensures that most money goes toward consumption rather than investment, regardless of income level.

The Alley Cat builds systems that automatically direct money toward investment before consumption is even considered. The decision is made once, then executed consistently, eliminating the internal negotiation that depletes willpower and sabotages progress.

This is why you see people making $30,000 a year building more wealth than others making $300,000. The amount matters less than the discipline applied to that amount.

When I started rebuilding with just $200 borrowed from Rance in Seattle, I didn't have the luxury of undisciplined spending. Every dollar had a specific purpose. Every expense was evaluated against potential return. I wasn't just being frugal; I was being strategic. I was using financial discipline to create leverage that would eventually generate substantially more than $200 in return.

The same principle applies to time. The most successful people I know aren't necessarily the most talented or the most intelligent. They're the most disciplined with their time. They don't allow their attention to be hijacked by distractions. They don't waste hours on activities that produce no meaningful outcome. They maintain ruthless focus on high-leverage actions that move them toward specific goals.

This level of discipline doesn't develop overnight. It's built through consistent practice, through small daily choices that eventually become automatic. It's built by setting clear boundaries and honoring them regardless of external pressure. It's built by prioritizing effectiveness over busyness, results over appearances.

The beautiful thing about discipline as currency is that it's accessible to everyone. You don't need special connections, advanced degrees, or family wealth to develop it. You just need consistent practice and a willingness to delay gratification for greater future returns.

But here's the difficult truth that most people don't want to hear discipline is earned through discomfort. There's no way around this reality. The capacity for discipline grows only when you deliberately choose harder paths when easier ones are available. When you complete tasks you could rationalize postponing. When you maintain standards that would be easier to lower.

The Buffoon avoids discomfort at all costs, not realizing that this avoidance ensures they'll experience even greater discomfort in the future. The Alley Cat embraces strategic discomfort, understanding that temporary challenges build the discipline that prevents permanent limitations.

Think about it this way: every time you choose momentary comfort over necessary discipline, you're spending future currency to purchase present ease. You're taking out a loan against your future self that will have to be repaid with interest.

The alternative is investing in discipline now to create freedom later. It's a choice between temporary ease followed by persistent limitations, or temporary challenge followed by expanded possibilities.

This investment doesn't mean living a joyless existence of constant deprivation. That's another Buffoon misconception. True discipline isn't about denying yourself everything pleasant; it's about consciously choosing which pleasures serve your larger purpose and which ones sabotage it.

The most disciplined people I know enjoy life intensely. They experience profound satisfaction from progress toward meaningful goals. They feel the deep pleasure of mastery developing through consistent practice. They know the unique joy of living in alignment with their highest values.

What they don't experience is the hollow pleasure of momentary indulgence followed by lasting regret. They don't know the bitter taste of potential squandered for temporary comfort. They haven't felt the gnawing emptiness of a life spent avoiding necessary challenges.

As you develop your own discipline currency, remember that the goal isn't perfection. It's progress. You won't maintain perfect discipline in every area simultaneously. No one does. The goal is continuous improvement through consistent practice, building capacity that compounds over time.

Start with one area. Maybe it's waking up at the same time every day regardless of how you feel. Maybe it's dedicating the first hour of each day to your most important project before any distractions. Maybe it's saving a specific percentage of every dollar that crosses your path, regardless of circumstances.

Whatever you choose, make it non-negotiable. Do it consistently until it becomes automatic. Then add another discipline. Then another. Eventually, you'll develop a portfolio of discipline currencies that can be exchanged for opportunities beyond conventional imagination.

That's when you'll truly understand discipline isn't just something you do. It's something you become. And once you become disciplined, nothing can stop you except yourself.

CHAPTER 5: MY FATE IS MINE TO DECIDE, NOT YOURS

After the manufacturing plant closed due to corporate mismanagement, I made a decision that would forever change my approach to earning. I would never again put myself in a position where someone else could terminate my income with a single decision.

Never again would I be laid off. Never again would someone have the power to fire me. Never again would my financial stability depend on another person's judgment, competence, or whims.

This wasn't about bitterness toward employers. It was about recognizing a fundamental truth that most people spend their entire lives avoiding when you work for others, you surrender control of your economic destiny.

You can be the most competent, dedicated, valuable employee in the organization and still lose everything because of factors completely beyond your control. Market downturns. Management changes. Corporate restructuring. Technological disruption. Political shifts. Global events. The Buffoon accepts this vulnerability as inevitable. They believe economic security comes from finding the right employer, the right position, the right industry. They seek stability through better dependence rather than through genuine independence.

The Alley Cat recognizes that true security can only come from controlling the source of your income not just the amount. They understand that who owns the resource matters more than who manages it. They build systems that generate revenue under their control rather than merely securing positions within systems controlled by others.

This distinction explains why some people with impressive credentials and prestigious positions remain perpetually vulnerable while others with minimal formal education and unconventional careers achieve genuine stability. The former depend on external systems they don't control. The latter create systems they do control. This isn't just theory. I've lived both sides of this reality.

When I was working at that manufacturing plant, my economic fate was determined by decisions made in corporate offices I would never visit, by executives I would never meet, based on factors I could never influence. Despite my exceptional performance, my promotion, my created systems that transformed efficiency I had no actual control over my continued employment or compensation.

The company's failure had nothing to do with my value. It had everything to do with the inherent vulnerability of depending on others to recognize and reward that value within systems designed primarily for their benefit, not mine.

After that experience, I began building businesses rather than seeking better jobs. I started delivering food not as a career but as a funding mechanism for ventures I controlled. I sacrificed immediate comfort for ultimate sovereignty. I chose independence over convenience, control over prestige. The Buffoon would look at someone delivering food and see limitation. The Alley Cat recognizes it as a self-funding pathway to something greater a means of generating immediate resources while building long-term assets without surrendering control.

This doesn't mean everyone needs to become an entrepreneur in the conventional sense. There are multiple pathways to economic sovereignty that don't involve launching traditional businesses:

1. Develop rare, high-demand skills that can't be easily replaced or automated. When you become genuinely irreplaceable, you shift from asking for compensation to setting your terms.
2. Create multiple income streams rather than depending on a single source. When no single entity controls your entire economic reality, you gain leverage and resilience.
3. Build assets that generate passive income without requiring your constant direct involvement. When your money works for you instead of you working for money, you break the direct connection between time and income.
4. Establish yourself as a recognized authority in a specific domain. When you own the expertise rather than just applying it within someone else's framework, you control its deployment and compensation.
5. Develop systems that can operate without your constant presence. When you build processes that create value whether you're physically present or not, you transcend the limitations of trading time for money.

All these approaches share a common theme shifting from being a resource within someone else's system to creating your own systems that generate, manage, and deploy resources according to your priorities.

But making this transition requires overcoming deeply ingrained programming about careers, success, and economic value. We've been conditioned to believe that "good jobs" with "stable employers" represent the pinnacle of economic achievement. We've been taught that traditional credentials, linear career progressions, and institutional affiliations are the primary markers of professional value.

This conditioning serves a specific purpose of maintaining a supply of compliant, qualified individuals willing to exchange their time, energy, and talent for less than the full value they create. It ensures that the primary beneficiaries of productive activity remain those who control systems rather than those who perform within them. Breaking free from this conditioning means recognizing that the conventional career path is designed primarily for the benefit of employers, not employees. The traditional professional progression optimizes for institutional interests, not individual sovereignty.

This doesn't mean traditional employment is inherently exploitative or that all employers are intentionally limiting their employees. Many organizations genuinely value their people and strive to create mutually beneficial relationships. But the fundamental structure remains the same: one party controls the resource (employment), while the other depends on access to it.

The Alley Cat understands this dynamic and works to reverse it to become the controller of resources rather than the dependent seeker of access. This reversal doesn't happen overnight. It requires strategic planning, deliberate skill development, and consistent investment in building alternative systems.

When I started rebuilding after setbacks, I didn't immediately achieve complete independence. I used conventional employment as a funding mechanism for developing assets that would eventually provide real sovereignty. I leveraged existing systems while building my own. I maintained multiple income streams to ensure that no single point of failure could devastate my economic reality.

This approach requires something most people aren't willing to give temporary sacrifice of convenience, status, and immediate gratification for long-term sovereignty. The Buffoon chooses the immediate comfort of traditional employment over the temporary discomfort of building genuine independence. The Alley Cat makes the opposite choice. Consider the practical implications of this difference in mindset and approach.

When economic conditions deteriorate, the Buffoon experiences genuine panic. Their entire financial reality depends on continued employment they don't control. Their skills are often specific to particular organizational contexts. Their professional identity is tied to institutional positions rather than transferable capabilities. Their income flows from a single source they can't direct or diversify.

When these same conditions affect the Alley Cat, they experience challenge rather than crisis. Their economic reality includes multiple streams they control directly. Their skills transcend specific organizations or industries. Their professional identity exists independent of institutional affiliations. Their income flows from diverse sources they can adjust, expand, or redirect. This isn't just about financial stability it's about personal sovereignty. When your economic fate belongs to someone else, every other aspect of your life becomes similarly vulnerable. Your residence, healthcare, education, recreation, relationships all become contingent on continued approval from those controlling your income.

True freedom begins with economic independence. Not necessarily enormous wealth, but genuine control over how you generate and deploy resources. Not freedom from effort, but freedom to direct that effort according to your priorities rather than someone else's requirements. This form of independence rarely comes from traditional paths. You don't achieve economic sovereignty by getting better jobs, higher salaries, or more prestigious positions within systems others control. You achieve it by building your own systems, developing your own assets, creating your own opportunities.

The path to this sovereignty isn't identical for everyone. Some will build traditional businesses. Others will develop specialized expertise deployed on their terms. Others will create intellectual property that generates ongoing returns. Others will build investment portfolios that provide passive income. What these diverse approaches share is a common principle: shifting from being an asset within someone else's system to developing systems that generate assets under your control.

Making this shift requires overcoming not just external obstacles but internal resistance. We've been trained to seek security through dependence rather than through capability. We've been conditioned to fear independence rather than embrace it. We've been taught to measure success by institutional validation rather than by actual sovereignty. The Buffoon internalizes these lessons completely, seeking slightly better positions within fundamentally limiting systems. The Alley Cat recognizes them as programming designed to maintain compliance rather than to facilitate freedom.

I'm not suggesting everyone should quit their jobs tomorrow without preparation or planning. That would be reckless rather than strategic. What I'm advocating is a fundamental shift in how you view employment as a temporary funding mechanism for building real independence rather than as a destination or identity.

Use your current position to develop skills, resources, connections, and insights that will allow you to create your own economic reality. Build side projects that could eventually become primary sources of income. Develop capabilities that transcend your current role or industry. Create assets that generate value whether you're employed or not.

Most importantly, recognize that genuine security never comes from finding the right employer or position. It comes from developing the ability to create value under your own direction, deployed according to your priorities, compensated according to terms you influence rather than merely accept.

Your fate is yours to decide not your employer's, not the market's, not the economy's. But claiming this sovereignty requires more than declaration; it demands deliberate development of systems that actually place control in your hands rather than in someone else's. The choice is simple but profound: Will you spend your life seeking better positions within systems designed for someone else's benefit, or will you build systems aligned with your own priorities and values?

Will you continue being a resource deployed according to external directives, or will you become the director of resources aligned with your authentic purpose? Your fate is yours to decide. But only if you actually decide it, rather than surrendering that decision to those who profit from your dependence.

21

CHAPTER 6: LIVING EXPENSES AS BUSINESS OPERATION EXPENSES

If you want to create extraordinary wealth, you need to fundamentally change how you think about your expenses.

Most people, even those with substantial incomes treat their living costs as something separate from their wealth-building strategies. They earn money, then decide what portion to save or invest after covering their living expenses. Their financial equation looks like this:

Income - Living Expenses = Available for Wealth Building

This approach guarantees that wealth building becomes optional something you do with "leftover" money after funding your lifestyle. And human nature being what it is, expenses inevitably expand to consume available resources, leaving little for creating actual prosperity.

The Alley Cat thinks differently. They approach personal finances with the same strategic discipline that successful businesses apply to operational expenses. Their financial equation looks like this:

Income - Wealth Building = Available for Living Expenses

This subtle shift changes everything. Wealth building becomes mandatory rather than optional. Living expenses become strategic decisions rather than automatic outcomes. Each cost is evaluated based on its return rather than merely its affordability.

When I was rebuilding after business setbacks, this principle wasn't just theory it was survival. Every dollar had to serve a specific purpose aligned with my larger strategy. Nothing was spent without clear understanding of its return. Nothing was purchased based merely on preference or convenience.

This doesn't mean living in perpetual deprivation. It means applying business thinking to personal finances: maximizing value while minimizing costs, investing in appreciating assets rather than depreciating liabilities, focusing on productivity rather than appearance.

Consider how businesses approach expenses versus how most individuals handle their finances:

Successful businesses carefully analyze the return on every expenditure. They don't purchase equipment, space, or services based on preferences or status; they invest in resources that generate more value than they cost. They regularly review expenses to eliminate anything not producing adequate return. They negotiate aggressively to secure optimal terms. They structure operations to maximize tax efficiency.

Most individuals do the opposite. They purchase based on preference rather than return. They rarely analyze whether expenses actually generate value exceeding their cost. They accept standard terms without negotiation. They structure finances based on convenience rather than optimization. They make tax decisions reactively rather than strategically.

The Buffoon earns $100,000 and immediately upgrades their lifestyle to consume $95,000, leaving $5,000 for nominal investing. They believe they deserve immediate gratification as reward for their work. They mistake consuming wealth for building wealth.

The Alley Cat earns $100,000 and immediately allocates $50,000 to wealth-building vehicles investments, business development, skill acquisition before determining what lifestyle can be supported with the remainder. They understand that wealth comes from ownership and appreciation, not from consumption and depreciation.

Let me illustrate this principle through concrete examples.

When most people increase their income, their first impulse is upgrading housing moving to larger, more impressive homes in more prestigious neighborhoods. This typically represents their largest expense, often consuming 30-40% of their income.

The Alley Cat approaches housing as a business operation decision rather than a status marker. They prioritize functionality, efficiency, and financial impact over appearance and prestige. They choose locations that minimize commuting costs and time rather than maximizing status. They select spaces that serve their actual needs rather than projecting desired images.

This doesn't mean living in unpleasant conditions. It means making housing decisions based on strategic value rather than emotional satisfaction or social validation. It means recognizing that housing beyond functional requirements represents consumption rather than investment, expense rather than asset.

The same principle applies to transportation. Most people select vehicles based on appearance, status, and emotional satisfaction rather than functional requirements and financial impact. They accept substantial depreciation and operating costs to project desired images rather than to serve actual needs.

The Alley Cat approaches transportation as a business operation expense. They analyze total cost against actual utility. They distinguish between vehicles as necessary tools versus vehicles as conspicuous consumption. They make decisions based on long-term financial impact rather than immediate emotional satisfaction.

Again, this doesn't mean driving unpleasant vehicles. It means making transportation decisions based on strategic value rather than social signaling. It means recognizing that transportation beyond functional requirements represents consumption rather than investment.

This business operation mindset extends to every expense category food, clothing, technology, entertainment, education. Each is evaluated based on its contribution to your larger strategy rather than merely its immediate satisfaction or social signaling value.

When you eat at expensive restaurants, are you making a strategic investment in relationship building with potential partners, or are you merely consuming resources that could be deployed toward wealth creation? When you purchase premium clothing, are you investing in professional presentation that creates tangible opportunities, or are you consuming resources to project status without corresponding return?

The Buffoon never asks these questions. They assume that increased income automatically justifies increased consumption. They mistake the appearance of prosperity for actual wealth creation. They treat expenses as entitlements rather than as strategic decisions.

The Alley Cat constantly evaluates every expenditure against potential alternatives. Not from a scarcity mentality that fears spending, but from a strategic perspective that maximizes return on every resource. They understand that every dollar directed toward non-appreciating consumption represents compounded wealth permanently forgone.

This perspective becomes particularly powerful when applied to major life decisions. Consider how most people approach education, both for themselves and for their children. They select institutions based primarily on prestige and social validation rather than on specific value creation relative to cost.

The Alley Cat approaches education as a business investment decision. They analyze actual return (skills developed, networks accessed, opportunities created) against total cost (tuition, time investment, opportunity cost). They distinguish between education that creates specific value versus education that merely signals conformity. They make decisions based on verifiable outcomes rather than institutional reputations.

This doesn't mean avoiding higher education or selecting only vocational training. It means approaching education with the same strategic discipline that would apply to any other major investment with clear understanding of expected return, careful analysis of alternatives, and ongoing assessment of actual value creation.

The same principle applies to geographical decisions. Most people select living locations based on familiarity, convenience, or preference rather than on strategic advantage. They remain in suboptimal environments because moving seems disruptive or challenging.

The Alley Cat approaches location as a business operation decision. They analyze environments based on opportunity concentration, regulatory advantage, network quality, and cost efficiency. They select locations that maximize specific opportunities aligned with their strategy rather than locations that merely feel comfortable or familiar.

This strategic discipline doesn't mean living without enjoyment or treating every decision as purely transactional. It means recognizing that resources directed toward wealth creation rather than immediate consumption eventually produce substantially greater enjoyment and satisfaction both financial and emotional.

When I was at my lowest point financially, sleeping in my car in Seattle, I wasn't functioning from deprivation. I was making strategic decisions about resource allocation and directing every available dollar toward rebuilding rather than toward temporary comfort. This wasn't punishment; it was investment. It wasn't sacrifice; it was strategy.

The temporary discomfort of minimizing living expenses while maximizing wealth-building investments eventually produces freedom that no amount of consumption can match. The Buffoon never experiences this freedom because they can't delay gratification long enough to create it. The Alley Cat prioritizes lasting sovereignty over temporary satisfaction.

To implement this principle in your own life, start by conducting a business-style audit of your current expenses. Analyze each cost category not based on whether you can afford it, but on whether it generates return exceeding its cost. Distinguish between expenditures that create future value versus those that merely provide immediate satisfaction.

Next, restructure your financial flow to prioritize wealth building over consumption. Before allocating a single dollar to living expenses, direct a specific percentage of every income source toward investments, business development, or skill acquisition. Make wealth building mandatory rather than optional.

Then, rebuild your lifestyle based on what remains after these wealth-creating allocations. This doesn't mean living in misery. It means designing a life that maximizes value while minimizing cost focusing resources on elements that create genuine satisfaction rather than on signaling prosperity to others.

As wealth begins accumulating through this strategic approach, resist the natural urge to immediately expand lifestyle proportionally. Instead, maintain the same discipline that created initial prosperity. Continue treating living expenses as business operation costs requiring justification rather than as entitlements automatically scaling with income.

This discipline eventually creates options unavailable to those who consume their way through life regardless of income level. I know people earning six figures who remain perpetually vulnerable because they consume everything they earn. I also know people with modest incomes who have achieved genuine financial sovereignty because they consistently prioritize wealth building over consumption.

The difference isn't income. It's strategy. It's understanding that living expenses aren't merely costs of existence they're strategic decisions that either advance or undermine your larger objectives. They're business operation expenses in the enterprise of your life.

Treat them accordingly, and watch as resources previously consumed begin generating prosperity that eventually exceeds anything temporary gratification could provide.

CHAPTER 7: RESPECT IS THE AXIS

Without respect, nothing functions properly. Not business partnerships. Not personal relationships. Not teams. Not communities. Not even internal dialogue with yourself.

Respect is the axis around which all meaningful interaction revolves. When it's missing, even situations with every other advantage will eventually collapse. When it's present, even challenging circumstances can produce extraordinary outcomes.

I've experienced both scenarios throughout my journey. I've been in business partnerships with abundant resources but insufficient respect they inevitably failed despite financial potential. I've also built relationships with minimal initial resources but foundation of genuine respect they consistently produced value exceeding apparent possibilities.

The difference wasn't capital, connections, or credentials. It was the presence or absence of this fundamental element that most people discuss but few truly understand.

Real respect isn't about politeness, though civility often accompanies it. It isn't about admiration, though appreciation may develop from it. It isn't about deference, though appropriate acknowledgment of capability reflects it.

At its core, respect is recognition of legitimate value, capability, and sovereignty both in yourself and in others. It's the authentic acknowledgment that someone (including yourself) possesses inherent worth independent of usefulness to your immediate objectives.

The Buffoon simulates respect through superficial behaviors using appropriate titles, maintaining expected courtesies, performing standardized rituals of acknowledgment. But these external performances without internal recognition create fundamentally unstable relationships that inevitably collapse when tested.

The Alley Cat demonstrates respect through consistent behaviors reflecting genuine recognition. They acknowledge capability without requiring credentials. They recognize value without demanding conformity. They honor sovereignty without imposing unnecessary control.

This distinction becomes immediately apparent in how each approach leadership.

The Buffoon attempts to lead through position, authority, and compliance. They believe respect comes from title, status, or power. They demand acknowledgment rather than earning recognition. They measure their importance by others' deference rather than by mutual value creation.

27

The Alley Cat leads through demonstration, capability, and collaboration. They understand respect must be earned through consistent value creation. They generate recognition through results rather than requirements. They measure their effectiveness by outcomes rather than by others' responses to their position.

I learned this principle through direct experience rather than theoretical exploration.

When I transformed that manufacturing plant from dysfunction to efficiency, I didn't have official leadership authority initially. I couldn't demand compliance through position power. I couldn't require cooperation through hierarchical privilege.

Instead, I earned respect by demonstrating value solving problems others couldn't solve, creating systems others hadn't developed, producing results others hadn't achieved. My effectiveness came from recognition earned through capability rather than from compliance demanded through authority.

Even after formal promotion and positional authority, this foundation remained unchanged. People followed my direction not because they had to, but because they recognized the legitimate value of my approach. They respected capability rather than merely complying with authority.

The same principle applies in every domain business, personal relationships, community involvement. Genuine respect creates possibilities that positional authority alone can never achieve.

Consider how this manifests in business partnerships. The Buffoon approach creates superficially impressive but fundamentally unstable arrangements. They select partners based on credentials, resources, or connections rather than on character, capability, and alignment. They structure relationships to maximize control rather than to optimize collaborative potential.

The Alley Cat builds partnerships founded on mutual respect for genuine capability. They select partners based on demonstrated value creation rather than on impressive appearances. They structure relationships to maximize collaborative potential rather than to protect against potential exploitation.

When I was rebuilding after setbacks, I couldn't offer potential partners impressive resources, established platforms, or extensive track records. What I could offer was genuine respect for their capabilities and authentic commitment to their success alongside my own.

This approach attracted partners who recognized these qualities as more valuable than superficial advantages. Together, we built relationships that produced extraordinary outcomes precisely because they were founded on mutual recognition of legitimate value rather than on transactional exploitation of temporary resources.

The same principle applies within teams. The Buffoon creates environments of compliance rather than commitment. People perform required functions without engaging their full capability. They withhold discretionary effort because they experience position power rather than earned authority.

The Alley Cat builds teams founded on genuine respect flowing in all directions leaders respecting team members' capabilities, team members respecting leaders' vision, everyone respecting the collective mission. This mutual recognition creates engagement that position power alone can never generate.

When I led manufacturing teams, I demonstrated respect for each person's potential contribution regardless of their formal role or background. I acknowledged insights from production staff with the same seriousness as those from management. I recognized capability wherever it appeared rather than only where organizational charts suggested it should exist.

This approach created environments where people contributed far beyond minimal requirements. They engaged fully because they experienced genuine recognition rather than merely positional demands. They committed to outcomes because they were respected as capable contributors rather than as interchangeable resources.

The axis of respect extends beyond external relationships to internal dialogue. How you relate to yourself specifically, whether you respect your own capability, value, and sovereignty determines your effectiveness in every other domain.

The Buffoon lacks genuine self-respect despite often projecting arrogance. They seek external validation precisely because they don't truly recognize their own legitimate value. They demand acknowledgment from others because they haven't developed authentic recognition of their own capability.

The Alley Cat operates from foundation of genuine self-respect. They recognize their own legitimate value without requiring constant external validation. They acknowledge their capabilities without either inflating or diminishing them. They honor their own sovereignty while respecting others' boundaries.

This internal alignment creates remarkable stability regardless of external circumstances. When I was sleeping in my car in Seattle, delivering food to survive while rebuilding my business, my external situation appeared desperate by conventional standards. But internally, my self-respect remained intact.

I didn't confuse temporary circumstances with fundamental value. I didn't mistake challenging situations for personal limitation. I maintained respect for my own capabilities even when external results hadn't yet manifested. This internal alignment allowed me to make decisions based on long-term potential rather than on immediate pressure.

The respect axis functions equally in both positive and negative directions. Just as genuine respect creates extraordinary possibilities, its absence generates devastating consequences often invisible until critical moments reveal fundamental instability.

Business partnerships lacking authentic respect eventually collapse when facing inevitable challenges, regardless of how impressive they appear initially. Teams without mutual recognition ultimately underperform despite abundant resources and talent. Individuals without genuine self-respect eventually make devastating decisions regardless of apparent success or intelligence.

This principle becomes particularly important during challenging circumstances. When resources are limited, competition intense, and pressures substantial, respect often determines survival versus failure.

In difficult environments, the Buffoon abandons respect in favor of expedience. They sacrifice recognition of others' sovereignty for immediate advantage. They discard acknowledgment of others' legitimate value for temporary gain. They trade mutual benefit for exploitative extraction.

The Alley Cat maintains the respect axis especially during challenges. They recognize that abandoning this foundation for short-term advantage creates long-term vulnerability far exceeding any temporary benefit. They understand that respect isn't a luxury for comfortable circumstances but an essential element for sustainable success.

When I faced legal challenges stemming from business dealings gone wrong, I maintained respect even for those who had treated me unfairly. Not from naivety or weakness, but from recognition that allowing circumstances to compromise this fundamental principle would create greater long-term damage than any temporary situation.

This wasn't about being nice or avoiding conflict. It was about maintaining the axis around which everything else revolves. Without respect for others, for legitimate processes, for myself no solution would create sustainable positive outcomes regardless of apparent immediate advantage.

Implementing this principle requires both internal development and external demonstration. Internally, cultivate genuine recognition of your own legitimate value, capability, and sovereignty without either inflation or diminishment. Acknowledge your actual strengths without exaggeration, your real limitations without shame, your authentic sovereignty without overreach.

Externally, demonstrate respect through consistent behaviors rather than occasional performances. Recognize capability wherever it appears rather than only where credentials suggest it should exist. Acknowledge value in its various forms rather than only in conventional manifestations. Honor sovereignty through boundaries rather than through control.

Most importantly, maintain this axis especially when circumstances create temptation to abandon it. When someone treats you disrespectfully, when resources become scarce, when pressure intensifies these moments reveal whether respect represents your fundamental operating system or merely a situational performance.

The Buffoon displays respect when convenient and discards it when advantageous. The Alley Cat recognizes it as the essential foundation without which nothing else functions properly, regardless of temporary circumstances or apparent advantage.

Which approach will you choose?

CHAPTER 8: YOU CAN'T STEAL FROM ALLEY CATS

Let me tell you something that might initially sound counterintuitive: When you betray an Alley Cat, you're not stealing from them you're stealing from yourself. This isn't some inspirational platitude or philosophical abstraction. It's a practical reality I've observed repeatedly throughout my journey.

When someone with positive intentions and team-oriented mindset gets crossed, the person committing the betrayal isn't gaining an advantage they're creating a formidable adversary while simultaneously losing an invaluable ally. They're not "winning" at someone else's expense; they're damaging themselves in ways they typically can't recognize until it's too late.

To have a calculated, coordinated, strategic enemy who previously understood your strengths, weaknesses, and vulnerabilities from the inside is a problem far exceeding any short-term gain from betrayal. To lose an ally who could have helped you navigate challenges, identify opportunities, and overcome obstacles represents an opportunity cost no temporary advantage can justify.

The Buffoon doesn't understand this dynamic. They approach relationships transactionally, evaluating each interaction based on immediate extraction potential rather than on long-term collaborative value. They view partnerships as zero-sum competitions where advantage comes from maximizing personal gain regardless of mutual outcomes.

The Alley Cat recognizes that genuine prosperity comes through alignment rather than exploitation. They build relationships founded on mutual benefit, shared growth, and collaborative advantage. They understand that betrayal creates damage exceeding any temporary benefit, regardless of who appears to "win" the immediate exchange.

I learned this principle through direct experience sometimes painfully.

When my business partner and I built that company from deep losses to consistent profits, we achieved this transformation through aligned vision, complementary capabilities, and mutual commitment to shared success. We weren't competing for larger pieces of a limited pie; we were collaboratively expanding the pie itself through coordinated effort.

The subsequent business collapse didn't come from external market forces or competitive pressure. It came from internal betrayal from someone calculating that they could extract more value by sacrificing mutual benefit for personal advantage. They believed they were "winning" at someone else's expense.

What they didn't recognize was that this apparent victory actually represented devastating self-sabotage. By betraying an aligned partner committed to mutual success, they didn't just damage someone else they destroyed the very system generating their own prosperity. They didn't just lose an ally; they created an adversary with intimate knowledge of their operation, approach, and vulnerabilities.

The temporary advantage they extracted paled in comparison to the long-term opportunity cost of this miscalculation. The resources they gained through betrayal represented a fraction of what continued collaboration would have generated for everyone involved, including themselves.

This dynamic extends beyond business partnerships to every form of relationship and collaboration. When you betray someone genuinely committed to mutual benefit, you're not gaining at their expense you're damaging yourself by destroying systems that would have generated substantially greater value through continued alignment.

This principle operates with particular intensity when the betrayed party embodies the Alley Cat mentality. Unlike the Buffoon, who might respond to betrayal with ineffective emotional reactions or misguided retribution, the Alley Cat maintains strategic perspective even when personally impacted.

They recognize betrayal not as an emotional injury requiring vengeance but as a strategic miscalculation revealing fundamental character limitations. They respond not from wounded ego but from clear assessment of changed circumstances. They redirect energy previously committed to mutual benefit toward their own objectives without wasting resources on pointless retaliation.

This isn't about being nice or avoiding conflict. It's about maintaining strategic effectiveness regardless of others' behavior. The Alley Cat doesn't seek revenge; they simply stop investing in collaborative possibilities with those who've demonstrated inability to maintain alignment.

This strategic redirection often creates consequences far more significant than any intentional retribution could achieve. The person who betrayed collaborative potential loses access to capabilities, insights, and opportunities that would have generated substantial ongoing value. They forfeit future benefits far exceeding whatever temporary advantage they extracted through betrayal.

Consider this in practical terms. When you betray someone committed to mutual success:

1. You lose access to their capabilities, insights, and resources that would have generated ongoing value exceeding whatever you extracted through betrayal.
2. You transform a potential ally into someone with no incentive to support your objectives and intimate knowledge of your vulnerabilities.
3. You demonstrate character limitations that reduce your attractiveness to other potential high-value collaborators who recognize these patterns.

4. You reinforce internal patterns that diminish your capacity for building genuinely prosperous relationships, ensuring you repeat this self-limiting cycle.

The Buffoon never recognizes these consequences until it's too late. They mistake temporary resource extraction for actual advantage without understanding the value destruction their approach creates for everyone involved, including themselves.

The Alley Cat recognizes that genuine prosperity comes from alignment rather than exploitation. They build collaborative relationships that generate expanding value rather than extractive interactions that produce diminishing returns. They understand that the most valuable resource isn't what you can take from others but what you can create together.

This principle becomes particularly important when selecting partners, teammates, and collaborators. The Buffoon evaluates potential relationships based on what they can extract from others regardless of mutual benefit. The Alley Cat selects partners based on capacity for sustained value creation through genuine alignment.

When I rebuilt after setbacks, I was extraordinarily careful about who I allowed into my innermost circle. This wasn't from bitterness or distrust but from recognition that collaboration requires capability for sustained alignment rather than merely temporary advantage. I assessed potential partners based on character fundamentals rather than on superficial resources or apparent opportunities.

This approach might initially seem limiting compared to pursuing every possible connection regardless of alignment potential. But this selectivity actually enabled substantially greater prosperity by ensuring that collaborative energy went toward genuinely productive relationships rather than toward managing misalignment or recovering from betrayal.

The most successful people I know share this perspective. They're extremely selective about their closest collaborators not from arrogance or exclusivity but from recognition that genuine alignment creates exponentially greater value than mere transactional association. They understand that one deeply aligned partner generates more prosperity than dozens of superficially connected associates.

This principle extends beyond formal business relationships to every collaborative context. The team member who prioritizes personal credit over collective results isn't "winning" at the team's expense they're damaging themselves by undermining systems that would generate substantially greater opportunity through continued alignment. The colleague who exploits shared information for individual advantage isn't gaining at others' expense they're limiting their own potential by destroying trust that would have created expanding possibilities.

Implementing this principle requires both selection criteria and response strategies. In selecting collaborators, evaluate character fundamentals rather than merely apparent resources or credentials. Assess capacity for sustained alignment rather than just immediate contribution. Prioritize mutual benefit orientation over short-term extraction capability.

In responding to betrayal, maintain strategic perspective rather than emotional reaction. Recognize misalignment as information about character limitations rather than as personal injury requiring retribution. Redirect energy previously committed to mutual benefit toward objectives aligned with demonstrated integrity.

Most importantly, understand that you can't actually steal from someone committed to creation rather than extraction. You can only damage yourself by forfeiting collaborative potential exceeding whatever temporary advantage you might gain through misalignment.

The old saying that "you never lose people chasing money, but you do lose money chasing people" captures an important aspect of this principle. When your priorities focus on extraction rather than creation, on personal advantage rather than mutual benefit, you inevitably damage systems that would generate substantially greater prosperity through continued alignment.

The Buffoon never grasps this reality. They continue pursuing short-term advantage at long-term expense, extraction at the cost of creation, individual gain at the expense of mutual benefit. They remain trapped in diminishing returns while wondering why genuine prosperity remains elusive despite apparent success in individual transactions.

The Alley Cat builds prosperity through alignment rather than extraction. They create expanding value through collaborative relationships rather than diminishing returns through exploitative transactions. They understand that genuine advantage comes not from taking bigger pieces of limited pies but from building bigger pies through coordinated capability.

This approach requires more than superficial behavior adjustment. It demands fundamental orientation toward creation rather than extraction, toward mutual benefit rather than personal advantage, toward expanding systems rather than exploitative transactions. It requires recognizing that genuine prosperity comes through alignment rather than through zero-sum competition.

When you embrace this principle fully, you understand why the statement "you can't steal from Alley Cats" represents practical reality rather than philosophical idealism. The true value of the Alley Cat isn't in what they temporarily possess but in what they consistently create. Stealing possessions doesn't diminish their creative capability it only reveals the thief's limitation to extraction rather than creation.

In the long game that truly matters, this orientation toward creation rather than extraction determines who prospers sustainably versus who experiences temporary advantage followed by inevitable decline. The Buffoon remains trapped in cycles of diminishing returns while the Alley Cat builds expanding systems of genuine prosperity.

The choice between these approaches isn't just moral it's practical. Creating aligned systems that generate expanding value simply produces better results than extracting temporary advantage from exploitative transactions. Building collaborative relationships focused on mutual benefit creates more prosperity than pursuing personal gain at others' expense.

Which approach will you choose?

CHAPTER 9: THE IMAGE OF THE ALLEY CAT

You can't easily categorize an Alley Cat by appearance alone. That's part of what makes us so effective that we defy conventional expectations and visual stereotypes.

Walk into any high-end establishment in America and you'll find people carefully dressed to project wealth, success, and importance. Designer suits, luxury watches, meticulously maintained appearances. Meanwhile, the actual owners of these establishments and the true wealth creators often dress in ways that would shock those trying so desperately to appear successful.

I've personally witnessed billionaires in casual t-shirts and jeans being treated dismissively by staff catering to customers wearing borrowed finery and living paycheck to paycheck. I've seen extraordinarily successful entrepreneurs mistaken for delivery personnel because they didn't match predetermined images of what "success" should look like.

The true Alley Cat creates a visual juxtaposition that confuses those trained to judge by appearance rather than substance. They disregard conventional signals of status and success in favor of functionality, authenticity, and personal preference.

My own appearance represents this principle perfectly. On any given day, you might find me in a baseball cap, hoodie, shorts or sweats, with crazy, colorful socks that stand out from an otherwise casual ensemble. Nothing about my clothing suggests extraordinary success by conventional standards.

Yet I consistently step out of luxury convertibles from Mercedes-Benz, BMW, and Audi vehicles that would typically be associated with formal business attire and conventional markers of professional achievement. I've watched people's expressions shift from dismissal to confusion as they try to reconcile their appearance-based expectations with contradictory evidence.

Some Alley Cats are draped in jewelry and designer clothes while driving exotic vehicles. Others wear simple attire while surrounded by visible markers of substantial wealth. Some display no external signals of prosperity while quietly building empires. There's no single "uniform" because we're defined by mindset rather than by appearance. I personally know a multi-million dollar Alley Cat who drives a 10 year old economy car as his primary vehicle. He also owns a 1972 Ferrari 365 GTB/4 Daytona that is in excellent condition which stays in his garage with only a little over 1200 miles on the odometer.

The only constant is the disruption of conventional expectations about how success should manifest visually. We confound those who expect successful people to look a certain way, drive certain vehicles, wear certain clothes, display certain status symbols. We reject the unwritten rule that prosperity must be signaled through standardized visual cues.

This isn't about being intentionally misleading or playing mind games. It's about liberation from superficial judgment systems that prioritize appearance over substance, perception over reality, signaling over creating. It's about the freedom to express authentic preferences rather than conforming to predetermined expectations.

When people describe me, they typically mention four things: my socks (always distinctive), my vehicles (always premium), my politeness (always consistent), and my work ethic (always evident). The contrast between casual appearance and quality vehicles creates a memorable impression precisely because it contradicts conventional associations.

This contradiction sparks curiosity. People wonder how someone who appears so casual can drive vehicles typically associated with formal success. They can't immediately categorize me within familiar frameworks of wealth display or status signaling. I don't fit neatly into predetermined boxes of "successful person" or "ordinary worker."

The Buffoon finds this uncertainty uncomfortable. They need clear visual signals to determine someone's worth, position, and potential value to their objectives. They rely on superficial markers because they lack capacity to assess actual substance. They mistake appearance for reality because they themselves are more appearance than substance.

The Alley Cat recognizes this psychological dynamic and uses it strategically. Not through deliberate deception, but through authentic disregard for conventional signaling systems. They understand that confusion created by contradicting appearance expectations often reveals more about observers than about the observed.

When I'm delivering food in a luxury convertible, people inevitably ask what I "really" do they can't reconcile casual work with premium vehicles. This question reveals their underlying assumption that success must manifest in standardized ways that certain activities are incompatible with certain prosperity levels. Their confusion exposes their limited understanding of how wealth is actually created.

I answer honestly: I'm building businesses while generating immediate income through practical activity. I'm creating long-term assets while meeting short-term needs. I'm thinking like an owner while performing necessary functions without ego attachment. Their confusion results not from deception but from encountering a mindset beyond their current understanding.

Some Alley Cats have numerous tattoos. Some have colored hair. Some have multiple piercings. Some maintain conventional appearances. Some adopt extreme minimalism while others embrace visible luxury. The specific manifestation varies widely because it reflects authentic individuality rather than standardized conformity.

This authentic expression frees substantial energy otherwise consumed by maintaining appearances. Consider how much mental bandwidth, emotional energy, and financial resources most people dedicate to controlling how others perceive them. The clothes carefully selected to project specific impressions. The possessions strategically displayed to signal particular associations. The behaviors meticulously managed to create desired perceptions.

The Alley Cat redirects this energy toward actual value creation. Instead of managing appearances, they develop capabilities. Instead of controlling perceptions, they build systems. Instead of signaling status, they generate results. This redirection creates substantial advantage compared to those exhausting themselves through constant impression management.

I've experienced this advantage directly. While others spend hours curating Instagram-worthy outfits and environments, I'm solving real problems creating actual value. While they're selecting accessories to project desired appearances, I'm developing skills that generate tangible results. While they're managing perceptions, I'm building prosperity.

This freedom from appearance preoccupation represents liberation rather than limitation. It doesn't mean neglecting physical presentation entirely or deliberately projecting slovenliness. It means approaching appearance functionally rather than performatively selecting what serves actual purposes rather than what creates desired impressions.

My choice of casual, comfortable clothing serves practical functions: it allows unrestricted movement, minimizes maintenance requirements, and enables continuous activity without distraction. My distinctive socks provide personal enjoyment without sacrificing functionality. My premium vehicles deliver specific driving experiences aligned with personal preferences while simultaneously serving transportation needs.

None of these choices aims primarily at managing others' perceptions. None prioritizes signaling over substance. None values appearance over reality. Each represents authentic preference expressed without preoccupation with external judgment.

This authenticity creates another powerful advantage: it attracts people responding to genuine value rather than to manufactured appearances. When you present yourself primarily through actual substance rather than curated signals, you naturally filter for relationships based on real recognition rather than on superficial assessment.

The Buffoon surrounds themselves with others equally focused on appearances people responding to status signals rather than to actual capability, to visible markers rather than to genuine value. They build networks as superficial as their own self-presentation, relationships founded on mutual performance rather than on authentic recognition.

The Alley Cat naturally connects with others capable of recognizing substance beyond appearance. They build relationships with those who assess value directly rather than through predetermined proxies. They create networks based on mutual capability recognition rather than on shared performance of predetermined success scripts.

This distinction explains why some people with impressive-looking networks struggle to activate those connections for actual value creation. Their relationships depend on maintained appearances rather than on recognized capability. When circumstances prevent continued performance, these superficial connections reveal their fundamental emptiness.

I've witnessed supposedly "successful" people with thousands of social media connections unable to mobilize genuine support during actual challenges. Meanwhile, those with fewer but more substantive relationships access meaningful assistance through authentic recognition rather than through maintained appearances.

The Alley Cat approaches networking through value demonstration rather than through appearance management. They build connections through capability recognition rather than through status signaling. They develop relationships based on mutual value creation rather than on shared performance of predetermined success scripts.

This approach requires courage the willingness to be assessed based on actual substance rather than on carefully curated appearances. Many people find this prospect terrifying because they've invested more in how they appear than in what they can actually create. They fear direct evaluation because they suspect their capability may not match their presentation.

The Alley Cat embraces this authentic assessment. They welcome being judged by results rather than by appearances because they've invested primarily in substance rather than in signals. They prefer relationships founded on genuine recognition rather than on mutual performance because they value actual connection over superficial association.

This preference shapes their entire approach to self-presentation. They don't adopt distinctive appearances to create specific impressions. They express authentic preferences without preoccupation with how those expressions might be perceived. They don't select possessions to signal particular associations. They choose based on genuine preferences and functional requirements.

In practice, this creates the visual juxtaposition that confuses the Buffoon. The luxury vehicle with the casually dressed driver. The successful entrepreneur in a t-shirt and jeans. The wealthy investor without visible status symbols. The prosperity that doesn't announce itself through standardized signals.

You can't judge these books by their covers. You must engage with their content directly. You must assess their value through actual substance rather than through superficial signaling. You must recognize capability through demonstration rather than through declaration.

That's precisely what makes the Alley Cat approach so powerful. It filters for relationships based on authentic recognition rather than on mutual performance. It attracts connections capable of assessing actual value rather than merely responding to familiar signals. It builds networks founded on genuine capability rather than on shared conformity to predetermined appearance expectations.

So when you see someone in casual clothes stepping out of a premium vehicle, or someone without conventional success markers creating extraordinary results, or someone whose appearance contradicts traditional prosperity associations, pay attention. You might be observing an Alley Cat whose substance exceeds their signaling, whose capability transcends their conformity, whose reality surpasses their appearance.

Don't judge these books by their covers. Read their actual content instead.

CHAPTER 10: LET YOUR ACCOMPLISHMENTS SAY HOLIER THAN

THOU, NOT YOUR ATTITUDE

I've seen it a thousand times. The wealthy executive who treats the waiter like garbage. The attractive woman who responds to basic courtesy with contempt. The successful business owner who dismisses young entrepreneurs without even glancing at their proposals. The luxury car driver who acts as if sharing the road is beneath them.

These people believe their external markers of success entitle them to treat others poorly. They've confused having things with being worthy. They've mistaken temporary advantages for inherent superiority.

In other words, they've become the Buffoon.

True Alley Cats understand a fundamental truth is that greatness never requires announcement. Real power never demands acknowledgment. Genuine value never needs external validation. If you have to tell people you're important through your attitude, you've already revealed that you're not.

Let me tell you about two types of people I've encountered while delivering food.

The first drives an entry-level luxury car they can barely afford. They live in an apartment complex with fancy amenities but paper-thin walls. When I arrive with their food, they barely make eye contact. They speak as if each word costs them something. They make sure I notice their watch, their phone, their clothes, all the props in their performance of success. They leave no tip.

The second lives in a modest house in an unassuming neighborhood. Their car is practical, perhaps even a few years old. When I arrive, they greet me by name. They ask how my day is going and actually listen to the answer. They thank me sincerely. They tip generously. Later, I discover they're worth millions, they own multiple businesses, investment properties, have genuine financial freedom.

The first person wants to be perceived as successful. The second person actually is successful. The difference is immediately apparent in how they treat others.

This principle extends beyond individual interactions. I've observed it in business settings throughout my career. The companies that constantly advertise their excellence usually deliver mediocrity. The professionals who continually emphasize their expertise typically offer ordinary results. The organizations that relentlessly promote their values often violate them in practice.

Meanwhile, true excellence speaks for itself. Genuine expertise demonstrates its value without declaration. Authentic values manifest in actions rather than announcements.

Consider two scenarios I've experienced.

In the first, I approached a successful investor about partnering on a real estate deal. His office was designed to intimidate with expensive artwork, elaborate furniture, strategic lighting to emphasize his position of power. Before I could finish explaining my proposal, he interrupted to tell me about his past successes, his connections, his brilliant insights. He made it clear that meeting with me was a favor he was graciously extending. He dismissed my proposal without truly considering it, explaining that someone at my level couldn't possibly understand the sophisticated strategies he employed.

In the second scenario, I met with another investor in a simple office with functional furniture. She listened carefully to my entire proposal, asked insightful questions, pointed out genuine flaws in my analysis, and suggested specific improvements. She shared relevant experiences without making them the focus of our discussion. She treated me as a potential peer rather than an inevitable inferior. Though she ultimately declined the specific deal, she offered to introduce me to others who might be interested and provided valuable advice that improved my next proposal.

The first investor needed his environment and attitude to convince me of his importance. The second investor's knowledge and behavior did that work for her.

The difference between these approaches reveals something profound about confidence. True confidence doesn't need to announce itself because it exists independent of others' acknowledgment. False confidence constantly seeks external validation because it lacks internal foundation.

The Buffoon in the Suit develops an arrogant attitude precisely because they're insecure about their actual value. They create an inflated persona to compensate for a deflated reality. They treat others poorly to create artificial elevation for themselves.

The Alley Cat has no need for such performances. Their accomplishments speak volumes while their attitudes remain humble. They understand that treating others with dignity costs nothing but creates everything like trust, respect, loyalty, opportunity.

I've applied this principle throughout my life, even when my circumstances were at their most challenging. When I was sleeping in my car and delivering food in Seattle, I maintained the same level of courtesy with everyone I encountered. I didn't allow my difficult situation to become an excuse for negative behavior.

This approach wasn't just morally correct, it was strategically advantageous. Those positive interactions eventually led to the $200 loan from Rance that helped me rebuild. They created connections that became partnerships. They established a reputation that opened doors when my financial situation couldn't.

Think about it pragmatically: if you're truly successful, what do you gain from treating others poorly? If you're genuinely attractive, what do you gain from responding to courtesy with contempt? If you're actually wealthy, what do you gain from flaunting it through arrogance?

The answer is nothing. You gain nothing. In fact, you lose potential allies, opportunities, and connections. You sacrifice strategic advantages for momentary ego gratification. You trade long-term prosperity for short-term power trips.

That's a terrible exchange rate. Only the Buffoon would consider it worthwhile.

Consider how this principle applies to appearance and presentation. I know people who spend enormous sums on designer clothes, luxury accessories, and status symbols while struggling to pay basic bills. Their external presentation screams success while their bank accounts whisper desperation.

Meanwhile, I know genuinely wealthy individuals who dress simply, drive modest vehicles, and maintain humble homes. Their resources are directed toward income-producing assets rather than status-signaling liabilities. They let their financial statements express their success rather than their outfits.

The first group needs their appearance to convince others of their worth because they lack substantive accomplishments. The second group lets their accomplishments speak for themselves while their appearance remains understated.

This doesn't mean successful people can't enjoy nice things. I drive luxury vehicles and appreciate quality. But there's a critical difference between enjoying prosperity you've earned and pretending to prosperity you haven't achieved. There's a fundamental distinction between quality as a preference and luxury as a personality.

The Buffoon uses external symbols to create the impression of success. The Alley Cat focuses on creating actual success, allowing appropriate symbols to follow naturally when they serve a purpose beyond impression management.

This principle becomes particularly important as you achieve genuine success. When you do attain wealth, power, or status, you face a critical choice: Will you use these advantages to elevate yourself above others, or will you use them to elevate others alongside you?

The Buffoon chooses the former, creating distance and distinction. The Alley Cat chooses the latter, creating connection and community. One approach leads to isolation despite prosperity; the other leads to meaningful impact beyond financial success.

I've encountered both paths in my journey. I've met wealthy individuals who use their resources primarily to emphasize the gap between themselves and "ordinary" people. They collect exclusive experiences, memberships, and possessions not for inherent enjoyment but for the separation these things create.

I've also met wealthy individuals who use their resources to create opportunity for others, to solve meaningful problems, to build bridges rather than barriers. They measure their success not by what they have but by what they enable.

The first group, despite their wealth, remains fundamentally poor spiritually and relationally impoverished regardless of financial prosperity. The second group experiences richness beyond financial measures their lives overflow with purpose, connection, and meaningful impact.

As you develop your own success, remember that your attitude often reveals more about you than your accomplishments ever could. It's not what you have but how you carry it that ultimately determines your character and legacy.

This applies regardless of your current circumstances. Whether you're struggling like I was in Seattle or succeeding beyond your initial goals, how you treat others remains the truest measure of who you are.

The provocatively dressed woman who responds to basic courtesy with contempt reveals her own insecurity, not her desirability. The wealthy person who treats service workers poorly demonstrates their own smallness, not their importance. The successful executive who dismisses young entrepreneurs exposes their own fear of replacement, not their superior judgment.

Let your work speak. Let your results testify. Let your accomplishments declare your value while your attitude communicates your character.

True Alley Cats don't need to tell the world they're special through arrogance, they show the world they're exceptional through achievement combined with humility. They don't use attitude as a shortcut to respect they haven't earned through action. They allow their consistent performance to create a reputation that speaks volumes while they remain approachable, humble, and kind.

After all, if you have to tell people you're important through your behavior, you've already revealed that you're not.

CHAPTER 12: WHEN AN ALLEY CAT SAYS IT, AN ALLEY CAT

MEANS IT

Words have become increasingly cheap in contemporary society. People make promises they have no intention of keeping. They express commitments they abandon at the first sign of inconvenience. They declare values they violate when adherence becomes challenging. They articulate principles they discard when circumstances change.

We've created a culture where speaking is disconnected from meaning, where declarations represent impression management rather than genuine commitment, where statements reflect desired perceptions rather than actual intentions.

The Buffoon participates enthusiastically in this disconnection. They say what sounds good in the moment without concern for subsequent follow-through. They make commitments based on immediate advantages without considering long-term implementation requirements. They express values that create favorable impressions without integrating those values into actual decisions.

The Alley Cat operates differently. When they speak, they mean exactly what they say. Not as performance, not as impression management, not as social positioning, but as genuine expression of actual intention that will be implemented regardless of convenience or changing circumstances.

This alignment between statement and meaning, between declaration and commitment, between expression and implementation creates a level of integrity increasingly rare in contemporary culture. It generates credibility that carefully crafted impressions can never match. It builds trust that strategic communication alone cannot establish.

I've maintained this principle throughout my life, even when adherence created short-term disadvantages or required uncomfortable honesty. When I tell someone I'll do something, they can consider it already done. When I express commitment to an objective, that commitment will be fulfilled regardless of obstacles. When I articulate a value, that value genuinely guides my decisions rather than merely enhancing my image.

This isn't self-righteous posturing. It's practical recognition that integrity creates alignment between words and meaning, between statements and intentions, between expressions and implementations. It also creates advantages exceeding any benefits from strategic misrepresentation or convenient flexibility.

Consider how this principle operates in various contexts.

In business relationships, the Buffoon makes commitments they can't fulfill, promises deadlines they can't meet, guarantees outcomes they can't ensure creating initially favorable impressions that inevitably dissolve when subsequent reality contradicts prior declarations. They generate short-term advantages through appealing misrepresentations that create long-term disadvantages through eroded credibility.

The Alley Cat makes only commitments they genuinely intend to fulfill, promises only deadlines they realistically expect to meet, guarantees only outcomes they can reasonably ensure sometimes creating less initially favorable impressions that consistently strengthen when subsequent reality confirms prior declarations. They generate sustainable advantages through accurate representations that build enduring credibility.

In personal relationships, the Buffoon expresses sentiments designed to create desired responses, declares feelings calculated to produce specific effects, articulates intentions shaped to generate particular impressions without genuine commitment to meaning behind these statements. They treat communication as performance rather than as authentic expression.

The Alley Cat expresses only sentiments they genuinely feel, declares only feelings they actually experience, articulates only intentions they truly maintain regardless of how these authentic expressions might be received initially. They treat communication as representation of reality rather than as manipulation of perception.

In self-development contexts, the Buffoon announces ambitious objectives without genuine commitment to required implementation, declares transformative intentions without realistic assessment of necessary actions, articulates impressive goals without honest evaluation of personal consistency capabilities and setting themselves up for inevitable disappointment when declarations exceed execution.

The Alley Cat announces only objectives they've genuinely committed to implementing, declares only intentions they've realistically assessed requirements for fulfilling, articulates only goals they've honestly evaluated consistency capabilities for achieving/creating foundation for sustainable progress through alignment between declaration and implementation.

This integrity between statement and meaning requires unusual discipline in contemporary culture, where strategic misrepresentation often provides immediate advantages exceeding short-term benefits of uncomfortable honesty. Telling people what they want to hear typically produces more favorable immediate responses than expressing accurate assessments that contradict desired narratives. Making impressive commitments usually generates more positive initial reactions than acknowledging realistic limitations that contradict preferred impressions.

Maintaining alignment between declaration and meaning despite these incentives demands genuine commitment to long-term credibility over short-term advantage, to sustainable trust over temporary favorability, to enduring integrity over momentary impression.

The Alley Cat maintains this commitment by applying specific principles to their communication:

1. They speak only after careful consideration of implementation capability. Before making statements, they assess whether expressed intentions can be fulfilled regardless of changing circumstances or unexpected challenges. They commit only to actions they're genuinely prepared to complete despite potential inconvenience or evolving conditions.
2. They recognize that silence represents valid option when integrity would require statements contradicting desired impressions or challenging recipients' preferences. Rather than choosing between misrepresentation and unproductive confrontation, they often select measured non-expression while maintaining internal clarity about actual reality.
3. They distinguish between speculative exploration and definitive commitment in their communication patterns, using clear linguistic markers to separate consideration from decision, possibility from intention, exploration from determination. They ensure recipients understand which statements represent definitive commitments versus tentative considerations.
4. They acknowledge changing assessments when new information genuinely alters previous conclusions rather than maintaining outdated positions for appearance consistency. They prioritize accuracy over perceived stability, updating expressed positions when underlying reality shifts while clearly communicating reasoning behind these adjustments.
5. They accept responsibility for implementation gaps when execution falls short of expressed intentions, viewing these instances as opportunities for realignment rather than as justifications for retroactive redefinition of initial commitments. They maintain integrity even when acknowledging shortfalls creates momentary discomfort.

Applying these principles creates extraordinary credibility over time. When an Alley Cat makes a commitment, people recognize that this statement represents genuine intention rather than mere impression management. When they express assessment, others understand that this declaration reflects honest evaluation rather than strategic positioning. When they articulate objection, recipients recognize that this expression represents actual concern rather than tactical maneuver.

This credibility generates practical advantages exceeding any benefits from strategic misrepresentation or convenient flexibility. People preferentially collaborate with those whose statements reliably reflect actual intentions. They preferentially trust information from sources whose declarations consistently align with subsequent realities. They preferentially engage with individuals whose expressions authentically represent underlying meanings.

When I was rebuilding after business setbacks, this established integrity created opportunities despite challenging external circumstances. People who knew me understood that my statements represented genuine intentions rather than desperate positioning. They recognized that my assessments reflected honest evaluation rather than wishful projection. They trusted that my commitments would be fulfilled regardless of difficulties or changing conditions.

This trust enabled critical relationships when conventional credentials or resources couldn't establish credibility. The $200 loan from Rance in Seattle came partly from recognition that my stated intentions for using those funds and my commitment to repayment represented genuine meaning rather than convenient declarations. Our connection formed through mutual recognition of this integrity despite brief acquaintance.

Maintaining this alignment between statement and meaning sometimes requires uncomfortable honesty when more appealing misrepresentation would create short-term advantages. It occasionally necessitates acknowledging limitations when exaggerated capabilities would generate preferred impressions. It sometimes demands declining commitments when accepting them would produce favorable immediate responses despite implementation impossibility.

These momentary discomforts represent investments in long-term credibility that consistently generate returns exceeding any temporary advantages from convenient misalignment between declaration and meaning. The Alley Cat accepts these short-term costs for sustainable long-term benefits created through established integrity.

This principle applies equally to interactions with yourself. The Buffoon lies to themselves as casually as they misrepresent reality to others. They make personal commitments they have no intention of fulfilling. They declare self-improvement objectives without genuine implementation plans. They express aspirational identities disconnected from actual behaviors.

The Alley Cat maintains integrity in internal dialogue with the same discipline applied to external communication. They make only personal commitments they genuinely intend to implement. They declare only self-improvement objectives aligned with realistic action plans. They express only identities connected to actual behaviors rather than merely to aspirational self-concepts.

This internal integrity creates psychological alignment that generates extraordinary implementation consistency. When you mean what you say even in private thoughts, you create foundation for sustained action regardless of external validation or accountability. Your own declarations represent genuine commitments rather than temporary inspirational statements disconnected from subsequent behavior.

Implementing this principle requires conscious attention to both statement and meaning. Ensuring alignment between what you express and what you genuinely intend, between what you declare and what you're genuinely committed to implementing, between what you articulate and what accurately represents your actual assessment.

This attention sometimes means saying less than you could, expressing fewer commitments than might create favorable impressions, articulating more measured assessments than might generate preferred responses. It occasionally requires explicitly distinguishing between definitive positions and speculative explorations, between certain commitments and tentative considerations, between established conclusions and developing perspectives.

The discipline required for maintaining this alignment exceeds capabilities of those primarily focused on impression management rather than on integrity establishment. The Buffoon inevitably sacrifices meaning alignment for preferred perception when circumstances create tension between these objectives. They instinctively prioritize advantageous impression over uncomfortable accuracy when situations force choosing between conflicting priorities.

The Alley Cat consistently prioritizes integrity over impression, meaning alignment over perception management, accurate representation over advantageous presentation. They understand that short-term advantages from strategic misrepresentation inevitably create long-term disadvantages through eroded credibility that momentary benefits from convenient flexibility ultimately produce sustained costs through diminished trust.

This prioritization doesn't mean ignoring strategic communication considerations or disregarding presentation impact. It means ensuring that strategic elements enhance rather than contradict underlying meaning, that presentation considerations clarify rather than distort actual intentions. It requires making foundations authentically aligned with expressed positions rather than merely creating appealing facades concealing contradictory realities.

When an Alley Cat says something, they mean exactly what they say. Not as performance. Not as positioning. Not as manipulation. But as genuine expression of actual intention that will be implemented regardless of convenience or changing circumstances.

In a world of increasingly meaningless words, this integrity becomes extraordinary competitive advantage creating credibility that carefully crafted impressions can never match, establishing trust that strategic communication alone cannot generate, building relationships that convenient misrepresentations inevitably undermine.

Which approach will you choose?

CHAPTER 13: YOU ARE NOT OWED ANYTHING YOU HAVEN'T

LENT TO SOMEONE ELSE FIRST

When I started working at that manufacturing plant for minimum wage, living in a hotel room with my family, my coworkers couldn't understand my approach. They'd watch me arrive at 2:00 AM to count inventory, stay until 2:00 PM creating systems, work harder than anyone had ever worked in that facility all for seven dollars and twenty-five cents an hour.

"Why are you killing yourself for this company?" they'd ask. "They don't pay you enough for all this extra work. You're making them money they're not giving you."

What they couldn't grasp was a fundamental principle that separates those who advance from those who remain stuck: You don't get paid for your worth until you've first demonstrated your worth. You can't demand what you haven't yet earned. You're not owed compensation for value you haven't yet created.

The Buffoon approaches relationships both professional and personal with an entitlement mindset. They believe they deserve respect before they've given it, loyalty before they've shown it, compensation before they've earned it. They think the world owes them opportunity, recognition, and reward simply because they exist or because they possess certain credentials.

The Alley Cat understands that everything valuable must be earned through contribution before it can be claimed through expectation. They lead with value creation rather than with demands for recognition. They demonstrate capability before requesting compensation. They show loyalty before expecting it in return.

This isn't about being naive or allowing exploitation. It's about recognizing that the universe operates on principles of reciprocity rather than entitlement. It's about understanding that investment precedes return, that contribution creates claims, that demonstration establishes desert.

At that manufacturing plant, I wasn't working for the company's benefit. I was working for my own future. I was building skills, creating systems, establishing reputation, and demonstrating capability that would eventually be recognized and rewarded. I was making deposits in a value account that I could later withdraw from with interest.

Those deposits didn't just include the tangible improvements I made to operations. They included the loyalty I showed when others were disloyal, the respect I demonstrated when others were disrespectful, the commitment I maintained when others were casual. I was lending positive energy to an environment that desperately needed it.

Within months, those investments began generating returns. Promotion. Substantial pay increases. Additional responsibilities. Recognition from management. Opportunities that never would have materialized if I'd insisted on being paid first before demonstrating value.

The greatest return wasn't immediate compensation. The greatest return was the capabilities I developed, the reputation I established, the confidence I gained from knowing I could transform dysfunctional situations through sheer determination and strategic effort. These assets couldn't be taken away when the company eventually closed due to corporate mismanagement.

This principle extends far beyond employment relationships. It applies to every form of human interaction where value exchange occurs.

In friendships, the person who demands loyalty without first demonstrating it rarely receives genuine commitment from others. The individual who expects support without offering it typically finds themselves isolated when they need assistance most. The friend who takes without giving eventually discovers their relationships are as shallow as their contributions.

Meanwhile, those who consistently show up for others, who offer support before needing it, who demonstrate loyalty before requiring it, build networks of genuine relationships that provide meaningful support throughout their lives.

In romantic relationships, the person who demands love without giving it, who expects commitment without demonstrating it, who requires trust without earning it, typically creates relationships based on transaction rather than on genuine connection. They approach partnership as extraction rather than as mutual contribution.

Those who lead with love, who demonstrate commitment before demanding it, who build trust through consistent action rather than through requirements, create relationships that strengthen under pressure rather than dissolving at the first sign of challenge.

In business contexts, the employee who demands promotion before proving competence, who expects compensation increases before demonstrating additional value, who requires recognition before contributing beyond minimum requirements, typically remains stuck in positions that reflect their contribution level rather than their expectation level.

Meanwhile, those who consistently exceed expectations, who solve problems without being asked, who create value before seeking compensation, typically find opportunities pursuing them rather than having to chase opportunities themselves.

This principle doesn't mean accepting permanent under compensation or allowing chronic exploitation. It means understanding the proper sequence: contribution before compensation, demonstration before demand, investment before return. It means recognizing that leading with value creation establishes foundation for legitimate claims that leading with expectations never can.

When I was sleeping in my car in Seattle, I could have approached potential partners and investors with demands based on my past successes, my experience, my need for assistance. I could have emphasized what others should do for me rather than what I could contribute to mutually beneficial arrangements.

Instead, I led with what I could offer. Even with minimal resources, I focused on how I could create value for others rather than on how they could solve my problems. I approached Rance not as someone seeking charity but as someone capable of generating returns on investment through demonstrated capability and reliable character.

This approach, leading with contribution rather than with need created the foundation for a relationship that became genuinely beneficial for both parties. Rance didn't help me because he felt sorry for my circumstances; he partnered with me because he recognized potential for mutual benefit based on demonstrated capability rather than on asserted entitlement.

The same principle applies to developing respect in any environment. You can't demand respect; you can only earn it through consistent demonstration of worthy behavior. You can't require others to treat you well; you can only influence that treatment by consistently treating others well yourself.

Respect flows to those who first show respect. Loyalty gravitates toward those who first demonstrate loyalty. Trust develops around those who first prove trustworthy. This isn't just moral philosophy, it's practical psychology that determines who receives what they seek versus who remains frustrated by what they expect but never obtain.

The Buffoon misunderstands this dynamic completely. They believe respect should automatically accompany their position, credentials, or apparent achievements. They think loyalty should flow toward them because of who they are rather than because of what they consistently do. They expect trust based on their claims rather than on their demonstrated reliability.

When these expectations aren't met, the Buffoon typically responds with resentment, blame, or demands for what they believe they deserve. They might become indignant about lack of recognition, bitter about insufficient appreciation, or angry about inadequate compensation. They externalize responsibility for outcomes they internally control through their own contribution patterns.

The Alley Cat approaches these same situations by examining their own contribution level before evaluating others' response patterns. When respect seems lacking, they assess whether they've consistently demonstrated respectful behavior. When loyalty feels absent, they evaluate whether they've reliably shown loyalty themselves. When trust appears missing, they examine whether they've consistently proven trustworthy.

This internal focus doesn't mean accepting inappropriate treatment or tolerating genuine exploitation. It means recognizing that the most reliable path to receiving what you want involves first giving what you want to receive. It means understanding that influence flows through example more effectively than through expectation.

At the manufacturing plant, I didn't just work harder than others I worked differently. I treated everyone with respect regardless of their position or background. I showed up consistently regardless of how I felt. I solved problems without waiting for permission or instruction. I contributed to collective success rather than just pursuing individual advancement.

These behaviors weren't calculated to manipulate specific responses. They reflected genuine commitment to being the type of person I wanted to work with, creating the type of environment I wanted to work in, contributing to the type of success I wanted to be part of.

The returns came naturally from this approach. Not because I demanded them, but because the value I created became undeniable and the positive energy I contributed became indispensable. People began seeking my input because I consistently offered valuable perspectives. Management began trusting my judgment because I consistently demonstrated sound decision-making. Opportunities began pursuing me because I consistently created value beyond my immediate responsibilities.

This is how the principle works in practice: you lend value to your environment through consistent positive contribution, and that environment eventually returns value to you with interest. But the investment must come first. The demonstration must precede the demand. The contribution must establish the foundation for legitimate expectation.

Understanding this sequence prevents the chronic frustration that comes from expecting returns on investments you haven't yet made. It eliminates the resentment that develops when you demand compensation for value you haven't yet created. It removes the confusion that results from expecting respect you haven't yet earned, loyalty you haven't yet demonstrated, or trust you haven't yet built.

Instead, it creates clear pathway to obtaining what you want: become the type of person who naturally attracts those outcomes through consistent positive contribution. Give what you want to receive. Demonstrate what you want to experience. Create what you want to claim.

The manufacturing plant experience taught me that this approach works regardless of starting circumstances. I began with minimal formal qualifications, no relevant experience, and every reason to expect limited opportunity. But by leading with maximum contribution rather than with minimum expectations, I created advancement that credentials alone never could have generated.

This doesn't mean working without appropriate compensation or accepting exploitative conditions indefinitely. It means understanding that negotiating power comes from demonstrated value rather than from asserted entitlement. It means recognizing that the strongest position for claiming what you deserve comes from first providing what others need.

When you consistently contribute beyond expectations, you eventually gain leverage to set terms rather than merely accepting them. When you reliably solve problems others can't solve, you create demand for your capabilities that enables premium compensation. When you demonstrate consistent loyalty and respect, you build relationships that provide support and opportunity exceeding anything you could demand through entitlement.

The Buffoon never grasps this dynamic. They remain trapped in cycles of expectation without contribution, demand without demonstration, requirement without reciprocity. They wonder why their careers stagnate, their relationships disappoint, their opportunities remain limited and not once recognizing that they're trying to withdraw from accounts they haven't funded.

The Alley Cat understands that life operates like a bank: you must make deposits before you can make withdrawals. The larger your deposits of value, respect, loyalty, and positive contribution, the larger the returns available when you need to draw on those investments.

Which approach will you choose? Will you lead with expectations and wonder why they're rarely met? Or will you lead with contributions and discover that returns exceed anything you could have demanded through entitlement alone?

You are not owed anything you haven't first lent to someone else. But when you consistently lend value, respect, loyalty, and positive energy to your environment, that environment typically returns far more than you initially invested.

That's not just moral philosophy, it's practical strategy for creating the life you want.

CHAPTER 14: IF YOU CAN SELL DRUGS SUCCESSFULLY, YOU CAN RUN A BUSINESS SUCCESSFULLY

This statement might shock some readers, but it represents a fundamental truth about business capability that conventional thinking refuses to acknowledge: the skills required for successful drug dealing are essentially identical to those required for legitimate business success.

Let me be absolutely clear: I'm not advocating drug dealing. I'm not encouraging illegal activity. I'm not glorifying criminal behavior. What I'm doing is recognizing that the strategic thinking, customer psychology understanding, risk management, supply chain coordination, and financial discipline required for successful illegal enterprises are precisely the same capabilities that create legitimate business success.

The difference isn't capability, it's application.

When I was twelve years old and got involved in dealing crack cocaine, I was forced to develop skills that most MBA programs never teach. I had to understand market dynamics in real time. I had to assess customer psychology without formal training. I had to manage supply chains without textbooks. I had to coordinate financial flows without accounting systems. I had to evaluate risks without business insurance.

I learned to read people quickly and accurately. I developed capability to assess market demand and adjust supply accordingly. I understood pricing strategies that maximized profit while maintaining customer loyalty. I mastered inventory management in environments where mistakes had serious consequences. I built customer relationships that generated repeat business and referrals.

These skills weren't theoretical knowledge acquired in classroom settings. They were practical capabilities developed through direct experience where mistakes created immediate consequences and success required genuine competence rather than merely impressive credentials.

The Buffoon can't acknowledge this reality because it contradicts their belief that success comes primarily through formal education, conventional credentials, and socially approved pathways. They can't admit that someone from a disadvantaged background who never attended business school might possess capabilities exceeding those of formally trained professionals.

The Alley Cat recognizes that capability transcends circumstances. They understand that survival in challenging environments often develops skills more valuable than anything acquired through conventional education. They realize that practical experience in high-stakes situations creates competencies that theoretical knowledge alone can never match.

This isn't about romanticizing difficult circumstances or suggesting that illegal activity represents optimal preparation for legitimate success. It's about recognizing that capability development isn't limited to conventional channels and that skills transfer across contexts regardless of their original acquisition environment.

Consider the specific capabilities developed through successful drug dealing:

Market Analysis: Understanding customer demand patterns, identifying underserved segments, recognizing market opportunities, assessing competitive positioning. These skills apply directly to legitimate business market research and strategic positioning.

Customer Psychology: Reading human motivation, predicting behavior patterns, understanding decision-making processes, building relationships that generate loyalty and repeat business. These capabilities translate directly to sales, marketing, and customer service excellence.

Financial Management: Managing cash flow, tracking profitability, controlling expenses, reinvesting proceeds strategically. These skills form the foundation of business financial competence regardless of industry or scale.

Risk Assessment: Evaluating potential threats, developing contingency plans, making decisions under uncertainty, managing downside exposure while pursuing upside opportunity. These capabilities prove essential for successful entrepreneurship in any context.

Supply Chain Coordination: Managing procurement, coordinating delivery, ensuring quality control, optimizing distribution networks. These skills apply directly to operations management in legitimate businesses.

Negotiation: Securing favorable terms, resolving conflicts, building mutually beneficial arrangements, maintaining relationships despite disagreements. These capabilities prove valuable in every business context.

Stress Management: Performing effectively under pressure, making clear decisions during crises, maintaining composure when stakes are high. These skills become essential for leadership in challenging business environments.

The specific context where these capabilities were developed doesn't diminish their transferability to legitimate applications. A skill is a skill regardless of where it was acquired. Competence transcends circumstances. Capability transfers across contexts.

When I eventually transitioned to legitimate business activities, I didn't have to learn these fundamental capabilities I just had to apply them in different environments with different constraints and different consequences. The strategic thinking remained the same. The psychology remained identical. The financial principles remained constant.

This transferability explains why some people from challenging backgrounds can rapidly build successful legitimate businesses while others with impressive formal qualifications struggle with basic entrepreneurial requirements. The former have developed practical capabilities through direct experience; the latter have acquired theoretical knowledge without corresponding competence.

It also explains why some individuals with questionable backgrounds can transform into extraordinarily successful legitimate entrepreneurs. They're not starting from zero, they're redirecting established capabilities toward legal objectives. They're not learning new skills; they're applying existing competencies in different contexts.

My uncle taught me to deal drugs because he recognized that young people could operate "under the radar" more effectively than adults, generating higher profits with lower risk. This is a lesson in market positioning, identifying competitive advantages based on unique characteristics that applies directly to legitimate business strategy.

He showed me how to process cocaine into crack because purchasing base product and adding value through processing generated higher margins than simply reselling someone else's finished product. This lesson in value-added manufacturing and profit margin optimization applies to countless legitimate business models.

He taught me to establish regular customers who would return repeatedly rather than focusing only on one-time transactions. This lesson in customer lifetime value and relationship building forms the foundation of sustainable business success in any industry.

These weren't lessons in criminal behavior but they were lessons in business fundamentals taught within a criminal context. The specific application was illegal, but the underlying principles were identical to those that drive legitimate business success.

The challenge was recognizing this transferability and having the courage to redirect these capabilities toward legal objectives. This required overcoming the external skepticism of society's assumption that criminal capability can't translate into legitimate success or internal conditioning that suggested legal opportunities weren't accessible to someone with my background.

Both obstacles proved false. The capabilities developed through challenging circumstances proved extraordinarily valuable in legitimate business contexts. The assumption that conventional paths represent the only routes to success proved incorrect. The belief that background determines destiny proved limiting rather than realistic.

When I started building legitimate businesses, I applied the same market analysis skills I'd developed selling drugs. I used the same customer psychology understanding. I implemented the same financial management disciplines. I employed the same risk assessment frameworks. I utilized the same relationship building approaches.

The results validated this transferability. Businesses I built using these redirected capabilities consistently outperformed those created by individuals with conventional business education but limited practical experience. The strategic thinking proved more valuable than theoretical knowledge. The practical competence proved more effective than credentialed expertise.

This doesn't mean criminal experience represents optimal business preparation. Legal pathways for developing these same capabilities obviously exist and typically involve fewer risks and negative consequences. But it does mean that capability acquired through any source can be redirected toward legitimate objectives when properly applied.

The key insight is recognizing that skills transfer across contexts regardless of their original acquisition environment. Street intelligence translates to business intelligence. Survival skills transform into entrepreneurial capabilities. Adaptive thinking proves valuable regardless of application domain.

This principle applies beyond criminal contexts to any challenging environment that develops practical capabilities through direct experience. Military veterans often possess leadership, planning, and execution skills that translate directly to business management. Athletes frequently develop discipline, performance optimization, and competitive strategies applicable to entrepreneurial success. Artists typically possess creativity, problem-solving, and aesthetic capabilities valuable in numerous business contexts.

The specific source matters less than the competence developed. The particular circumstances matter less than the capabilities acquired. The original application matters less than the transferability potential.

For those who have acquired capabilities through unconventional or challenging circumstances, this recognition can be liberating. Your background doesn't disqualify you from legitimate success but it may have prepared you better than conventional pathways ever could. Your experience isn't a barrier to overcome, it's an asset to leverage. Your skills aren't limited to their original context, they're transferable to legal applications that can generate extraordinary results.

For those who have followed conventional paths exclusively, this recognition should be humbling. Don't underestimate capabilities that don't come with formal credentials. Don't dismiss competence that wasn't acquired through approved channels. Don't assume that unconventional backgrounds represent disadvantages rather than different types of preparation.

The most successful teams combine diverse experience bases that include both conventional expertise and unconventional competence. The most effective businesses leverage capabilities regardless of their original acquisition source. The most profitable ventures recognize skill and competence wherever they're found rather than only where they're expected.

If you've developed business capabilities through challenging circumstances either legal or otherwise you should recognize that these skills represent genuine assets that can be redirected toward legitimate objectives. Don't allow others' assumptions about your background to limit your assessment of your own potential. Don't let conventional expectations constrain unconventional capabilities.

If you can successfully navigate complex markets, manage difficult relationships, coordinate resource flows, assess risks accurately, and generate profits consistently then regardless of context you possess fundamental business competencies that can create success in legal enterprises.

The question isn't whether your capabilities are legitimate, it's whether you'll apply them legitimately. The issue isn't whether your skills are valuable, it's whether you'll deploy them valuably. The challenge isn't whether you can succeed, it's whether you'll choose to succeed legally.

Capability is capability. Competence is competence. Skills are skills.

Their value doesn't depend on their source but only on their application.

CHAPTER 15: NO ONE CAN STOP ALLEY CATS, THEY CAN ONLY

BE STOPPED BY THEMSELVES

Throughout my life, I've faced obstacles that would have permanently derailed most people. Business failures that wiped out years of effort. Legal challenges that could have ended everything. Financial setbacks that left me sleeping in cars and truck yards. Personal betrayals that destroyed partnerships and relationships.

Each time, people around me expected these circumstances to define permanent limitations. They assumed these setbacks would create lasting barriers. They believed these challenges represented endpoints rather than transition points. They were wrong.

Not because the obstacles weren't real or significant, but because they fundamentally misunderstood the nature of Alley Cat resilience. External circumstances can create temporary challenges, but they cannot create permanent limitations unless internal surrender allows them to do so.

The difference between those who recover from setbacks and those who remain defined by them isn't resources, connections, or even opportunity. It's internal response to external pressure. It's the fundamental choice between accepting limitations or finding pathways around them. It's the decision to be shaped by circumstances or to shape circumstances through persistent action.

The Buffoon allows external setbacks to become internal limitations. When they face business failures, they conclude they're not entrepreneurial material. When they encounter financial difficulties, they accept reduced expectations as permanent reality. When they experience relationship betrayals, they decide trust is too risky to attempt again. They internalize temporary circumstances as permanent constraints.

The Alley Cat treats external setbacks as temporary obstacles requiring creative solutions. Business failures become learning experiences that improve future strategies. Financial difficulties become motivation to develop new income streams. Relationship betrayals become filters that improve partner selection criteria. They refuse to internalize temporary circumstances as permanent limitations.

This distinction explains why some people remain stuck for years after single setbacks while others rebuild repeatedly from similar or worse circumstances. The difference isn't external, it's internal. It's not what happens to them, it's how they respond to what happens to them.

When my business collapsed and I found myself homeless in Seattle, the external circumstances appeared devastating. No stable housing. No reliable transportation.

Minimal resources. No local network. No obvious pathway forward. Most observers would have concluded that recovery would require external assistance or extraordinary external opportunity.

But the most significant factor determining eventual outcome wasn't external, it was internal. It was my refusal to accept homelessness as permanent condition rather than temporary circumstance. It was my commitment to rebuild regardless of current constraints. It was my determination to create solutions rather than simply endure problems.

The pathway forward didn't require external rescue or extraordinary external opportunity. It required internal commitment to persistent action despite discouraging circumstances. It demanded maintaining belief in eventual success despite current evidence suggesting otherwise. It necessitated taking daily actions aligned with long-term objectives despite short-term futility.

That $200 loan from Rance represented catalyst rather than salvation. The critical element wasn't the external resource, it was internal readiness to leverage any available opportunity for maximum progress. The money mattered, but the mindset mattered more. The assistance helped, but the approach proved decisive.

This dynamic repeats across every significant challenge I've faced. Legal difficulties created external pressure but couldn't force internal surrender. Financial setbacks generated external constraints but couldn't dictate internal response. Business failures produced external consequences but couldn't determine internal commitment to eventual recovery.

In each case, the primary determining factor wasn't external circumstances but internal response to those circumstances. External events created temporary challenges; internal choices determined permanent outcomes.

The Alley Cat understands this fundamental truth: the greatest threats are internal rather than external. Self-doubt poses more danger than market conditions. Surrender represents greater risk than competition. Internal limitation creates more barriers than external obstacles.

This doesn't mean external circumstances don't matter. They absolutely do. Market conditions, legal constraints, financial resources, available opportunities. All of these factors influence possible pathways and required strategies. But they don't determine ultimate outcomes unless internal choices allow them to do so.

Consider how this principle operates across different domains.

In business, external market downturns create challenges for everyone, but they don't affect everyone equally. Some companies collapse during difficult conditions while others emerge stronger. Some entrepreneurs abandon efforts during setbacks while others discover opportunities hidden within challenges. The external circumstances are identical; the internal responses differ dramatically.

The companies and entrepreneurs who thrive during difficult conditions share common characteristics: they refuse to accept external circumstances as permanent limitations, they adapt strategies rather than abandoning objectives, they view obstacles as temporary barriers requiring creative solutions rather than as permanent constraints requiring acceptance.

In personal development, external disadvantages, limited formal education, challenging family backgrounds, and resource constraints affect starting conditions but don't determine final destinations. Some individuals use these disadvantages as excuses for permanent limitation while others use them as motivation for extraordinary achievement.

Those who overcome disadvantageous starting conditions consistently demonstrate specific internal characteristics: they refuse to accept background as destiny, they take responsibility for current circumstances regardless of past influences, they focus on available options rather than on missing advantages.

In relationships, external betrayals, disappointments, and conflicts affect everyone who engages authentically with others. Some people withdraw permanently after negative experiences while others learn to engage more effectively. Some become cynical and isolated while others become wiser and more selective.

Those who build satisfying relationships despite past disappointments share internal approaches: they refuse to allow past experiences to dictate future possibilities, they learn from difficulties without becoming defined by them, they maintain openness while improving judgment.

The pattern remains consistent across domains: external circumstances create conditions, but internal responses determine outcomes. External events generate challenges, but internal choices determine whether those challenges become permanent limitations or temporary obstacles.

Understanding this distinction changes everything about how you approach difficulties. Instead of asking "Why is this happening to me?" you ask "How can I respond to create positive outcomes?" Instead of focusing on external factors beyond your control, you concentrate on internal factors within your influence. Instead of accepting circumstances as destiny, you treat them as current conditions requiring strategic response.

This shift doesn't eliminate external challenges or make them less significant. It redirects attention toward elements you can actually influence rather than elements you can only endure. It focuses energy on response strategies rather than on circumstance analysis. It emphasizes capability development rather than situation lamentation.

The Alley Cat approaches every setback with this internal focus. When businesses fail, they analyze decision-making processes rather than just market conditions. When relationships disappoint, they examine selection criteria and interaction patterns rather than just other people's behavior. When financial difficulties arise, they evaluate spending decisions and income strategies rather than just economic conditions.

This internal focus doesn't mean accepting responsibility for everything that occurs but some external events are genuinely beyond individual influence. It means taking responsibility for response to everything that occurs since response is always within individual control regardless of external circumstances.

When I faced legal challenges stemming from business dealings gone wrong, I couldn't control prosecution decisions, court procedures, or ultimate outcomes. But I could control how I responded to these circumstances. I could choose to learn from mistakes rather than just endure consequences. I could decide to maintain long-term perspective rather than succumb to short-term pressure. I could commit to building better systems rather than just accepting current limitations.

These internal choices didn't eliminate external challenges or guarantee specific outcomes. But they ensured that whatever outcomes emerged would contribute to long-term improvement rather than permanent limitation. They transformed unavoidable difficulties into voluntary development opportunities.

This transformation requires specific internal disciplines:

Refusing victim mentality: Recognizing that past influences don't determine current capabilities or future possibilities. Accepting that current circumstances represent starting points rather than permanent constraints. Taking responsibility for response patterns regardless of external triggers.

Maintaining problem-solving orientation: Approaching obstacles as puzzles requiring creative solutions rather than as barriers requiring acceptance. Focusing on available options rather than on missing resources. Emphasizing action possibilities rather than action limitations.

Preserving long-term perspective: Treating current difficulties as temporary phases rather than permanent conditions. Maintaining belief in eventual progress despite immediate evidence suggesting otherwise. Making decisions based on desired destinations rather than current positions.

Developing adaptive strategies: Adjusting approaches based on changing circumstances rather than abandoning objectives. Learning from setbacks rather than being defined by them. Using obstacles as information for improving methods rather than as justification for reducing goals.

Building incremental momentum: Taking small positive actions consistently rather than waiting for major opportunities. Creating forward progress regardless of pace. Maintaining movement despite temporary reversals.

These disciplines don't guarantee external success or eliminate external challenges. They ensure that internal capability continues developing regardless of external circumstances. They maintain forward progress despite temporary obstacles. They prevent external setbacks from becoming permanent internal limitations.

The most important recognition is this: every significant limitation you'll ever face will ultimately be internal rather than external. External circumstances create temporary challenges; internal choices determine permanent outcomes. External events may slow your progress, but they cannot stop it unless you allow them to do so.

You can only be stopped by yourself. Everyone else can only create temporary obstacles that require creative solutions. External circumstances can only generate challenges that demand adaptive responses. Other people can only create difficulties that test internal commitment rather than eliminate external possibilities.

This understanding places ultimate responsibility exactly where it belongs: with you. Not with circumstances. Not with other people. Not with external conditions beyond your control. With your internal response to whatever circumstances, people, and conditions you encounter.

That responsibility represents burden and liberation simultaneously. Burden because you cannot blame external factors for permanent limitations. Liberation because external factors cannot create permanent limitations without your internal permission.

No one can stop you. They can only challenge you. Challenges either strengthen capability or reveal its absence, they never eliminate possibility unless internal surrender allows them to do so.

Which will you choose? External focus that emphasizes what you cannot control, or internal focus that develops what you can influence? Victim mentality that accepts limitations imposed by circumstances, or problem-solving orientation that creates solutions despite obstacles?

The choice is yours. No one can make it except you.

CHAPTER 16: ACTION ONLY COMES FROM ACTION

One of the most dangerous misconceptions in modern society is the belief that preparation leads to action. That planning leads to execution. That thinking about something leads to doing something. The uncomfortable truth is this: Action only comes from action.

Not from thinking about action. Not from planning action. Not from discussing action. Not from researching action. Not from getting ready for action. Only from action itself.

I've watched countless people spend years "getting ready" to start businesses they never launch. I've seen innumerable "entrepreneurs" perfect business plans for ventures that never materialize. I've observed endless "preparation" that never culminates in actual performance.

These are the Buffoons in Suits. They are people who mistake motion for progress, activity for achievement, and preparation for performance.

Meanwhile, Alley Cats understand a fundamental principle: momentum can only be created through movement. The first step doesn't come from thinking about stepping; it comes from moving your foot forward, however imperfectly.

When I got that $200 loan from Rance in Seattle, I didn't spend it on courses about business. I didn't invest it in seminars about success. I didn't use it to buy books about wealth building.

I immediately put it into action. I used it to solve immediate problems that were preventing forward motion. I created momentum through direct, immediate action, however small.

That small action led to slightly larger action, which led to more substantial action, which eventually led to significant results. None of it would have happened if I'd used that $200 to "prepare" rather than to act.

This principle became clear to me during my time at the manufacturing plant. When I first arrived, I found most employees standing around talking about what needed to be done. They had meetings about inefficiencies. They had discussions about problems. They created reports about issues. Nothing was actually happening.

Instead of joining these conversations, I simply started working. I moved from station to station, building products, solving problems as I encountered them, improving processes through direct experience rather than theoretical analysis.

The result? I single-handedly produced more than entire shifts of workers who were "preparing" to be productive.

This wasn't because I was inherently more capable. It was because I understood that production comes from producing, not from talking about producing. Results come from action, not from analysis.

The Buffoon mentality says: "I need to get all my ducks in a row before I start."

The Alley Cat mentality says: "I'll start with the ducks I have and collect more as I go."

One leads to perpetual preparation; the other leads to actual progress.

Think about the most successful people you know personally. Not celebrities you've read about, but actual humans whose lives you've observed directly. I guarantee they share one common characteristic: they take consistent action without requiring perfect conditions.

They start businesses before they feel "ready." They make offers before they're certain of acceptance. They create opportunities through direct action rather than waiting for opportunities to be presented.

This approach appears risky to the Buffoon mindset. After all, what if you take action before you're fully prepared? What if you make mistakes that could have been avoided with more research? What if you fail because you moved too quickly?

These fears sound reasonable, but they're based on a fundamental misconception: the idea that additional preparation significantly reduces risk.

In reality, the opposite is often true. The longer you wait to take action, the higher the risk becomes. Markets change. Opportunities disappear. Motivation fades. Resources deplete. The perfect conditions you're waiting for never materialize, and the preparation you're accumulating becomes increasingly irrelevant to evolving circumstances.

The Alley Cat understands that the greatest risk isn't taking imperfect action; it's taking no action at all.

When I decided to start delivering food to rebuild after business setbacks, I didn't wait until I had a perfect vehicle or an optimized strategy. I started immediately on foot as necessary, using public transportation when available, figuring out the most efficient routes through direct experience rather than theoretical planning.

Was this approach perfect? Of course not. I made countless mistakes. I wasted time on inefficient deliveries. I accepted orders that barely covered my costs.

But through this imperfect action, I generated immediate income. I learned the business from the inside. I discovered opportunities invisible from the sidelines. I built relationships that created additional possibilities.

Most importantly, I created momentum that carried me forward into progressively better circumstances. That momentum would never have developed if I'd waited until conditions were ideal or my strategy was perfect.

This principle applies universally, from starting businesses to developing relationships to improving health. Action creates results. Everything else is just preparation for action that often never occurs.

Consider fitness. The Buffoon approaches physical transformation by researching optimal workout plans, purchasing perfect equipment, scheduling ideal training times, and discussing effective strategies.

The Alley Cat simply starts moving. Today. With whatever is available. Even if that means basic bodyweight exercises in a hotel room. Even if that means walking when running would be more efficient. Even if that means improvised equipment instead of perfect machines.

Six months later, the Buffoon is still perfecting their approach while the Alley Cat has already transformed their body through consistent, imperfect action.

This isn't about being reckless. It's about recognizing that perfect conditions are an illusion that prevents progress. It's about understanding that action itself reveals what works and what doesn't far more effectively than theoretical analysis.

When I was rebuilding my business network after setbacks, I didn't wait until I had impressive business cards, a perfect pitch, or ideal introductions. I started conversations with whoever was in front of me. I created connections through direct engagement rather than strategic positioning.

Many of these conversations led nowhere. Some created modest opportunities. A few developed into significant partnerships. But none of them would have happened if I'd waited until conditions were perfect.

The Buffoon mindset says: "I'll act when I feel confident."

The Alley Cat mindset says: "I'll become confident through action."

One waits for an emotional state that never arrives autonomously; the other creates that emotional state through direct experience. This principle becomes particularly important when facing challenging circumstances. When you're struggling financially, the natural tendency is to retreat, to wait until conditions improve before taking significant action. This is precisely the opposite of what creates transformation.

When I was sleeping in my car in Seattle, I could have reasonably concluded that conditions weren't right for rebuilding. I could have waited until I had stable housing, reliable transportation, and adequate resources before pursuing meaningful opportunities.

Instead, I recognized that these improved conditions would only come through immediate action, however limited. I used the circumstances I had rather than waiting for the circumstances I wanted. I created momentum through direct engagement with whatever was available.

The key insight is understanding that action generates its own energy. Movement creates momentum. Progress produces motivation. Each step forward, however small, makes the next step easier and more obvious.

This is why successful people often seem to have abundant energy while unsuccessful people complain about lacking motivation. The successful people aren't naturally more energetic they've learned to generate energy through action rather than waiting for energy to arrive before taking action.

When you're not sure what to do, do something. When you don't have perfect information, act on the information you have. When conditions aren't ideal, work with the conditions available. When resources are limited, maximize what you possess rather than lamenting what you lack.

The action doesn't need to be perfect. It doesn't need to be comprehensive. It doesn't need to solve every problem or address every concern. It just needs to move you forward, however incrementally, toward your desired outcome.

That movement will reveal information, create opportunities, generate resources, and produce momentum that static preparation can never match. Each action will inform better actions. Each step will illuminate next steps. Each forward movement will build capacity for faster, more effective future movement.

The Buffoon waits for perfect conditions that never arrive. The Alley Cat creates better conditions through imperfect action that eventually produces perfect results. Action only comes from action. Not from intention. Not from preparation. Not from perfect conditions. Not from complete confidence. Only from the decision to move forward with whatever you have, wherever you are, however you can.

Start today. Start now. Start with whatever is available. The momentum you create will carry you toward the resources, opportunities, and circumstances you need to achieve your larger vision. That momentum only comes from movement. And movement only comes from moving.

Action only comes from action.

CHAPTER 17: BELIEF IN A STRANGER

Sometimes the most transformative force in your life comes from someone you've never met in person, someone who has no obligation to care about your success, someone who gains nothing from your transformation except the satisfaction of helping another human being rise.

This chapter explores both the extraordinary benefits and potential dangers of placing belief in strangers. Those unexpected mentors who appear when you need guidance most, who see potential in you that others have missed, who invest their time and wisdom in your development despite having no personal stake in your outcome.

I experienced this phenomenon during one of the darkest periods of my life. I was living in government housing, feeling trapped in circumstances that seemed to offer no legitimate exit. The only way I could see to generate income was selling drugs. Not because I wanted to, but because it appeared to be the only option available in my environment.

What I really wanted was to produce music. That was my passion, my dream, my true calling. But dreams don't pay rent when you're living in poverty. Dreams don't put food on the table when opportunities seem nonexistent. Dreams don't solve immediate problems when survival takes priority over aspiration.

Then I met someone online who would fundamentally change my perspective on what was possible.

This stranger was someone I'd never met in person, someone who owed me nothing, someone who had every reason to focus on their own objectives rather than investing in mine but began providing me with encouragement, wisdom, and most importantly, a different way of seeing my circumstances.

They didn't offer me money. They didn't provide material assistance. They didn't solve my immediate problems. Instead, they gave me something far more valuable: they helped me see possibility where I'd only seen limitation. They showed me pathways where I'd only seen dead ends. They demonstrated through their own transformation that extraordinary change was possible from ordinary starting points.

I watched this person go from zero to having substantial resources. I observed them transition from isolation to networking with people whose names I recognized from celebrity culture. I witnessed them build something significant from nothing more than vision, commitment, and strategic action. Most importantly, they consistently told me that I could do the same thing.

"It starts with belief," they would say. They didn't just talk about belief, they demonstrated it. They believed in me when I wasn't sure I believed in myself. They saw potential in me that I couldn't yet recognize. They invested time in my development when no one else was paying attention.

Here's what made this relationship truly transformative: they didn't just encourage me, they educated me. They didn't just motivate me, they mentored me. They didn't just inspire me, they informed me about realities I hadn't understood.

When I initially approached our relationship with a handout mindset and hoping they might provide shortcuts or direct assistance. They quickly reshaped my thinking. They showed me the downsides and pitfalls of expecting others to solve problems I needed to solve myself. They made me understand that without a plan, any handout would only be consumed rather than invested. They taught me that dependency, even on well-meaning assistance, creates weakness rather than strength.

They shifted me from a consumer mindset to a merchant mindset. They helped me see that time was my most valuable resource because of everything I could accomplish with it if I approached it strategically. They showed me how to think differently about debt, about opportunity, about the relationship between effort and outcome.

Most importantly, they constantly warned me against seeking external validation. They emphasized that believing in myself was all I needed and if it helped, they definitely believed in me too. That combination of personal responsibility and external support created fuel that continues powering my efforts today.

The knowledge they shared covered so many different areas and provided so many alternative ways of looking at situations that I can never fully repay them. I'm forever grateful for their investment in my development, even though they gained nothing tangible from helping me succeed.

This experience taught me both the extraordinary benefits and potential dangers of believing in strangers.

The Benefits:

Strangers often see your potential more clearly than people close to you because they're not influenced by your history, your past mistakes, or preconceived notions about your limitations. They evaluate you based on present capability rather than past performance. They judge potential rather than pattern.

Strangers who choose to invest in your development typically do so because they genuinely recognize something valuable in you. They're not motivated by obligation, guilt, or manipulation. They're responding to authentic recognition of your potential. This makes their encouragement particularly meaningful and their insights particularly valuable.

Strangers can provide perspectives unavailable within your current environment. They bring external viewpoints that challenge local assumptions, alternative strategies that weren't obvious within your circumstances, different frameworks for understanding problems and opportunities.

Strangers who have achieved what you're trying to accomplish can provide roadmaps based on actual experience rather than theoretical knowledge. They can show you what's actually possible rather than what's theoretically achievable. They can demonstrate real pathways rather than hypothetical approaches.

The Dangers:

Not every stranger who offers guidance has genuine intentions. Some people pose as mentors to create dependency, to gather information for their own advantage, or to manipulate others for purposes that aren't immediately obvious. Distinguishing between authentic mentors and manipulative exploiters requires careful evaluation.

Believing in strangers can sometimes replace the essential work of believing in yourself. If you become dependent on external validation and encouragement, you may struggle when that support isn't available. The goal should be using external belief as catalyst for internal confidence rather than as permanent replacement for self-reliance.

Strangers may provide advice that worked in their circumstances but doesn't apply to your situation. What succeeds in one environment may fail in another. What works for one personality type may not work for another. External guidance should be adapted rather than adopted wholesale.

Some strangers may have hidden agendas that only become apparent after you've invested significant trust and effort based on their advice. They may be building networks for their own benefit, gathering information about your activities, or positioning themselves for future advantage at your expense.

How to Navigate This Dynamic Safely:

Evaluate the consistency between what strangers say and what they do. Authentic mentors demonstrate through their own behavior the principles they encourage in others. They practice what they preach rather than merely preaching what sounds good.

Look for evidence of genuine care for your development rather than just interest in your usefulness to their objectives. Real mentors want you to succeed independently rather than remain dependent on their guidance. They encourage your growth rather than requiring your continued need for their input.

Verify the track record of strangers who offer guidance. Have they actually achieved what they claim? Can you observe evidence of their success rather than just accepting their self-presentation? Do their results match their recommendations?

Maintain your own decision-making authority regardless of how valuable external guidance becomes. Use insights from strangers to inform your choices rather than to replace your judgment. Accept responsibility for outcomes regardless of whose advice influenced your decisions.

Build internal capability for self-motivation and self-validation while appreciating external encouragement. Use stranger's belief in you as fuel for developing stronger belief in yourself rather than as permanent substitute for self-confidence.

The stranger who transformed my perspective didn't try to create dependency, they worked to eliminate it. They didn't want me to need them permanently, they wanted me to develop independent capability. They didn't seek to control my decisions, they provided tools for making better decisions myself.

That's the mark of authentic mentorship from strangers: they aim to make themselves unnecessary by building your capability for independent success. They provide guidance that enables self-reliance rather than encouragement that creates dependency. They share knowledge that empowers your judgment rather than advice that replaces your thinking.

When you encounter strangers who offer belief in your potential, evaluate their intentions carefully but don't automatically reject their support. Some of the most transformative relationships in life come from unexpected sources and people who have no obligation to care about your success but choose to invest in your development anyway.

The key is distinguishing between strangers who genuinely want to help you succeed and those who want to use your trust for their own purposes. The former will encourage your independence, the latter will cultivate your dependence. The former will provide tools for self-reliance; the latter will create need for continued support.

In my case, that stranger's belief in me became catalyst for stronger belief in myself. Their encouragement didn't replace my motivation, it amplified it. Their guidance didn't dictate my decisions, it informed them. Their investment in my development didn't create obligation, it inspired gratitude that motivates me to help others in similar ways.

Sometimes belief in a stranger and their belief in you can change everything. Approach these relationships with wisdom, maintain your independence, and remember that the ultimate goal is developing such strong belief in yourself that external validation, while appreciated, is never necessary for your continued progress.

The stranger who believed in me helped me discover something crucial: I didn't need anyone else to believe in me, I just needed to believe in myself. Having someone else's belief as fuel for that journey made all the difference in reaching that realization.

That's the paradox and the power of belief in strangers: when done wisely, it leads to independence rather than dependence, to self-reliance rather than reliance on others, to internal confidence rather than external validation.

Choose your strangers wisely. But when you find authentic mentors, appreciate their investment in your development and use it to build the strongest possible belief in your own unlimited potential.

CHAPTER 18: WIN BY DISASSOCIATION AND DISBANDING

When the goals are clear for the entire group, there will always be times when stealth becomes necessary. There will always be moments when you need to keep plans concealed from the world. You cannot let the world know your strategies before they're implemented, or those plans can be foiled before they have chance to succeed.

But here's the challenge: if your group is not willing to go into stealth mode when necessary, if they cannot operate quietly when the situation demands it, sometimes you must silence the group. And the most effective way to silence a group is through disassociation and disbanding.

This isn't about being cruel or manipulative. This is about strategic necessity when continued association threatens your ability to achieve objectives that matter. This is about recognizing when loyalty to individuals conflicts with commitment to purposes that transcend those individuals.

Some people in your circle may exhibit overly belligerent behavior that draws unnecessary attention. Some may act with such arrogance that they create enemies where none needed to exist. Some may carry themselves in ways that damage your group's reputation or effectiveness. Some simply may not be carrying themselves in any manner beneficial to your goals or your cause.

When these dynamics emerge, you must disassociate from these individuals because association with them can ruin your plans, destroy your image, undermine your goals, and create devastating damage to what you're trying to build.

They can be so loud, so reckless, so undisciplined that they give others information without trying. This information that can be deadly to your objectives. They can create exposure that compromises strategies requiring discretion. They can generate conflicts that drain energy from productive activities.

It becomes imperative to avoid those with mental issues they cannot control. It becomes essential to distance yourself from those who have accepted the disease of drug usage that impairs their judgment and reliability. Some people may be best taken care of from a distance to maintain your highest capabilities. Some people have mentalities so limiting and negative that you must avoid them because their perspectives will contaminate your own thinking.

This principle isn't about abandoning people callously or discarding relationships carelessly. It's about recognizing that certain associations can become liabilities that prevent you from serving your higher purpose. It's about understanding that sometimes helping people means creating distance that protects both them and you from mutual destruction.

Loyalty must come from every angle inside your inner circle. Your core team must be completely built on structure of loyalty and respect but not in a ruthless sense, but in the sense of serving the greater good. Not everyone can meet these standards, and not everyone should be expected to do so. For those in your immediate orbit, these qualities are non-negotiable.

Not everyone is an Alley Cat, and you will recognize this through many indicators. An Alley Cat is born through being put through enormous pressure and being squeezed out the other end like a diamond from a diamond cutter. They are aware of how to manage setbacks. They have experienced disappointments throughout life. They have faced betrayals and learned from them. They are built for what's coming because they've already survived what's passed.

True Alley Cats have naturally had to commandeer ships that were coasting without guidance and headed toward icebergs. They have faced challenges alone and made it out stronger. They truly understand that all of their driving force comes from themselves. They make themselves happy. They are comfortable with independence. They don't look to anyone for validation or support they can't provide for themselves. They don't need external approval to maintain internal confidence.

These are the people you want in your inner circle. These are the individuals whose association strengthens rather than weakens your position. These are the allies whose loyalty and capability you can depend on when situations become challenging.

But identifying true Alley Cats requires careful evaluation. It means looking beyond surface presentations to understand fundamental character. It means assessing how people respond to pressure, disappointment, and setbacks rather than just how they behave during comfortable circumstances.

Some people appear strong during easy times but crumble when facing real challenges. Some seem loyal when loyalty costs nothing but betray when loyalty becomes inconvenient. Some project confidence when everything is going well but become liabilities when circumstances become difficult.

The process of disassociation and disbanding serves multiple purposes:

Protection of Mission: Your primary objectives deserve protection from those who might compromise them through indiscretion, incompetence, or malicious intent. Sometimes continued association with certain individuals threatens mission success regardless of personal feelings or historical relationships.

Maintenance of Standards: By removing those who don't meet essential criteria, you maintain high standards for those who remain. This creates environment where excellence becomes normal expectation rather than exceptional achievement.

Energy Conservation: Dealing with problematic personalities, managing conflicts, and compensating for others' limitations drains energy that could be directed toward productive activities. Disassociation frees this energy for better purposes.

Strategic Flexibility: Smaller, more reliable teams can move faster and adapt more effectively than larger groups containing unreliable elements. Strategic situations often require rapid response that becomes impossible when you're managing internal problems.

Clear Communication: When everyone in your circle shares similar values, capabilities, and commitment levels, communication becomes more efficient and effective. You don't waste time explaining obvious principles or managing conflicting agendas.

The decision to disassociate isn't made lightly or hastily. It requires careful evaluation of whether problems can be addressed through direct communication, whether improvements are possible through coaching or mentoring, whether issues represent temporary challenges or permanent incompatibilities.

When evaluation reveals fundamental misalignment that cannot be corrected, when continued association threatens your ability to serve larger purposes, when loyalty to individuals conflicts with commitment to principles, disassociation becomes not just strategic but ethical. It serves everyone's long-term interests, including those being disassociated from.

Some people thrive in different environments than the ones you're creating. Some have natural capabilities that align better with different objectives than yours. Some possess qualities that complement personalities different from yours. Disassociation allows them to find contexts where they can contribute more effectively while freeing you to work with those whose capabilities complement your mission.

This process requires honest self-assessment as well. Are you someone worth associating with? Do you bring value to relationships that equals or exceeds what you expect from others? Are you operating with the same standards of loyalty, reliability, and capability that you require from your circle?

The Alley Cat approaches these evaluations ruthlessly honestly. They don't maintain associations based on sentiment, convenience, or fear of confrontation. They prioritize effectiveness, alignment, and mutual benefit. They recognize that loyalty to individuals who undermine shared objectives represents disloyalty to those objectives and to other team members who are making sacrifices to achieve them.

Sometimes the kindest thing you can do for someone is refusing to enable their dysfunction through continued association. Sometimes the most helpful response to someone's limitations is creating distance that forces them to develop capabilities they've been avoiding. Sometimes protection requires separation.

77

The implementation of disassociation doesn't require dramatic confrontations or public announcements. Often, it involves gradual reduction of communication, systematic exclusion from important discussions, strategic creation of distance through schedule management and priority allocation.

The goal isn't punishment, it's protection. Protection of your mission, your other relationships, your energy, your effectiveness, and your ability to serve purposes larger than any individual association.

When you surround yourself only with those who inspire you, motivate you, and challenge you to become better, you create environment that amplifies everyone's capabilities. When you eliminate those who drain energy, create conflict, or undermine standards, you free resources for extraordinary achievement.

Your inner circle should consist entirely of people whose presence makes you more effective rather than less, whose association strengthens rather than weakens your position, whose loyalty and capability you can absolutely depend on when situations become challenging.

If that means a smaller circle, so be it. Better to have two loyal, capable allies than twenty questionable associates. Better to work with those who share your standards than to compromise those standards to accommodate those who don't. Better to achieve objectives with reliable partners than to fail with unreliable crowds.

The Alley Cat understands this principle intuitively. They naturally gravitate toward quality relationships rather than quantity associations. They prioritize depth over breadth, reliability over convenience, alignment over popularity.

This doesn't mean becoming isolated or rejecting everyone who doesn't meet impossible standards. It means being strategic about your closest associations, protective of your inner circle, and honest about which relationships serve your highest purposes versus which ones merely consume energy without generating corresponding value.

Win by disassociation and disbanding when necessary. Sometimes the greatest victory comes not from adding the right people but from removing the wrong ones. Sometimes progress requires subtraction rather than addition. Sometimes winning means knowing when to let go.

Your mission deserves protection. Your standards deserve maintenance. Your energy deserves strategic deployment. Your future deserves associations that support rather than undermine your highest potential.

Choose accordingly.

CHAPTER 19: SOBRIETY IS A SUPERPOWER

I have witnessed people cover more progress and ground in a year of being sober than they achieved in their entire lifetime while under the influence. This isn't hyperbole or moral judgment, it's observable reality based on watching numerous individuals transform their capabilities through the simple act of maintaining consistent mental clarity.

Sobriety isn't just about avoiding alcohol or drugs. It's about operating at your maximum cognitive capacity, maintaining emotional stability, and accessing your full intellectual potential without chemical interference. It's about being present for your own life rather than observing it through the filter of altered consciousness.

The Buffoon approaches sobriety as deprivation seen as something that removes enjoyment, reduces social acceptance, or eliminates coping mechanisms. They see it as giving up pleasure rather than gaining power. They view it as restriction rather than liberation.

The Alley Cat recognizes sobriety as competitive advantage as something that enhances capability, improves decision-making, and increases effectiveness. They understand it as multiplying existing strengths rather than simply removing weaknesses. They approach it as optimization rather than sacrifice.

This difference in perspective creates entirely different outcomes. The Buffoon struggles with sobriety because they're focused on what they're losing. The Alley Cat thrives in sobriety because they're focused on what they're gaining.

The gains from sustained sobriety are extraordinary and compound over time:

Enhanced Processing Power: Your brain operates at higher efficiency when not processing chemical interference. Complex problems become easier to solve. Multi-step thinking becomes more natural. Pattern recognition improves dramatically. Decision-making becomes faster and more accurate.

Superior Time Management: Sober individuals consistently demonstrate extraordinary time management capabilities. They accomplish more in hours than others achieve in days. They maximize productivity during peak mental performance periods. They eliminate time lost to recovery, regret, or impaired decision-making.

Emotional Stability: Consistent sobriety creates emotional equilibrium that allows for rational responses rather than reactive behaviors. You maintain composure during challenges. You think clearly under pressure. You make decisions based on logic rather than on temporary emotional states.

Improved Multitasking: The clear mind can handle multiple complex tasks simultaneously without becoming overwhelmed. You can maintain several projects, relationships, and objectives without confusion or neglect. Your cognitive bandwidth expands to accommodate increasing responsibilities.

Greater Control: Perhaps most importantly, sobriety provides complete control over your emotions, impulses, and actions. You respond to situations rather than reacting to them. You choose behaviors based on desired outcomes rather than immediate impulses. You maintain consistency regardless of external pressures.

I've observed this superpower effect repeatedly throughout my life. People who eliminate substance use from their routines consistently outperform their previous achievements by margins that seem impossible until you witness them directly.

The entrepreneur who stops drinking suddenly develops laser focus that allows them to build businesses they'd been "planning" for years. The student who eliminates party drugs discovers academic capabilities they never knew they possessed. The professional who quits social drinking finds they can work longer hours with greater effectiveness while still having energy for personal development.

Here's the crucial distinction: looking at sober people who are mediocre or unambitious doesn't disprove this principle, it simply demonstrates that sobriety without Alley Cat mentality produces different results than sobriety combined with focused ambition and strategic thinking.

Plenty of sober people live ordinary lives because they're applying ordinary thinking to their enhanced capabilities. They're using their superpower for routine activities rather than for extraordinary achievements. They're maintaining clarity without directing that clarity toward meaningful objectives.

The magic happens when you combine the Alley Cat mindset with the sustained clarity that sobriety provides. This combination creates capabilities that seem almost impossible to those operating under any form of chemical influence.

During my own periods of complete sobriety, I consistently achieved more in months than I had accomplished in years during times when my thinking was clouded by any form of substance use. The difference wasn't subtle, it was dramatic, obvious, and measurable.

Strategic thinking became clearer. Long-term planning became more natural. Complex problem-solving became easier. Relationship management became more effective. Financial decisions became more sound. Physical energy became more consistent.

Most importantly, I could maintain multiple priorities simultaneously without losing focus on any of them. I could build businesses while maintaining relationships while pursuing personal development while managing responsibilities without feeling overwhelmed or scattered.

This enhanced capability isn't just about avoiding negative effects of substance use, it's about accessing positive capabilities that remain dormant when your brain is processing any chemical interference, however minimal.

Even moderate alcohol consumption, occasional recreational drug use, or prescription medications that affect cognitive function can prevent you from accessing your full intellectual potential. The impact might not be immediately obvious, but it becomes apparent when you experience sustained periods of complete clarity.

The Alley Cat approaches sobriety strategically rather than morally. It's not about being "good" or conforming to social expectations, it's about optimizing performance and maximizing capabilities. It's about gaining every possible advantage in pursuits that matter.

This strategic approach makes sobriety easier to maintain because it's based on positive motivation rather than negative restriction. You're not giving up something you enjoy; you're gaining something more valuable than what you're releasing. You're not sacrificing pleasure; you're exchanging temporary gratification for enhanced capability.

The social challenges of sobriety also reveal important information about your environment and relationships. People who pressure you to drink or use substances after you've chosen sobriety are revealing their own dependencies and limitations. They're demonstrating that they need you to be impaired to feel comfortable with their own impairment.

True friends and valuable associates will support your decision to optimize your capabilities regardless of how that decision affects their comfort with their own choices. They'll respect your commitment to enhanced performance even if they don't make similar choices themselves.

Those who can't accept your sobriety are often those who relied on your impaired judgment to feel better about their own poor decisions. They needed you to be operating at reduced capacity to justify their own limitations. Your enhanced clarity threatens their rationalization for remaining impaired.

This filtering effect actually represents another advantage of sobriety, it helps identify relationships based on mutual growth versus relationships based on shared dysfunction. It attracts people interested in high performance while repelling those committed to mediocrity.

The competitive advantages of sobriety become even more pronounced in business contexts. While others are recovering from hangovers, managing mood swings, or dealing with clouded judgment, you're operating at peak capacity. While they're making decisions influenced by chemical interference, you're thinking with complete clarity.

This advantage compounds over time. Small improvements in decision-making create large differences in outcomes. Slightly better judgment leads to significantly better results. Marginally enhanced focus produces dramatically superior achievement.

The Buffoon never recognizes these advantages because they mistake temporary chemical euphoria for genuine satisfaction, artificial confidence for real capability, altered perception for enhanced insight. They don't realize that what they experience as enhancement is actually impairment compared to their natural potential.

The Alley Cat understands that any chemical that alters brain chemistry is by definition reducing optimal function. They recognize that their natural state represents their highest capability. They approach sobriety as returning to their superpower rather than giving up their pleasure.

This perspective makes sobriety not just sustainable but desirable. When you experience the enhanced capabilities that come from sustained clarity, returning to chemical interference feels like voluntarily handicapping yourself. It becomes obviously counterproductive rather than temptingly attractive.

If you're currently using any substances that affect your cognitive function, consider conducting an experiment: commit to complete sobriety for a specific period perhaps ninety days and honestly evaluate the differences in your capabilities, achievements, and overall life satisfaction.

Don't approach this as permanent sacrifice or moral improvement. Approach it as performance optimization and capability enhancement. Measure the results objectively rather than just emotionally.

Track your productivity, decision-making quality, relationship satisfaction, financial progress, and achievement of important objectives. Compare these metrics to your performance during periods when you were using substances, even moderately.

I believe you'll discover what I and many others have experienced: sobriety doesn't just eliminate negative effects, it unlocks positive capabilities that remain hidden when your brain is processing any chemical interference.

The question isn't whether you can afford to be sober, it's whether you can afford not to access your full intellectual and emotional potential during the limited time you have to achieve your most important objectives. Sobriety is a superpower. The only question is whether you'll choose to activate it.

Your dreams, goals, and responsibilities deserve your maximum capability. Your potential deserves complete expression. Your life deserves to be lived at full capacity rather than through the diminished lens of chemical interference.

That's not moral judgment, it's strategic reality. The choice, as always, is yours.

CHAPTER 20: TEAMMATES MAN THE TOWER WHEN YOU CAN'T

Real teammates don't leave unnecessary work for you to handle. They don't abandon problems for you to solve. They don't create messes for you to clean up. They don't step over issues and walk away as if they're normal, leaving burdens for others to bear.

True teammates understand that your team is a unit, and as a unit, you do not allow any member to go under unnecessary burden unless that burden is specifically requested by the teammate themselves. Then, and only then, will they honor that request and allow you to handle what you've chosen to handle.

The difference between genuine teammates and mere associates becomes crystal clear when challenges arise. When problems appear on the horizon, when obstacles threaten progress, when difficulties emerge that could derail objectives. This is when you discover who's actually on your team versus who's just along for the ride.

Genuine teammates see problems and solve them before those problems reach you. If they spot an issue developing, they address it proactively and then inform you that they've handled it. They don't wait for you to notice the problem. They don't bring it to your attention as something requiring your intervention. They take care of it and report resolution rather than identification.

Genuine teammates see messes and clean them up regardless of who created them, because they understand that team success requires collective responsibility. They don't analyze whose fault something is before determining whether to address it. They don't calculate whether solving problems falls within their specific job description. They handle what needs handling because the team's well-being depends on problems being solved rather than on problems being assigned blame.

Genuine teammates understand that strengthening the team makes everyone stronger, while allowing team members to struggle unnecessarily weakens the entire unit. They recognize that individual burden becomes collective burden if not addressed promptly. They know that helping teammates succeed helps everyone succeed.

The Buffoon approaches teamwork differently. They watch as problems develop and then point them out to others without offering solutions. They step over messes and continue walking, expecting someone else to clean up what they could have addressed themselves. They allow teammates to struggle with unnecessary burdens while focusing exclusively on their own immediate responsibilities.

Buffoons stand and watch as their ship burns, then tell everyone it's not their fault when the ship sinks. They prioritize avoiding blame overachieving success. They focus on protecting themselves rather than protecting the team. They measure their value by what they avoid doing rather than by what they accomplish.

The contrast becomes especially apparent during challenging periods. When teams face difficult circumstances, when resources become limited, when external pressures increase, these situations reveal true character and genuine commitment.

During my time at the manufacturing plant, I witnessed both approaches repeatedly. Some workers would notice problems developing and immediately address them, understanding that preventing small issues from becoming large crises served everyone's interests. They would spot inefficiencies and correct them, identify bottlenecks and eliminate them, recognize potential quality issues and resolve them all without being asked, assigned, or specifically compensated for these efforts.

Others would observe the same problems and either ignore them entirely or report them to management without attempting any solution themselves. They would walk past obvious inefficiencies, step around clear obstacles, and continue their routines while problems accumulated and eventually created crises that affected everyone.

The difference wasn't capability. Both groups possessed similar skills and knowledge. The difference was mindset. One group thought like owners, the other thought like renters. One group focused on collective success, the other focused on individual protection.

This distinction extends far beyond formal work environments. It applies to any collaborative relationship where shared objectives require mutual support and collective responsibility.

In personal relationships, genuine partners anticipate each other's needs and address them proactively. They don't wait for explicit requests when they can see obvious requirements. They don't calculate reciprocity before offering assistance. They understand that relationship success depends on mutual support rather than on transactional exchanges.

Buffoon partners keep score of who's doing what, wait for specific requests before offering help, and focus on ensuring they don't do more than their "fair share" even when additional effort would significantly benefit the relationship.

In business partnerships, genuine collaborators monitor shared objectives and address obstacles before those obstacles threaten collective success. They don't compartmentalize responsibilities so rigidly that they ignore problems outside their specific domains. They understand that business success requires comprehensive attention rather than just individual performance.

Buffoon partners focus exclusively on their designated areas while allowing shared objectives to suffer from problems they could easily address but choose not to handle because those problems fall outside their narrow definitions of responsibility.

The teammate mentality requires expanding your definition of "your job" to include whatever needs to be done for collective success. It means taking ownership of outcomes rather than just of activities. It means measuring success by team achievement rather than by individual task completion.

This doesn't mean becoming a doormat or allowing others to exploit your willingness to handle additional responsibilities. It means proactively addressing issues that affect shared objectives while ensuring that your extra efforts contribute to collective success rather than simply enabling others' laziness.

The key distinction is between helping teammates who are genuinely struggling despite their best efforts versus covering for teammates who are deliberately avoiding responsibilities they should be handling themselves. Genuine teammates help those who are trying; they don't enable those who are avoiding.

When teammates are overwhelmed by legitimate challenges, stepping in to provide assistance strengthens the entire team. When teammates are simply refusing to carry their fair share, taking over their responsibilities weakens the team by rewarding irresponsibility and creating unsustainable burden distribution.

Effective teams develop cultures where everyone naturally looks for ways to support collective success rather than just individual performance. Team members routinely ask themselves: "What can I do to help us succeed?" rather than just "What am I supposed to do?"

This culture creates environments where problems get solved quickly because multiple people are watching for issues and addressing them proactively. It generates momentum because obstacles get removed before they can slow progress. It builds trust because everyone knows that others are looking out for collective interests rather than just individual concerns.

The Alley Cat naturally adopts this teammate mentality because they understand that their own success is connected to their team's success. They recognize that helping others succeed creates environments where they can succeed more easily. They know that investing in collective capability generates returns that exceed the investment required.

The Buffoon resists this mentality because they view every situation as zero-sum competition where helping others necessarily reduces their own advantages. They can't see how strengthening the team strengthens their own position. They mistake selfishness for self-interest.

This limited perspective prevents them from accessing the extraordinary results that come from genuine collaboration. They remain stuck in individual performance while missing the exponential possibilities that emerge from coordinated team effort.

If you want to identify genuine teammates versus mere associates, observe how they respond when problems arise that affect the team but don't fall within their specific responsibilities. Do they address these issues proactively, or do they wait for someone else to handle them? Do they look for ways to help, or do they focus on avoiding blame?

Watch how they behave when team members are struggling with challenges. Do they offer assistance, or do they maintain distance to avoid additional responsibility? Do they share knowledge that could help others succeed, or do they hoard information that provides individual advantage?

Notice how they approach shared resources and common areas. Do they maintain and improve these resources, or do they use them without contributing to their upkeep? Do they leave things better than they found them, or do they extract value without adding value?

These behaviors reveal fundamental orientation toward collaboration versus exploitation, team success versus individual protection, collective responsibility versus narrow self-interest.

When you find genuine teammates, those who naturally man the tower when you can't, who solve problems before bringing them to your attention, who strengthen the team through their presence rather than burden it through their requirements you must protect these relationships carefully. These individuals are rare and valuable beyond their immediate contributions.

When you encounter Buffoons disguised as teammates, those who watch ships burn while claiming innocence, who create problems rather than solving them, who drain energy rather than contributing it. Recognize them quickly and either convert them through clear expectations or remove them before they damage team effectiveness.

Most importantly, become the type of teammate you want to work with. Man the tower for others when they can't. Solve problems before they reach your teammates. Clean up messes regardless of who created them. Strengthen your team through your presence rather than burdening it through your requirements.

The quality of your teammates will ultimately reflect the quality of your own teamwork. Become indispensable through your willingness to ensure collective success, and you'll naturally attract others who share that commitment.

That's how extraordinary teams are built. One genuine teammate at a time, through consistent demonstration of collective responsibility and mutual support.

The tower always needs someone watching. Make sure you're the type of person others can count on to man it when they can't.

CHAPTER 21: AN EXCELLENT CREDIT SCORE IS LIKE A

NUCLEAR POWER SUPPLY

Most people think about credit scores as simple numbers that determine whether they can get loans or credit cards. They treat credit as a convenience for purchasing things they can't immediately afford. They view good credit as something nice to have rather than as something essential to build.

This limited understanding prevents them from accessing one of the most powerful wealth-building tools available in modern society: the ability to leverage excellent credit as a nuclear power supply for business development, investment opportunities, and wealth creation.

An excellent credit score doesn't just give you access to money, it gives you access to cheap money. It provides leverage that can multiply your capabilities exponentially. It creates opportunities for compound growth that simply aren't available to those with poor or mediocre credit.

The difference between having excellent credit and having poor credit isn't just convenience, it's access to an entirely different economic reality. It's the difference between paying cash for everything and having strategic access to capital when opportunities arise. It's the difference between being limited by your current resources and being able to leverage future earnings for present opportunities.

When I was rebuilding after setbacks, I understood that credit would be crucial for scaling whatever I built beyond what personal resources alone could achieve. I wasn't just thinking about buying cars or houses, I was thinking about having access to capital for business development, investment opportunities, and strategic positioning.

Excellent credit creates what I call "nuclear power supply" because it provides massive capability that can be deployed when needed. Just like nuclear power generates enormous energy from relatively small inputs, excellent credit provides access to substantial capital from the relatively small effort required to maintain perfect payment history and strategic credit utilization.

The Buffoon approaches credit reactively. They apply for loans when they need money, then wonder why they're declined or offered unfavorable terms. They focus on monthly payments rather than total cost. They prioritize immediate gratification over long-term optimization. They treat credit as emergency resource rather than as strategic tool.

The Alley Cat approaches credit proactively, they build excellent credit systematically before they need to use it, positioning themselves to access optimal terms when opportunities arise. They focus on total cost rather than just monthly payments. They prioritize strategic positioning over immediate consumption. They treat credit as power supply for wealth creation rather than just convenience for consumption.

This strategic approach creates access to opportunities unavailable to those with mediocre credit:

Business Development: Excellent credit enables business lines of credit, equipment financing, and expansion capital at favorable rates. You can grow businesses faster than cash flow alone would allow. You can take advantage of time-sensitive opportunities that require immediate capital deployment.

Real Estate Investment: Superior credit provides access to investment property financing, refinancing opportunities, and portfolio expansion. You can build wealth through real estate appreciation and cash flow without requiring massive initial capital.

Arbitrage Opportunities: Excellent credit creates possibilities for financial arbitrage. This allows borrowing at low rates to invest in higher-yielding opportunities. You can benefit from interest rate spreads that generate passive income.

Emergency Positioning: Perfect credit provides financial security during challenging periods. Rather than being forced to sell assets or accept unfavorable terms during difficulties, you have access to capital that maintains your strategic positioning.

Negotiating Power: Excellent credit improves your negotiating position in numerous contexts. Sellers know you can secure financing quickly. Partners know you can access capital when needed. Suppliers know you represent low-risk business.

But building nuclear power supply credit requires understanding principles that most people never learn:

Payment History Perfection: Never, ever miss payments or pay late. Set up automatic payments for at least minimum amounts. Treat payment dates as sacred deadlines. Understand that payment history represents 35% of your credit score and forms the foundation of everything else.

Strategic Utilization Management: Keep credit utilization below 10% of available limits, and ideally below 5%. This requires either limiting spending or increasing available credit. Understand that utilization represents 30% of your credit score and dramatically affects your access to premium terms.

Account Age Optimization: Keep old accounts open to maintain lengthy credit history. Don't close your oldest cards even if you don't use them regularly.

Understand that credit age represents 15% of your score and demonstrates long-term reliability.

Credit Mix Development: Maintain diverse credit types, revolving credit, installment loans, possibly mortgage debt. This demonstrates ability to manage different payment structures and represents 10% of your score.

Inquiry Management: Limit hard inquiries to strategic applications. Shop for rates within concentrated time periods when seeking loans. Understand that inquiries represent 10% of your score and excessive applications suggest desperation or poor planning.

Building excellent credit requires patience because improvements compound over time. Once established, excellent credit becomes self-reinforcing. It provides access to better terms that make maintaining excellent credit easier while creating opportunities that generate income to support continued optimization.

The nuclear power analogy extends beyond just capacity, it includes the responsibility that comes with such power. Just as nuclear energy requires careful management to remain beneficial rather than destructive, excellent credit requires strategic deployment to create wealth rather than debt.

Many people with access to substantial credit destroy their financial futures by using that access for consumption rather than investment. They leverage their excellent credit to purchase depreciating assets, luxury cars, expensive homes, vacation properties that create ongoing expenses rather than income.

The Alley Cat uses credit strategically to acquire appreciating assets or income-producing opportunities. They leverage credit to build businesses that generate cash flow exceeding debt service. They use credit to purchase real estate that appreciates while providing rental income. They deploy credit for investments that compound over time rather than for consumption that provides temporary satisfaction.

This strategic approach requires discipline because credit makes poor decisions easier to execute. The same credit line that could fund profitable business expansion could also finance expensive lifestyle inflation. The same excellent score that provides access to favorable investment property loans could also enable purchase of luxury items that drain cash flow.

The difference lies in maintaining long-term perspective despite short-term temptations. Excellent credit should enhance your wealth-building capability rather than enable consumption that undermines wealth creation. It should provide strategic flexibility rather than facilitate financial overextension.

Building nuclear power supply credit also requires understanding credit as system rather than collection of individual accounts. Your overall credit profile includes:

Credit Reports: Monitor all three credit bureaus monthly. Dispute any inaccuracies immediately. Understand that different lenders use different bureaus and scoring models.

Credit Scores: Track multiple scoring models since different lenders use different versions. FICO scores matter most for major purchases like mortgages and auto loans.

Credit Relationships: Build relationships with multiple lenders including banks, credit unions, and specialized financial institutions. Different lenders offer different products and terms.

Credit Strategies: Understand advanced strategies like authorized user arrangements, credit line increases, product change options, and optimal application timing.

Most people treat credit as reactive necessity rather than proactive strategy. They apply for credit when they need money rather than building credit when they don't need it. They focus on getting approved rather than optimizing terms. They manage credit casually rather than strategically.

This reactive approach limits access to the nuclear power supply benefits that excellent credit can provide. By the time they need capital for opportunities, their credit isn't positioned to provide optimal access.

The Alley Cat builds credit infrastructure during periods when they don't need it, positioning themselves for periods when they do need it. They optimize credit during stable times so it's available during challenging times. They treat credit building as ongoing strategy rather than occasional necessity.

If your credit isn't currently excellent, begin systematic improvement immediately. Perfect payment history from this point forward. Reduce utilization through increased payments or credit line increases. Monitor reports for inaccuracies. Plan long-term optimization rather than seeking quick fixes.

If your credit is already excellent, begin leveraging it strategically for wealth creation rather than just convenience. Explore business credit lines, investment property financing, and arbitrage opportunities. Use your nuclear power supply to generate returns rather than just to facilitate consumption.

Remember that excellent credit represents one of the few advantages available regardless of background, connections, or initial capital. Anyone can build excellent credit through consistent application of straightforward principles. Anyone can access nuclear power supply benefits through strategic credit optimization.

The question isn't whether you can afford to build excellent credit, it's whether you can afford to continue operating without access to the nuclear power supply that excellent credit provides.

Your wealth-building strategy should include credit optimization as fundamental component rather than optional consideration. Your business development should assume access to capital rather than dependence on accumulated cash. Your investment opportunities should include leverage possibilities rather than just cash purchases.

Excellent credit isn't just convenient, it's powerful. Nuclear power supply powerful.

Build it. Maintain it. Deploy it strategically.

Your future self will thank you for having access to this power when extraordinary opportunities arise.

CHAPTER 22: THE MANUFACTURING PLANT STORY

Sometimes the most profound transformations happen in the most unlikely places. For me, that place was a dysfunctional manufacturing plant where I started working the night shift for minimum wage while my family lived in a hotel room. What began as desperation would become one of the most important learning experiences of my life a masterclass in how individual excellence can transform entire systems.

When I first arrived at the plant, I was assigned to the night shift, working from 8:30 PM to 6:00 AM for seven dollars and twenty-five cents an hour through a temporary staffing agency. My circumstances were dire: my family was living in a hotel room, I had just lost a job that paid three times more because they discovered my criminal record, and I couldn't bring more bad news home while we were already struggling for basic stability.

I had a simple goal: earn enough to move us out of that hotel into a place of our own. I quickly realized that achieving even this modest objective would require an extraordinary approach.

The night shift was chaos. Most workers treated it as an opportunity to avoid real work rather than as a chance to contribute meaningfully. They would arrive, punch in, and immediately head outside to smoke cigarettes, drink alcohol, and smoke marijuana in the parking lot. The person who was responsible for training us was usually outside participating in these activities rather than providing instruction.

Meanwhile, production targets were being missed, quality standards were ignored, and the entire operation was losing money. The day shift would arrive to find minimal progress from the previous night, creating frustration and inefficiency that compounded throughout the facility.

I could have joined the prevailing culture of minimal effort and maximum avoidance. No one would have questioned it. No one expected excellence from the night shift. The bar was set so low that simply showing up sober would have been considered above average. Instead, I made a different choice. I decided to work as if my life depended on it.

While others gathered in the parking lot, I stayed inside learning the production processes. I studied the diagrams, examined the products, and figured out how each station contributed to the overall manufacturing flow. I started building products from the first station through the final quality control checkpoint, following each piece through the entire assembly process.

Initially, I worked slowly because I was learning. But as I understood the systems better, I began moving faster. I brought large cups of coffee to maintain energy throughout the long shifts. I created personal challenges to increase my speed and accuracy. I developed routines that maximized efficiency.

Soon, I was single-handedly producing more during the night shift than the entire day shift was producing with full crews. When the day shift arrived, they would ask if the night shift had actually accomplished anything. I would tell them it was all me, and initially they didn't believe it until management reviewed security cameras and confirmed my claims. The first 2 weeks at the plant I had worked a solid 242 hours. 119 hours one week and 123 hours the next. This provided me with enough money to immediately move out of that hotel into an apartment and to activate all of my utilities.

The transformation was so dramatic that they had to hire an additional forklift driver because the single driver was overwhelmed by the volume of finished products I was generating. Workers who had been sitting around with nothing to do suddenly had more work than they could handle.

As my individual productivity became undeniable, other night shift workers began to take notice. Some started joining me, asking how they could help and what they could contribute. I showed them how to match my pace, how to move efficiently between stations, how to maintain quality while increasing speed.

Eventually, a small core of us was working at such a high level that management decided to eliminate the night shift entirely and move the productive workers to the day shift. We carried our momentum into the new environment, where we continued outperforming established teams who had been working together for years.

My efforts didn't go unnoticed by upper management. The plant manager approached me one day and asked about my goals, my background, and my intentions. I explained my situation honestly. I was trying to create stability for my family and had never experienced stable life myself.

He told me that if I maintained my current attitude and work ethic, I would have a stable life that no one could take away from me. A few days later, a corporate representative arrived and began asking about my management skills, supervisory experience, and capabilities beyond production work.

They handed me a radio to communicate with plant staff and told me that my last day working on the production line had arrived unless I chose to go out there occasionally to maintain familiarity with operations. Instead, they assigned me to count and manage all inventory throughout the entire facility.

This was when I discovered the plant's biggest problem: they had no idea what materials they had, when they were running out of supplies, or how to predict material requirements. Inventory was scattered, unorganized, and completely untracked. Parts were mixed together, shelves were chaotic, and no systematic approach existed for managing materials.

94

I brought my Microsoft Excel skills to bear on this challenge. I created comprehensive spreadsheets that catalogued every component, every part, every piece of material in the facility. I developed what amounted to a bill of materials that separated items by department, categorized components by type, and organized everything down to individual screws and bolts.

I implemented a material requirement planning system that tracked usage patterns and predicted future needs. Through trial and error, I determined that maintaining three days of inventory on hand provided the optimal balance between cost efficiency and operational security. Any more created excess holding costs, any less risked production interruptions.

This wasn't just about spreadsheets and organization. I physically reorganized the entire warehouse, arranging parts in numerical order, separating items by color and type, creating systematic storage that corresponded to my digital tracking systems. I knew the location, quantity, and usage rate of every item in the facility.

My responsibilities expanded beyond inventory management. I began coordinating with vendors, managing supplier relationships, and negotiating purchasing terms. I tracked customer relationships, monitored quality issues, and managed feedback from the receiving end of our finished products. I essentially managed the entire supply chain from raw material procurement to customer satisfaction.

Management created an office for me with climate control, a large desk, a comfortable chair, and a 48-inch screen that provided access to every security camera in the facility. I could monitor all operations while managing the systems that kept everything flowing smoothly.

Corporate representatives began training me in Six Sigma principles, lean manufacturing techniques, and advanced supply chain management. They weren't trying to replace me, they were developing my capabilities to handle even greater responsibilities.

My schedule evolved to support these expanded duties. Instead of the traditional day shift, I worked from 2:00 AM to 2:00 PM to optimize inventory management and production coordination. This allowed me to conduct morning cycle counts before the day shift arrived, plan daily production requirements, and coordinate with suppliers during business hours.

I hosted morning meetings with production staff to discuss daily objectives and priorities. I then met with management to provide updates and coordinate strategic decisions. I had become the liaison between operations and administration, ensuring everyone had the information and resources needed for optimal performance.

Under my inventory management and production scheduling, the plant eliminated days when workers were sent home due to material shortages. We stopped missing shipment deadlines. We began accumulating finished product inventory that provided flexibility for handling unexpected orders or delivery challenges.

The transformation was comprehensive and measurable. The facility went from chronically dysfunctional to consistently productive. Costs decreased while output increased. Quality improved while efficiency accelerated. Customer satisfaction enhanced while employee morale stabilized.

Here's the critical detail that shaped my perspective on value and compensation: despite transforming the entire operation, despite essentially functioning as plant manager, despite working 12-hour days six days a week, I was paid $18 per hour, not a salary, not management compensation, just hourly wages for extraordinary management responsibilities.

I held the title of fabrication manager and production scheduler, but I performed all the duties of a plant manager without receiving plant manager compensation. I built systems that saved the company thousands of dollars while increasing revenue substantially, yet my personal compensation remained minimal compared to the value I created.

This experience taught me crucial lessons about the relationship between value creation and value capture. You can create extraordinary value within someone else's system, but capturing proportional compensation requires either negotiating power that comes from being genuinely irreplaceable or building your own systems where you control value distribution.

The plant eventually closed due to irresponsible spending, poor strategic decisions made by corporate leadership and factors completely beyond my control or influence. All the efficiency improvements, cost savings, and revenue increases I'd generated couldn't overcome fundamental mismanagement at levels above my authority.

When the closure was announced, I was disappointed but not because I loved the job, but because I had built something meaningful from complete dysfunction. I had proven to myself that individual excellence could transform entire systems. I had demonstrated capabilities I didn't know I possessed.

I was also angry. Angry that my extraordinary contribution had been compensated minimally while others who contributed far less received far more. Angry that corporate mismanagement had destroyed something I had worked so hard to build. Angry that being an excellent employee provided no protection against decisions made by others.

This experience crystallized my commitment to never again putting myself in a position where someone else could terminate my income with a single decision. I would never again create substantial value within systems I didn't control. I would never again accept minimal compensation for extraordinary contribution.

The skills I developed during this experience proved invaluable: inventory management, supply chain coordination, vendor relationship management, production scheduling, quality control, and systematic organization. But more important than specific skills was the confidence that came from knowing I could transform dysfunctional situations through determination, strategic thinking, and consistent excellence.

The manufacturing plant story became proof that extraordinary results are possible regardless of starting circumstances. It demonstrated that individual initiative can overcome systemic dysfunction. It showed that excellence creates its own opportunities even within the most challenging environments.

It also revealed the limitations of creating value within systems controlled by others. It exposed the danger of depending on external recognition and compensation for value you create. It highlighted the importance of building your own platforms rather than just improving others' operations.

The lessons from this experience continue guiding my approach to business, relationships, and value creation. Work as if your life depends on it, because it does. Create systems rather than just improving them. Build assets you control rather than just contributing to assets others control.

Most importantly: never underestimate your capacity to transform dysfunction into excellence through strategic effort, systematic thinking, and relentless commitment to creating value.

Sometimes the most unlikely places provide the most important education. Sometimes the most challenging circumstances develop the most valuable capabilities. Sometimes the experiences that seem like setbacks actually prepare you for breakthroughs.

The manufacturing plant story represents all three. It was education disguised as employment, capability development disguised as crisis, and preparation disguised as punishment.

I'm grateful for every difficult hour of that experience. Not because it was pleasant, but because it was necessary for becoming who I needed to be.

CHAPTER 23: AVOID BEING THE CHARITY CASE

It's natural to want to surround yourself with people who motivate you, who have achieved what you're trying to achieve, who possess the wealth, status, or success you're working toward. These relationships can provide inspiration, guidance, and opportunities that accelerate your progress beyond what you could accomplish alone.

But there's a crucial distinction between building mutually beneficial relationships with successful people and becoming their charity case. The difference determines whether these associations strengthen your position or weaken it, whether they accelerate your growth or create dependency that ultimately limits your potential.

The Buffoon approaches successful people with a mindset of extraction. They want to be around wealth without creating wealth. They seek to benefit from others' success without contributing equivalent value. They hope that proximity to achievement will somehow transfer achievement to them through osmosis or association.

This approach creates relationships where they're always the one receiving rather than giving, always the one seeking rather than providing, always the one needing rather than contributing. They become the charity case, someone tolerated out of sympathy or obligation rather than someone valued for their contribution.

The Alley Cat approaches successful people with a mindset of exchange. They understand that sustainable relationships require mutual benefit, that valuable people have limited time and attention, that access to high-achieving individuals must be earned through demonstrated value rather than requested through personal need.

When you become the charity case, several damaging dynamics emerge that ultimately undermine your objectives:

You're Treated According to Your Perceived Value: Even well-meaning successful people will unconsciously treat you at the level they perceive you contribute. If you're consistently the one receiving without giving, you'll be treated as a recipient rather than as a peer, regardless of your potential or intentions.

You Develop Dependency Rather Than Capability: When someone else consistently provides solutions to your problems, resources for your challenges, or opportunities for your advancement, you develop dependency on their assistance rather than capability for independent achievement. This dependency ultimately limits your growth rather than accelerating it.

You Attract the Wrong Type of "Successful" People: Genuinely successful people with healthy boundaries typically avoid those who consistently take without giving. The "successful" people who do maintain relationships with chronic takers often have their own issues. They may enjoy the power dynamic, need validation through helping others, or benefit from having people around who make them feel superior.

You Undermine Your Own Confidence: When you consistently position yourself as someone who needs help rather than someone who provides value, you reinforce internal narratives about your own inadequacy. You begin to believe your own presentation of yourself as someone who lacks rather than someone who contributes.

You Miss Opportunities for Genuine Growth: Real growth comes from stretching beyond your current capabilities, solving problems you haven't solved before, creating value you haven't created previously. When someone else consistently handles challenges for you, you miss the developmental opportunities those challenges represent.

The alternative is ensuring that your work ethic, drive, and capability match the wealth/accomplishments of those you want to associate with. This doesn't mean you need to have achieved identical results it means you need to demonstrate equivalent commitment, effort, and value creation within your current circumstances.

Ask yourself: What am I bringing to benefit everyone around me? How does my association create value for others rather than just extracting value from them? What can others learn from me, gain from knowing me, or accomplish through partnership with me that they couldn't achieve alone?

Everyone wants to be attached to people with substantial resources, impressive networks, high status, or extensive experience. But most people approach these relationships with a taking mindset rather than a giving mindset. They focus on what they can gain rather than on what they can contribute.

This creates a fundamental imbalance that prevents genuine connection and mutual benefit. Successful people are constantly approached by those seeking assistance, opportunity, or access. What they rarely encounter is someone offering genuine value, bringing unique capabilities, or providing benefits that enhance their own objectives.

When you approach relationships from a contribution mindset rather than an extraction mindset, you immediately differentiate yourself from the majority who approach successful people as potential sources of help rather than as potential partners for mutual benefit.

This shift requires honest self-assessment: What unique value do you bring? What problems can you solve? What capabilities do you possess that might benefit others? What perspective, energy, or resources can you contribute to collaborative relationships?

If you struggle to identify specific value you bring, this reveals important development areas rather than reasons for avoiding successful people entirely. Use this awareness to build capabilities, develop resources, or create value that makes you genuinely beneficial to potential partners rather than just another person seeking assistance.

The goal isn't to avoid learning from those more successful than you or to reject help when it's offered. The goal is to structure these relationships as mutual exchanges rather than one-way assistance programs.

This might mean:

Offering Your Time and Energy: Even if you lack financial resources or extensive experience, you can contribute effort, research, organization, or execution support that valuable people need but lack time to handle themselves.

Providing Fresh Perspective: Your different background, younger viewpoint, or alternative experience might offer insights that established successful people can't access from their current positions.

Contributing Specialized Skills: You might possess technical capabilities, creative talents, or specific knowledge that complements their existing capabilities and enhances their projects or objectives.

Bringing Enthusiasm and Drive: Your motivation, energy, and commitment can add value to collaborative efforts, especially when that enthusiasm is channeled productively rather than just expressed emotionally.

Creating Future Value: Even if you can't contribute immediately, you might represent potential future partnerships where today's mutual investment creates tomorrow's mutual benefits.

The key is ensuring that every interaction provides some form of value exchange rather than purely value extraction. This might be subtle asking thoughtful questions that stimulate their thinking rather than just seeking answers to your problems. It might be indirect sharing information or connections that benefit their objectives rather than only discussing your own needs.

When I was rebuilding after setbacks, I was extremely careful to approach potentially valuable relationships with a contribution mindset despite my challenging circumstances. Even with minimal resources, I looked for ways to provide value rather than just seek assistance.

I offered to handle tasks that required time and effort rather than just expertise or resources. I shared insights from my unusual background that provided perspectives they couldn't access elsewhere. I demonstrated work ethic and reliability that made me valuable as an execution partner even when I couldn't contribute financially.

This approach attracted people who recognized potential for mutual benefit rather than just people who felt sorry for my circumstances. It created relationships based on exchange rather than charity, partnership rather than dependency, mutual value rather than one-way assistance.

The distinction becomes particularly important during networking events, industry gatherings, or situations where you have access to successful people but limited time to make impressions. How you approach these interactions determines whether you're remembered as someone with potential for future partnership or as someone seeking help who offered nothing in return.

Avoid leading with your needs, challenges, or requests for assistance. Instead, lead with curiosity about their work, genuine interest in their challenges, or insights that might benefit their objectives. Focus the conversation on their goals rather than on your goals, while naturally weaving in information about your capabilities and potential contributions.

This approach requires patience because mutual benefit relationships often develop slowly compared to charity relationships that might provide immediate assistance. But the long-term value of partnership-based relationships far exceeds the short-term benefits of dependency-based assistance.

Remember that successful people typically became successful by building mutually beneficial relationships rather than by depending on others' charity. They understand the value of exchange-based partnerships and naturally gravitate toward others who demonstrate similar understanding.

If you approach them with extraction mindset, you're essentially advertising that you don't understand the principles that created their success. If you approach them with contribution mindset, you're demonstrating that you share the values and approaches that enable sustainable achievement.

The choice between becoming a charity case versus becoming a valuable partner often determines whether your association with successful people accelerates your progress or limits your development. Choose contribution over extraction, partnership over dependency, mutual value over one-way assistance.

Your future self will thank you for building relationships based on strength rather than need, on capability rather than limitation, on what you bring rather than just what you hope to receive. That's how you avoid being the charity case while still benefiting from relationships with those who've achieved what you're working toward.

Be someone others want to partner with, not someone they feel obligated to help.

CHAPTER 24: BE THE CONDUCTOR

You cannot change people, but you can learn the sounds they make and use them as instruments to perfectly assemble your orchestra and play the songs you want to create.

This is one of the most liberating realizations you can have about leadership, relationships, and achieving objectives that require collaboration with others. Instead of exhausting yourself trying to transform people into what you wish they were, you learn to work with who they actually are while arranging them strategically to create the outcomes you want.

People, like instruments, have natural tendencies, inherent capabilities, and characteristic patterns of behavior. A trumpet will always sound like a trumpet, not a violin. A drum will always provide rhythm, not melody. A piano can play harmony or lead, but it cannot replicate the sustained notes of a flute.

Fighting these natural characteristics wastes energy and produces inferior results. Accepting them and arranging them strategically creates beautiful music that maximizes each instrument's contribution while achieving collective objectives that exceed what any individual instrument could accomplish alone.

The Buffoon approaches leadership by trying to make everyone the same. They want all their people to think identically, act uniformly, and contribute equally across all areas. When individuals don't conform to their preferred patterns, they become frustrated and attempt to force changes that go against natural tendencies.

This approach creates conflict, reduces efficiency, and wastes the unique capabilities that different personality types and skill sets can contribute to collective objectives. It's like trying to make violins sound like drums. This is possible with enormous effort, but counterproductive and inferior to simply using drums when you need percussion.

The Alley Cat approaches leadership by understanding each person's natural "sound" and positioning them where that sound contributes most effectively to the overall composition. They don't try to change fundamental characteristics, they arrange those characteristics strategically to create harmony and achieve objectives.

This doesn't mean accepting poor performance or problematic behavior. Just as instruments can be tuned, modified, and maintained to improve their performance while retaining their essential character, people can be developed, trained, and supported to optimize their contribution while working within their natural tendencies.

You can tune a guitar to improve its sound quality, change its strings to enhance its tone, or modify its setup to make it easier to play but you cannot make a guitar sound like a saxophone. Similarly, you can help people develop skills, improve habits, and optimize their approaches but you cannot change their fundamental personality, core motivations, or basic cognitive patterns.

Understanding this distinction prevents the frustration that comes from expecting people to become what they're not capable of becoming while enabling you to maximize what they are capable of contributing.

The conductor's role involves several key responsibilities:

Understanding Each Instrument: Effective conductors know the capabilities, limitations, and characteristics of every instrument in their orchestra. They understand which instruments can play which parts, which combinations create harmony versus discord, which arrangements produce the effects they want to achieve.

In human terms, this means understanding each person's strengths, weaknesses, motivations, communication style, and natural behavioral patterns. It means recognizing which people work well together versus which combinations create conflict. It means knowing who can handle which responsibilities effectively.

Strategic Arrangement: Conductors arrange instruments not randomly but strategically, positioning each where they can contribute most effectively to the overall composition. They don't place percussion in melody sections or expect woodwinds to provide the foundational rhythm.

In leadership terms, this means placing people in roles that align with their natural capabilities rather than forcing them into positions that require them to work against their strengths. It means creating teams where individual capabilities complement rather than conflict with each other.

Coordinated Timing: Conductors manage when different instruments enter and exit the composition, ensuring that each contributes at optimal moments rather than everyone playing constantly. They understand that silence from some instruments at certain times enhances rather than detracts from the overall effect.

In management contexts, this means knowing when to engage different people in various aspects of projects, when to have them lead versus support, when to give them prominent roles versus background functions. Not everyone needs to contribute equally to every aspect of every objective.

Adaptive Direction: Skilled conductors adjust their direction based on how the orchestra responds, making real-time modifications to optimize performance rather than rigidly adhering to predetermined plans when those plans aren't producing desired results.

103

Effective leaders similarly adapt their approach based on how their teams respond, modifying strategies and arrangements when initial approaches don't generate optimal outcomes. They remain flexible about methods while maintaining focus on objectives.

Clear Communication: Conductors provide clear signals that allow each instrument to understand their role, timing, and contribution to the larger composition. They communicate in ways that each section can understand and respond to effectively.

Leadership requires similar communication clarity, ensuring that each person understands their role, how their contribution fits into larger objectives, and what success looks like for both individual and collective performance.

The conductor analogy also highlights the importance of maintaining perspective about your role versus others' roles. The conductor doesn't play every instrument, they coordinate the playing of instruments by those who specialize in each one. They focus on arrangement, timing, and overall direction rather than on executing every individual part themselves.

Many leaders exhaust themselves trying to do everything personally rather than focusing on coordination and strategic direction. They micromanage individual contributions rather than optimizing collective performance. They lose sight of the larger composition while obsessing over individual notes.

Effective conducting requires trusting each instrument to play its part while maintaining responsibility for the overall performance. It means accepting that you cannot control every individual note while taking ownership of the collective result. It means understanding that your primary value lies in arrangement and coordination rather than in individual execution.

This approach becomes particularly valuable when working with challenging personalities or managing people whose natural tendencies create friction in traditional management structures. Instead of fighting their characteristics, you learn to position them where those same characteristics become assets rather than liabilities.

The person who naturally questions everything might be problematic in an execution role but invaluable in a quality assurance position. The individual who needs constant variety might struggle with routine tasks but excel in troubleshooting and problem-solving roles. The team member who works best independently might be counterproductive in collaborative environments but extraordinarily effective in specialized individual contributor positions.

By understanding these patterns and arranging people strategically, you can create high-performing teams from individuals who might seem incompatible or difficult to manage using conventional approaches.

The key insight is that your job as leader isn't to change people into what you wish they were, it's to arrange them strategically so that who they actually are contributes optimally to what you're trying to achieve.

This requires letting go of the fantasy that you can transform personalities, eliminate weaknesses, or make everyone equally capable across all areas. Instead, you focus on maximizing strengths, minimizing the impact of weaknesses through strategic positioning, and creating arrangements where individual limitations don't undermine collective objectives.

Some people will never be detail-oriented, but they might be excellent at generating creative solutions. Some will never be comfortable with uncertainty, but they might be exceptional at systematic execution. Some will never work well in groups, but they might produce extraordinary results when given independent projects.

The conductor's approach involves accepting these realities while arranging them strategically rather than fighting them unsuccessfully. It means playing to strengths rather than trying to eliminate weaknesses. It means creating compositions that sound beautiful despite or perhaps because of the unique characteristics of each instrument.

When you master this approach, leadership becomes less stressful and more effective. You stop wasting energy on impossible transformation projects and start investing energy in strategic arrangement that produces superior results with less effort and conflict.

You also develop better relationships with your team members because you're working with their natural tendencies rather than against them. People feel more valued when their genuine capabilities are utilized effectively rather than when they're constantly pressured to become something they're not.

Most importantly, you achieve better outcomes because you're leveraging the full range of human capabilities rather than trying to force everyone into narrow, standardized patterns that waste diverse talents and perspectives.

Be the conductor. Learn the sounds people make. Arrange them strategically. Create beautiful music through coordination rather than transformation.

The symphony you create will exceed anything you could accomplish by trying to make every instrument sound the same.

CHAPTER 25: AN ALLEY CAT CIRCLE WILL ALWAYS REMAIN

SMALL

If you keep your grass cut low, you can see the snake coming. This simple principle explains why genuine Alley Cats maintain deliberately small inner circles rather than surrounding themselves with large networks of casual associations. A small, carefully curated group allows you to know each member intimately from their character, capabilities, motivations, and potential areas of concern. A large group makes such intimate knowledge impossible, creating vulnerabilities that can prove devastating.

The Buffoon equates bigger circles with greater success. They collect contacts like trophies, accumulate social media followers like points in a game, and measure their importance by the size of their network rather than by the quality of their relationships. They believe that more connections automatically translate to more opportunities, more security, and more influence.

This approach creates dangerous illusions. Large circles inevitably include people whose loyalties are questionable, whose agendas are hidden, whose character is uncertain. They provide the appearance of support while potentially harboring threats you cannot adequately monitor or manage.

The Alley Cat understands that there are genuine dangers to having too many allies, because those "allies" often include hidden enemies disguised as friends. At least with declared enemies, you know their position, understand their agenda, and can prepare for their actions. Hidden enemies within your circle pose far greater threats because they have access, information, and opportunity that external enemies lack.

This creates a counterintuitive but crucial insight: it's often better to have two clear enemies and one loyal ally than to have two questionable allies and one unclear enemy. Two enemies and one ally means you know exactly who stands where, can prepare accordingly, and can trust your ally completely. Two allies and one enemy potentially means you have three enemies the declared one plus two hidden ones masquerading as support.

The mathematics of this principle become even more troubling when you consider that unclear relationships often break against you rather than for you during challenging moments. People who seemed supportive during easy times frequently reveal their true character when circumstances become difficult. Fair-weather friends become additional problems precisely when you most need reliable support.

Maintaining a small circle isn't about paranoia or antisocial behavior. It's about strategic relationship management that prioritizes depth over breadth, quality over quantity, loyalty over convenience. It's about recognizing that your inner circle represents your most valuable and vulnerable asset. Containing the people who know your plans, understand your weaknesses, and have access to information that could either support or sabotage your objectives.

The principle of keeping grass cut low applies to relationship management in several ways:

Transparency: In small circles, everyone's character, motivations, and behaviors are visible to everyone else. Hidden agendas become difficult to maintain when relationships are intimate rather than superficial. People cannot easily pretend to be what they're not when others have extensive, consistent exposure to their actual patterns.

Accountability: Small groups create natural accountability because each member's contribution (or lack thereof) is obvious to all other members. Free riders, problem creators, and hidden enemies cannot easily hide among small numbers of people who know each other well.

Communication: Clear, direct communication becomes possible in small circles where everyone understands context, history, and individual communication styles. Misunderstandings decrease while trust and efficiency increase.

Coordination: Small teams can move faster, adapt more quickly, and maintain secrecy more effectively than large groups. They can make decisions rapidly without extensive consultation or complex consensus-building processes.

Quality Control: It's possible to thoroughly vet and continuously evaluate a small number of relationships in ways that become impossible with large networks. You can invest the time and attention necessary to truly understand character, capabilities, and reliability.

The challenge lies in resisting the social pressure to expand your circle beyond optimal size. Many people interpret small circles as evidence of unpopularity, antisocial tendencies, or limited networking ability. They assume that successful people naturally have large networks and that small circles indicate some form of personal or professional limitation.

This misunderstanding causes many people to compromise the quality of their inner circle for the appearance of popularity or networking success. They include people they don't fully trust, maintain relationships they don't find genuinely valuable, and allow access to individuals whose character they haven't adequately assessed.

The Alley Cat resists these pressures because they understand that reputation for having many connections matters far less than reality of having reliable connections. They prioritize substance over appearance, effectiveness over perception, security over social validation.

This doesn't mean avoiding all professional networking, casual friendships, or broader social connections. It means distinguishing between your inner circle those with access to your plans, resources, vulnerabilities, your outer network of professional associates, casual acquaintances, and strategic connections.

Your outer network can and should be larger, more diverse, and less intimate. These relationships serve different purposes: professional opportunities, information gathering, industry connections, social activities, and strategic positioning. They don't require the same level of trust, scrutiny, or access that inner circle relationships demand.

The key distinction lies in understanding which relationships belong in which category and maintaining appropriate boundaries between them. Not everyone in your professional network needs to become a personal confidant. Not every casual friend needs to know your business strategies. Not every social acquaintance requires access to your private thoughts and plans.

Many people blur these boundaries, treating professional associates like intimate friends or sharing private information with casual acquaintances. This boundary confusion creates vulnerabilities that can be exploited by those with less honorable intentions.

The Alley Cat maintains clear distinctions between relationship categories and manages each type appropriately. They share information, grant access, and provide trust proportional to the relationship level rather than treating all connections identically.

Within the inner circle, loyalty becomes non-negotiable. Not blind loyalty that ignores problems or enables poor behavior, but thoughtful loyalty that prioritizes collective success while maintaining individual integrity. This means supporting each other during challenges, maintaining confidentiality about sensitive information, and addressing conflicts directly rather than allowing them to fester or be discussed with outsiders.

This loyalty must flow in all directions. If you expect loyalty from others, you must demonstrate loyalty to them. If you require confidentiality about your affairs, you must maintain confidentiality about theirs. If you need support during difficulties, you must provide support when others face challenges.

The small circle approach also requires accepting that not everyone can or should be included in your inner circle, regardless of their apparent qualifications or your personal feelings about them. Some people are wonderful individuals who simply don't fit within the tight coordination and deep trust that small circles require. Others may have valuable capabilities that don't align with your specific objectives or team dynamics.

This exclusion isn't personal rejection, it's strategic selection based on fit, capability, and alignment rather than on general worthiness or social compatibility. Just as professional sports teams don't include every talented athlete but select those whose capabilities complement team objectives, effective inner circles include those whose character and capabilities align with collective goals.

The process of building and maintaining small circles requires ongoing evaluation and occasional difficult decisions. People change with time. Circumstances evolve. What initially appeared to be good fit may prove problematic as relationships develop. What seemed like solid character may reveal weaknesses under pressure.

The Alley Cat approaches these evaluations honestly rather than sentimentally. They prioritize the integrity and effectiveness of the circle over individual relationships that no longer serve collective objectives. This might mean having difficult conversations about changed expectations, reduced access, or complete separation when necessary.

This isn't callousness, it's responsibility to those who remain committed and aligned. Allowing problematic individuals to compromise circle effectiveness punishes loyal members while rewarding those who don't maintain appropriate standards.

Remember that your inner circle represents both your greatest asset and your greatest vulnerability. Choose its members carefully, maintain its boundaries deliberately, and protect its integrity consistently. Quality always trumps quantity in relationships that truly matter.

The snake hiding in tall grass represents threats you cannot see coming. The small, carefully maintained circle with clear visibility represents security through strategic relationship management.

Keep your grass cut low. Maintain your circle small. Choose your allies carefully.

The safety and success of everything you're building depends on the wisdom of these choices.

CHAPTER 26: AI AS AN EXTENSION OF THE HUMAN MIND

We are living through the most significant technological transformation in human history, and most people are approaching it with the wrong mindset entirely. They see artificial intelligence as a threat to human capability rather than as an amplification of it. They view AI as a replacement for human thinking rather than as an extension of human intelligence.

This fundamental misunderstanding is creating a massive opportunity gap between those who embrace AI as a tool for enhancing their capabilities and those who resist it out of fear, ignorance, or misguided principles about "authentic" human achievement.

The Buffoon approaches AI with suspicion and resistance. They worry about being replaced, becoming dependent, or somehow "cheating" by using technological assistance to enhance their thinking and productivity. They cling to outdated methods because they feel more "authentic" or "human," not realizing they're voluntarily handicapping themselves in an increasingly competitive environment.

The Alley Cat recognizes AI as the ultimate power tool for the mind. Similar to how power tools revolutionized physical construction by amplifying human capability rather than replacing human creativity, planning, and strategic thinking. Just as no one today argues that using power tools makes you a "fake" carpenter, using AI tools doesn't make you a "fake" thinker.

Consider the analogy more deeply: Before power tools, construction was limited by human physical capability. Skilled craftsmen could create beautiful work, but it took enormous time and physical effort. Power tools didn't eliminate the need for skill, creativity, or strategic thinking, they amplified the craftsman's ability to execute their vision efficiently and effectively.

The craftsman still needs to understand materials, design structures, solve problems, and coordinate complex projects. The tools simply allow them to work faster, more precisely, and with less physical exhaustion. The most successful modern contractors are those who master both traditional skills and advanced tools, not those who refuse to use power equipment because they want to remain "authentic."

AI operates identically for mental work. It doesn't replace the need for human judgment, creativity, strategic thinking, or problem-solving capability. It amplifies your ability to process information, explore possibilities, generate alternatives, and execute ideas more efficiently and effectively.

The human mind remains the engine that provides vision, direction, values, and strategic oversight. AI becomes the transmission that amplifies and focuses that mental energy toward achieving objectives faster and more comprehensively than would be possible through unassisted human thinking alone.

Without human intelligence directing it, AI is merely sophisticated machinery like wheels, axles, chassis, and body of a car with an engine, and transmission, but without a driver. It can't determine where to go, what objectives to pursue, what values to prioritize, or what outcomes to create. It can only assist in achieving goals that human intelligence defines and directs.

When combined with focused human intelligence, AI creates exponential capabilities that transform what's possible for individuals willing to master these tools. The key insight is understanding AI as an IQ multiplier rather than an IQ replacement.

If you say that your friends are a picture of your future, then having AI in your back pocket means you're set to have access to virtually all available information, all known strategies, all documented approaches to any challenge you might face. You're essentially carrying the collective knowledge and analytical capability of humanity in your pocket.

But here's the crucial distinction that separates those who benefit from AI versus those who remain frustrated by it: information availability doesn't automatically translate to achievement. Having access to knowledge doesn't guarantee you'll use it effectively. Knowing what to do doesn't mean you'll actually do it.

The separating line isn't access to information, it's the drive, courage, and charisma to actually implement what you learn. You can have vast knowledge through AI assistance and still accomplish nothing if you lack the internal motivation to take action. You can have perfect strategies and comprehensive plans but remain unsuccessful if you don't possess the persistence to execute them consistently.

This is why AI amplifies existing human qualities rather than replacing them. If you're naturally driven, AI helps you pursue objectives more effectively. If you're intellectually curious, AI helps you explore ideas more comprehensively. If you're strategically minded, AI helps you develop better plans more efficiently.

But if you lack drive, curiosity, or strategic thinking, AI won't automatically provide these qualities. It will give you better information and more sophisticated analyses, but it won't give you the motivation to use them or the judgment to apply them wisely.

The Alley Cat understands this dynamic and approaches AI strategically:

Enhancement, Not Replacement: They use AI to amplify their existing capabilities rather than to replace their thinking. They maintain responsibility for decisions, direction, and values while using AI to improve the quality and speed of their analysis and execution.

Skill Development: They view AI proficiency as an essential modern skill, like literacy or computer competency in previous generations. They invest time in learning to use AI tools effectively rather than hoping to succeed without them.

111

Competitive Advantage: They recognize that mastering AI tools provides significant advantages over those who refuse to use them, similar to how mastering computers provided advantages in previous decades.

Quality Amplification: They focus on using AI to improve the quality of their thinking and work rather than just to increase quantity or speed. Better analysis, more comprehensive research, and more creative problem-solving become possible.

Strategic Integration: They integrate AI into their workflows systematically rather than using it sporadically. They develop consistent approaches for leveraging AI across different aspects of their personal and professional activities.

The practical applications are limitless and expanding rapidly:

Research and Analysis: AI can process vast amounts of information, identify patterns, and provide comprehensive analysis in minutes rather than hours or days. This allows for better-informed decisions and more thorough understanding of complex situations.

Creative Development: AI can generate multiple alternatives, suggest novel approaches, and help overcome creative blocks while the human mind provides direction, evaluation, and refinement of ideas.

Strategic Planning: AI can model scenarios, identify potential obstacles, and suggest optimization strategies while human judgment determines objectives and makes final decisions about implementation.

Communication Enhancement: AI can help refine writing, improve presentations, and develop more effective messaging while human authenticity and personality provide the genuine connection that technology cannot replicate.

Learning Acceleration: AI can customize educational content, provide personalized feedback, and create efficient learning paths while human motivation and application determine actual skill development.

The businesses being built today by AI-savvy individuals are outpacing traditional businesses by enormous margins. The professionals integrating AI into their workflows are producing higher quality results in less time than their peers who resist these tools. The creators using AI assistance are generating more content, exploring more possibilities, and reaching larger audiences than those working without technological amplification.

This isn't temporary disruption, it's permanent transformation. Just as societies that embraced previous technological revolutions (printing press, industrial machinery, computers, internet) gained lasting advantages over those that resisted them, individuals and organizations that master AI integration will maintain competitive advantages over those who refuse to adapt.

The resistance to AI often stems from misunderstanding about what intelligence and creativity actually involve. Many people believe that using external tools somehow diminishes the authenticity or value of human achievement. This perspective reveals limited understanding of how human intelligence has always operated.

Humans have always used external tools to amplify internal capabilities. Written language amplifies memory. Mathematics amplifies calculation. Scientific instruments amplify observation. Transportation amplifies mobility. Communication technology amplifies connection. AI simply represents the latest and most powerful tool for amplifying the most valuable human capability: intelligent thinking.

The question isn't whether AI will become integral to human achievement, it already has. The question is whether you'll master these tools to enhance your capabilities or allow others to gain advantages by embracing what you choose to resist.

My recommendation is simple: Start using AI tools immediately and systematically. Experiment with different applications. Develop workflows that integrate AI assistance naturally into your regular activities. Learn to collaborate effectively with artificial intelligence while maintaining human judgment and direction.

Most importantly, understand that AI isn't replacing human intelligence, it's extending it. The human mind remains the engine that provides creativity, values, judgment, and strategic direction. AI becomes the transmission that amplifies and focuses that mental energy toward achieving objectives more effectively than would be possible alone.

The future belongs to those who master this collaboration, not to those who resist it. The Alley Cat embraces every tool that enhances capability and provides competitive advantage. AI represents the most powerful such tool ever created.

Use it wisely, and it will amplify everything you're capable of achieving. Resist it, and you'll find yourself competing with diminished capabilities against those operating with enhanced ones.

The choice, as always, is yours. But the consequences of that choice are becoming more significant every day.

CHAPTER 27: INNOVATION AS THE CONSTANT

Throughout human history, the only constant has been change. The only predictable pattern has been innovation. The only certainty has been that the methods, technologies, and approaches that work today will eventually be replaced by methods, technologies, and approaches that work better tomorrow.

Yet most people approach change as an exception rather than as the rule. They seek stability as if it were achievable rather than adaptation as if it were necessary. They build their lives, careers, and strategies around the assumption that current conditions will persist rather than around the certainty that current conditions will evolve.

This fundamental misunderstanding of reality creates predictable patterns of obsolescence. Those who resist change eventually find themselves bypassed by those who embrace it. Those who cling to outdated methods eventually lose ground to those who master emerging approaches. Those who fight evolution eventually get left behind by those who participate in it.

The Buffoon treats innovation as disruption that threatens their position rather than as opportunity that enhances their potential. They invest enormous energy trying to preserve status quo rather than positioning themselves advantageously for inevitable change. They view evolution as a threat to their security rather than as a path to their advancement.

The Alley Cat recognizes innovation as the fundamental pattern of progress and positions themselves at the forefront of transformation rather than at the trailing edge of resistance. They understand that change creates opportunities for those who adapt quickly while creating problems for those who adapt slowly or not at all.

This distinction in perspective creates entirely different outcomes. The Buffoon gets overwhelmed by change because they're constantly fighting against it. The Alley Cat thrives during change because they're consistently working with it. One sees innovation as problem; the other sees it as solution.

Consider the historical pattern: Every generation faces technological, social, and economic changes that transform how work gets done, how value gets created, and how success gets achieved. The printing press disrupted scribes. Industrial machinery disrupted craft production. Computers disrupted manual information processing. The internet disrupted traditional communication and commerce.

In each case, those who embraced the new tools and methods prospered while those who resisted them struggled. The scribes who learned to operate printing presses thrived; those who insisted on hand-copying manuscripts became obsolete. The

114

craftsmen who adapted industrial techniques scaled their operations; those who refused to modernize lost market share to more efficient competitors.

The same pattern continues today with artificial intelligence, automation, global connectivity, and rapid technological advancement. Those who master these tools will gain advantages over those who resist them. Those who adapt their approaches will outperform those who cling to outdated methods.

The key insight is understanding that resistance to innovation doesn't prevent change, it only prevents you from benefiting from change. Evolution continues regardless of your participation. The question isn't whether innovation will occur, but whether you'll position yourself advantageously within that innovation.

This requires developing what I call "adaptation capability" the ability to recognize emerging trends, assess their implications, master new tools and methods, and integrate innovations into your existing activities in ways that enhance rather than disrupt your core objectives.

Adaptation capability involves several key components:

Trend Recognition: Developing sensitivity to emerging patterns in technology, market conditions, social behaviors, and economic structures. This means paying attention to early indicators rather than waiting until changes become obvious to everyone.

Opportunity Assessment: Evaluating which innovations represent genuine advantages versus temporary fads. Not every new development deserves adoption, but dismissing innovations too quickly can mean missing significant opportunities.

Strategic Integration: Learning to incorporate new tools and methods into existing workflows rather than allowing them to disrupt productive activities. The goal is enhancement through innovation rather than replacement of everything that currently works.

Continuous Learning: Maintaining intellectual curiosity and learning capability that allows for ongoing skill development rather than assuming that current knowledge will remain sufficient indefinitely.

Experimental Mindset: Being willing to test new approaches, learn from failures, and iterate toward better solutions rather than demanding immediate perfection from innovation attempts.

The biggest mistake people make with innovation is treating it as binary choice: embrace everything new or reject everything unfamiliar. This creates unnecessary extremes that prevent optimal integration of beneficial innovations while avoiding problematic ones.

The Alley Cat approaches innovation selectively rather than reflexively. They evaluate each potential change based on its likely impact on their objectives rather than accepting or rejecting it based on emotional reactions to change itself. They adopt innovations that enhance their capabilities while avoiding those that provide minimal benefit relative to implementation costs.

This selective approach requires developing judgment about which innovations represent genuine improvements versus which ones represent change for its own sake. Some new technologies, methods, and approaches provide substantial advantages that justify learning curves and transition costs. Others provide minimal improvements that don't warrant the effort required to implement them.

The key is maintaining openness to beneficial change while avoiding change that doesn't serve your larger purposes. This requires clear understanding of your objectives, honest assessment of your current capabilities, and realistic evaluation of potential improvements that specific innovations might provide.

My own experience illustrates this principle. When I was rebuilding after business setbacks, I consistently looked for new tools, methods, and approaches that could accelerate progress rather than relying exclusively on traditional methods that might have worked historically but weren't optimized for current conditions.

I embraced delivery apps when they emerged because they provided access to immediate income without requiring traditional employment relationships. I integrated digital tools for organization, communication, and business development because they enhanced efficiency beyond what manual methods could provide. I adopted AI assistance because it amplified analytical capabilities beyond what unassisted thinking could achieve.

But I didn't adopt every new technology or method indiscriminately. I evaluated each innovation based on its potential contribution to my specific objectives rather than accepting it simply because it was new or rejecting it simply because it was unfamiliar.

This selective approach allowed me to benefit from genuine improvements while avoiding distractions that would have consumed time and energy without producing proportional returns. It enabled strategic adaptation rather than reactive change management.

The same principle applies across domains. In business, innovations in marketing, operations, customer service, and product development create competitive advantages for those who implement them effectively. In personal development, innovations in learning methods, productivity systems, and skill development accelerate growth for those who integrate them wisely.

In relationship building, innovations in communication technology, networking platforms, and collaboration tools enhance connection capabilities for those who use

116

them strategically. In financial management, innovations in investment platforms, analytical tools, and opportunity identification improve wealth-building potential for those who master them appropriately.

The pattern remains consistent: innovation creates opportunities for those who participate in it and problems for those who resist it. The choice isn't whether innovation will occur, but whether you'll position yourself to benefit from it.

This requires overcoming natural human tendencies toward comfort with familiar patterns and resistance to unfamiliar approaches. It demands intellectual humility that acknowledges current methods might not represent optimal solutions. It necessitates courage to experiment with new approaches despite uncertainty about outcomes.

But the rewards for developing adaptation capability far exceed the costs of maintaining it. Those who consistently integrate beneficial innovations maintain competitive advantages that compound over time. They solve problems more effectively, achieve objectives more efficiently, and create opportunities that aren't available to those using outdated methods.

The Buffoon fights against innovation and eventually gets overwhelmed by it. The Alley Cat works with innovation and eventually gets amplified by it. One approach leads to obsolescence; the other leads to advancement.

The choice between these approaches often determines long-term success more than intelligence, education, initial resources, or other factors that people traditionally associate with achievement. Adaptation capability has become the meta-skill that enables all other capabilities to remain relevant and effective.

Embrace innovation selectively but consistently. Remain open to beneficial change while avoiding change for its own sake. Develop adaptation capability as core competence rather than as occasional necessity. Position yourself at the forefront of transformation rather than at the trailing edge of resistance.

The future belongs to those who participate in creating it, not to those who resist its arrival. Innovation is the constant the question is whether you'll work with it or against it.

Choose wisely. Your long-term effectiveness depends on that choice.

CHAPTER 28: THE HUMAN MIND AS THE ENGINE

Technology provides the vehicle, but human creativity, vision, and strategic thinking provide the engine that drives it toward meaningful destinations. Without human intelligence directing technological capability, even the most sophisticated tools become merely expensive machinery sitting idle in the garage.

This distinction becomes crucial as we navigate an era of rapidly advancing artificial intelligence, automation, and technological capability. Many people fear being replaced by machines, while others become overly dependent on technological solutions without maintaining their own intellectual development. Both approaches miss the fundamental truth: technology amplifies human capability but cannot replace human purpose, creativity, and strategic judgment.

The relationship between human intelligence and technological tools mirrors the relationship between an engine and a vehicle. The vehicle provides the mechanism for movement, but the engine provides the power that makes movement possible. The vehicle determines how efficiently that power gets translated into forward motion, but without the engine, even the most sophisticated vehicle remains stationary.

Similarly, technology provides the mechanism for amplifying human capability, but human intelligence provides the power that makes meaningful achievement possible. Technology determines how efficiently human intention gets translated into results, but without human vision and direction, even the most advanced technology produces nothing of lasting value.

The Buffoon misunderstands this relationship in both directions. Sometimes they fear technology will replace human intelligence, causing them to resist tools that could enhance their capabilities. Other times they expect technology to substitute for human intelligence, leading them to become passive consumers of technological solutions rather than active directors of technological resources.

The Alley Cat understands that human intelligence and technological capability work best in partnership, with human creativity and strategic thinking providing direction while technology provides amplification and execution support. They maintain responsibility for vision, values, and decision-making while leveraging technology to implement their intentions more effectively than would be possible through unassisted human effort alone.

This partnership requires understanding what humans do uniquely well versus what technology does uniquely well, then structuring collaboration that maximizes the advantages of both rather than trying to make either substitute for the other.

Humans excel at:

Vision and Purpose: Determining what's worth achieving, why it matters, and how it aligns with larger values and objectives. Technology can help implement vision but cannot create meaningful vision independently.

Creative Problem-Solving: Generating novel approaches to complex challenges, especially those requiring intuition, empathy, or understanding of human psychology. Technology can suggest alternatives but cannot create truly innovative solutions without human creativity.

Strategic Judgment: Making decisions under uncertainty, balancing competing priorities, and adapting strategies based on changing circumstances. Technology can provide analysis but cannot replace human judgment about complex strategic decisions.

Relationship Building: Creating authentic connections, inspiring trust, and coordinating collaborative efforts that require emotional intelligence and interpersonal skills. Technology can facilitate communication but cannot replace human relationship-building capabilities.

Values Integration: Ensuring that activities and outcomes align with ethical principles, personal values, and larger purpose. Technology can optimize for specified objectives but cannot determine what those objectives should be.

Contextual Understanding: Interpreting complex situations that require understanding of cultural nuances, historical patterns, and human motivations. Technology can process information but cannot fully comprehend context the way human intelligence can.

Technology excels at:

Information Processing: Analyzing vast amounts of data, identifying patterns, and performing complex calculations faster and more accurately than human cognitive ability alone.

Systematic Execution: Implementing detailed processes consistently, maintaining accuracy across repetitive tasks, and scaling operations beyond human capacity limitations.

Optimization: Finding efficiencies, eliminating redundancies, and improving performance through systematic analysis of variables and outcomes.

Storage and Retrieval: Maintaining perfect recall of information, accessing historical data instantly, and cross-referencing multiple sources simultaneously.

Simulation and Modeling: Testing scenarios, predicting outcomes, and exploring possibilities without requiring real-world experimentation that might be costly or risky.

24/7 Operation: Maintaining consistent performance without fatigue, emotion, or other human limitations that can affect consistency and reliability.

The most powerful combination emerges when human intelligence provides direction, creativity, and strategic oversight while technology provides amplification, execution support, and analytical enhancement. Neither replaces the other; both enhance what the partnership can achieve together.

Consider how this applies to business development. Human intelligence identifies market opportunities, understands customer psychology, creates compelling value propositions, and builds relationships that generate trust and loyalty. Technology amplifies these human capabilities by providing market analysis, automating customer interactions, optimizing marketing campaigns, and scaling operations beyond what manual effort could sustain.

The business succeeds not because technology replaced human judgment but because human judgment directed technological capability toward meaningful objectives that serve real human needs. The technology made implementation more efficient and effective, but human vision determined what was worth implementing.

The same principle applies across domains. In creative work, human imagination and artistic vision provide direction while technology provides tools for expression, distribution, and audience connection. In scientific research, human curiosity and theoretical thinking provide direction while technology provides analytical capability and experimental precision. In social impact, human empathy and values provide direction while technology provides scaling capability and implementation efficiency.

The key insight is maintaining human intelligence as the driving force while using technology as the amplifying mechanism. This requires several important disciplines:

Continuous Learning: Developing and maintaining intellectual capabilities rather than allowing technology to replace human thinking. Using technological assistance to enhance rather than substitute for mental development.

Purpose Clarity: Maintaining clear understanding of objectives, values, and desired outcomes rather than allowing technological capability to determine direction. Technology should serve human purposes, not create them.

Strategic Oversight: Remaining actively involved in important decisions rather than delegating judgment entirely to technological systems. Technology can inform decisions but shouldn't make them independently.

Creative Development: Nurturing imagination, intuition, and innovative thinking rather than relying exclusively on technological analysis. Human creativity provides the vision that technology implements.

Relationship Investment: Continuing to build authentic human connections rather than allowing technology to substitute for personal interaction. Technology can facilitate relationships but cannot replace them.

Ethical Integration: Ensuring that technological applications align with moral principles and social responsibility rather than optimizing purely for efficiency or profit.

The danger lies not in technology itself but in human abdication of responsibility for providing direction, maintaining judgment, and ensuring that technological capability serves meaningful human purposes. When humans stop thinking strategically, creating innovative solutions, or maintaining ethical oversight, technology becomes powerful machinery without purposeful direction.

This creates outcomes that might be technically sophisticated but humanly meaningless efficiency without purpose, optimization without values, capability without wisdom. The result is technological advancement that doesn't translate into human flourishing or meaningful progress.

The opportunity lies in maintaining human intelligence as the engine while leveraging technological capability as increasingly sophisticated vehicles for implementing human vision and achieving human objectives. This partnership can produce outcomes that exceed what either human intelligence or technological capability could achieve independently.

As I've integrated AI and other technological tools into my business development, creative projects, and strategic planning, I've maintained responsibility for setting objectives, making final decisions, and ensuring that outcomes align with my values and larger purposes. The technology has amplified my analytical capability, accelerated my implementation speed, and enhanced my creative possibilities but it hasn't replaced my judgment, vision, or strategic thinking.

This approach has produced better results faster than either unassisted human effort or purely technological solutions could have generated. The partnership leverages the unique strengths of both human intelligence and technological capability while avoiding the limitations that either would have when operating independently.

The future belongs to those who master this partnership rather than to those who try to choose between human intelligence and technological capability. The most successful individuals, organizations, and societies will be those that maintain human intelligence as the engine while leveraging technology as increasingly powerful vehicles for achieving meaningful human objectives.

This requires commitment to developing both technological proficiency and human intelligence rather than allowing one to substitute for the other. It demands maintaining agency over technology rather than allowing technology to determine your direction or replace your judgment.

Most importantly, it necessitates remembering that the ultimate goal isn't technological sophistication for its own sake but meaningful human achievement that improves lives, solves important problems, and creates lasting value for individuals and communities.

Technology provides extraordinary vehicles for achieving human objectives. But human intelligence must remain the engine that powers those vehicles toward destinations worth reaching.

Keep your engine well-maintained, properly fueled, and clearly directed. Let technology amplify your horsepower, but never let it replace your driver.

The road ahead requires both. Master the partnership, and you'll travel farther and faster than either could take you alone.

CHAPTER 29: IMPLEMENTING WITHOUT HESITATION

There's a massive gap between knowledge and application, between understanding what should be done and actually doing it. This gap explains why some people with minimal formal education achieve extraordinary results while others with impressive credentials remain stuck in mediocrity. It reveals why information abundance hasn't automatically translated to achievement abundance, why having access to all human knowledge doesn't guarantee personal success.

The separating factor isn't access to information, it's the ability to implement that information immediately and consistently without requiring perfect conditions, complete certainty, or external validation.

Most people treat implementation as the final step in a long preparation process. They believe they need to gather more information, develop better plans, secure ideal conditions, and feel completely confident before taking action. This approach guarantees that implementation never occurs because perfect conditions, complete information, and total confidence are illusions that prevent action rather than prerequisites for it.

The Buffoon falls into this preparation trap repeatedly. They attend seminars, read books, watch videos, and discuss strategies endlessly while producing minimal actual results. They mistake information consumption for progress, planning for achievement, and discussion for implementation. They accumulate knowledge without applying it, creating elaborate theoretical frameworks without testing them in reality.

The Alley Cat understands that implementation creates its own momentum, generates its own information, and develops its own confidence through direct experience rather than through extended preparation. They apply insights immediately, test strategies quickly, and adjust approaches based on real-world feedback rather than theoretical analysis.

This distinction explains dramatically different outcomes from similar starting points. Two people can attend the same educational program, receive identical information, and develop comparable understanding but only one will transform that information into tangible results through immediate implementation.

The implementer will discover what works through direct experience, develop practical skills through repeated application, and build confidence through accumulated successes and failures. The preparer will continue gathering information, refining plans, and waiting for better conditions while making minimal actual progress.

The abundance of available information actually makes this implementation gap more significant rather than less. When information was scarce, simply having access to knowledge provided substantial advantage. Now that information is abundant, the advantage goes to those who can sort through available knowledge quickly and implement valuable insights immediately.

Everyone has access to the same educational content, strategic frameworks, and success principles. The competitive advantage comes from speed and quality of implementation rather than from exclusive access to superior information. Those who implement quickly learn faster, adapt sooner, and achieve results while others are still planning.

This creates what I call the "implementation advantage". The exponential benefits that accrue to those who consistently translate knowledge into action without delay. Each implementation cycle generates experience that improves subsequent implementations. Each action creates momentum that makes future actions easier. Each result provides feedback that enables better future decisions.

The implementation advantage compounds over time because action generates information that preparation alone cannot provide. You discover what actually works versus what sounds good in theory. You identify obstacles that weren't obvious during planning stages. You develop practical skills that can't be acquired through study alone.

Most importantly, you build implementation capability itself the meta-skill of translating ideas into actions consistently and effectively. This capability becomes more valuable than any specific knowledge because it enables you to benefit from new information as soon as you encounter it rather than adding it to a pile of unused insights.

The key barriers to implementation aren't external they're internal psychological obstacles that create hesitation, delay, and eventual abandonment of potentially valuable initiatives:

Perfectionism: Waiting for ideal plans rather than implementing good-enough approaches that can be improved through experience. Perfect is the enemy of done, and done is infinitely better than perfect plans that never get executed.

Analysis Paralysis: Continuing to gather information and analyze options rather than making decisions based on available data. More analysis rarely leads to better decisions if fundamental information is already available.

Confidence Requirements: Waiting to feel certain before taking action rather than building confidence through successful implementation of uncertain initiatives. Confidence follows action more often than it precedes it.

Resource Perfectionism: Waiting for ideal resources rather than maximizing available resources. Implementation with limited resources often produces better results than waiting for abundant resources that may never materialize.

Timing Perfectionism: Waiting for perfect timing rather than creating momentum that improves timing through forward motion. Perfect timing is usually a retrospective assessment rather than a predictive one.

Approval Seeking: Requiring consensus or external validation before proceeding rather than implementing based on personal judgment and accepting responsibility for outcomes. External approval often reflects others' limitations rather than objective assessment of your capabilities.

Failure Avoidance: Preventing potential failures rather than learning from actual failures. The cost of failure during implementation is usually far less than the opportunity cost of not implementing at all.

Overcoming these barriers requires developing specific implementation disciplines:

Bias Toward Action: When uncertain between additional preparation and immediate implementation, choose implementation unless clear evidence suggests more preparation would provide substantial benefit. Most situations benefit more from action than from additional analysis.

Minimum Viable Implementation: Start with the smallest possible version of your idea rather than waiting to implement the complete vision. Small implementations provide feedback for improving larger implementations while generating immediate momentum.

Iterative Improvement: Implement quickly, gather feedback, and improve based on results rather than trying to perfect approaches before testing them. Real-world testing provides information that theoretical analysis cannot generate.

Time Boxing: Set specific deadlines for implementation rather than open-ended preparation periods. Limited time forces prioritization and prevents perfectionism from delaying action indefinitely.

Progress Metrics: Measure implementation progress rather than just planning progress. Track actions taken, tests completed, and results generated rather than just knowledge acquired or plans developed.

Feedback Integration: Actively seek and incorporate feedback from implementations rather than defending initial approaches. Implementation provides data for improvement, not validation for existing beliefs.

Momentum Maintenance: Use implementation successes to fuel additional implementations rather than celebrating completion and returning to preparation mode. Momentum makes subsequent implementations easier and more effective.

The most successful people I know share this implementation orientation. They don't wait for perfect conditions they create better conditions through consistent action. They don't require complete information they make decisions based on available data and adjust based on results. They don't need total confidence they build confidence through accumulated implementation successes.

When I was rebuilding after business setbacks, I couldn't afford extended preparation periods. Every day without income was a day closer to complete failure. This urgency forced immediate implementation of any potentially valuable strategy rather than careful analysis of optimal approaches.

This pressure created benefits that extended far beyond financial necessity. I developed rapid implementation capability that enabled me to test ideas quickly, discard ineffective approaches without significant investment, and scale successful strategies before competitors could respond. The urgency forced efficiency that became competitive advantage.

The same principle applies regardless of external pressure. Self-imposed urgency for implementation creates similar benefits like faster learning, quicker adaptation, and accumulated advantages from consistent action while others remain stuck in preparation mode.

Implementation without hesitation doesn't mean reckless action without consideration. It means making decisions quickly based on available information rather than indefinitely delaying decisions while gathering increasingly marginal additional data. It means accepting uncertainty as inherent in achievement rather than eliminating uncertainty as prerequisite for action.

It means understanding that implementation capability represents more valuable asset than knowledge accumulation, that action generates momentum more effectively than planning, and that results come from doing rather than from knowing what to do.

The vast majority of people already know what they need to do to improve their circumstances, achieve their objectives, and create the lives they want. They don't need more information, they need more implementation. They don't need better strategies, they need consistent application of adequate strategies. They don't need perfect conditions, they need action despite imperfect conditions.

The gap between where you are and where you want to be isn't filled with additional knowledge, it's filled with consistent implementation of knowledge you already possess. The distance between current results and desired results isn't covered through more preparation, it's covered through more action.

Stop waiting for better conditions, more information, greater confidence, or external permission. Start implementing what you already know with the resources you already have under the conditions that currently exist.

Implementation without hesitation isn't just about getting things done faster, it's about getting things done at all. It's about joining the small percentage of people who consistently translate knowledge into results rather than remaining in the large majority who accumulate insights without applying them.

The choice is simple but profound: continue preparing for action you may never take, or start taking action that will teach you everything you need to know.

Implement now. Improve later. But implement first.

Everything else is just preparation for implementation that may never occur.

CHAPTER 30: FOCUSED

Alley Cats are extraordinarily focused creatures. Every move they make serves a specific purpose. Every action they take aligns with deliberate intention. They don't waste energy on random activity or purposeless behavior. They don't create problems where none exist or seek conflict without clear justification.

This laser-focused approach stands in stark contrast to the chaotic, self-destructive patterns exhibited by the Buffoon, who often creates trouble specifically because they are trouble themselves. They search for problems in others to deflect attention from their own issues. They generate conflicts to provide cover for their own wrongdoing. They actively seek situations that allow them to project their guilt onto external circumstances.

Understanding this distinction becomes crucial for identifying when someone is approaching you with genuine concerns versus hidden agendas. It helps you recognize when someone is highlighting actual problems versus manufacturing distractions from their own problematic behavior.

The focused Alley Cat operates from a position of clarity about their objectives and strategic awareness about their actions. They don't make moves without reason because random action dissipates energy that could be directed toward meaningful progress. They don't search for trouble because creating unnecessary conflict interferes with productive activity.

When an Alley Cat does identify problems or raise concerns, these observations typically stem from legitimate issues that affect shared objectives or collective success. They're not seeking to create drama, they're highlighting obstacles that need addressing for everyone's benefit. They're not projecting guilt, they're providing information that serves mutual interests.

The unfocused Buffoon operates from internal guilt, fear, and consciousness of their own wrongdoing. They know they're engaging in problematic behavior, and this knowledge creates psychological pressure that demands relief. They seek this relief by finding or manufacturing evidence that others are equally problematic, equally guilty, equally wrong.

This psychological dynamic drives them to actively search for trouble in others, not because they genuinely care about identifying problems but because they need to feel less alone in their wrongdoing. They need to believe that "everyone does it" to justify their continued engagement in behavior they know is wrong. They need to find fault in others to avoid facing fault in themselves.

I've observed this pattern repeatedly throughout my journey. People who were engaging in questionable business practices would constantly scrutinize my activities, looking for any evidence of similar behavior. Not because they were concerned about business ethics, but because they needed to believe that my success came through questionable means rather than through legitimate capability and effort.

People who were violating trust in relationships would constantly question the loyalty and honesty of others. Not because they valued trust and honesty, but because they needed to believe that betrayal was universal rather than a choice they were making personally.

People who were cutting corners in their work would constantly point out imperfections in others' performance. Not because they cared about quality standards, but because they needed to believe that everyone was compromising standards rather than facing the reality that their shortcuts represented personal character flaws.

The pattern is always the same: those who know they're doing wrong actively search for evidence that others are doing wrong too. They need company in their guilt. They require validation that their problematic behavior is normal rather than exceptional. They seek justification that everyone is compromised rather than accepting responsibility for their own compromises.

This creates a specific type of danger for the focused Alley Cat. When you're operating with integrity, clarity, and legitimate purpose, you become a target for those who need to find fault in others to justify their own faults. Your clean behavior creates uncomfortable contrast with their problematic patterns. Your clear conscience highlights their guilty knowledge. Your legitimate success exposes their questionable methods.

Recognizing this dynamic allows you to identify when someone is approaching you with genuine concerns versus hidden agendas. Ask yourself these questions:

Does this person have a history of looking for problems in multiple people, or are their concerns specific and reasonable? Those projecting guilt cast wide nets, finding fault with many people. Those raising legitimate concerns focus on specific issues with specific individuals.

Do their accusations align with observable evidence, or do they seem to be fishing for confirmation of preconceived conclusions? Those seeking justification for their own behavior typically start with assumptions and look for supporting evidence. Those identifying actual problems typically start with evidence and draw logical conclusions.

Are they more interested in understanding the situation or in establishing that wrongdoing occurred? Those projecting guilt want confirmation that others are wrong rather than clarity about what actually happened. Those addressing legitimate concerns want accurate understanding regardless of where that understanding leads.

Do they seem relieved when they find problems, or concerned about resolving them? Those seeking company for their guilt feel better when they discover others' faults. Those identifying actual problems feel worse about the complications these problems create.

Are they offering solutions or just highlighting faults? Those projecting guilt rarely provide constructive suggestions because their goal is justification rather than resolution. Those addressing real problems typically offer ideas for improvement because their goal is actually solving the issues they've identified.

The focused Alley Cat responds to these dynamics strategically rather than emotionally. They don't become defensive when people search for problems in their behavior because they're confident in their own integrity. They don't try to prove their innocence to those who need to find guilt because they recognize this need has nothing to do with actual evidence.

Instead, they maintain their focus on legitimate objectives while protecting themselves from those whose agenda involves creating problems rather than solving them. They limit access to information that could be misinterpreted or manipulated. They avoid providing ammunition to those who are looking for reasons to feel better about their own questionable behavior.

This doesn't mean becoming secretive or paranoid. It means being strategic about transparency and sharing information with those who can use it constructively while protecting it from those who might use it destructively. It means recognizing that openness is a privilege earned through demonstrated good faith rather than an obligation owed to everyone regardless of their intentions.

The focused Alley Cat also understands that their clear purpose and clean behavior may make others uncomfortable. Some people feel judged by the mere existence of those operating with higher standards, even when no judgment is being expressed. Some feel pressured to elevate their own behavior when surrounded by examples of excellence, even when no pressure is being applied.

This dynamic isn't the Alley Cat's responsibility to manage. They can't lower their standards to make others feel better about maintaining lower standards. They can't compromise their integrity to reduce others' discomfort with their own lack of integrity. They can't sacrifice their focus to accommodate others' scattered approaches.

What they can do is maintain their course while remaining compassionate toward those struggling with internal conflicts. They can model better behavior without preaching about it. They can demonstrate that integrity and focus produce better results without explicitly criticizing alternative approaches. They can show through example what's possible when someone commits fully to legitimate objectives pursued through ethical means.

The key insight is this: when someone approaches you looking for problems without clear justification, investigate their own behavior before accepting their concerns about yours. When someone seems determined to find fault regardless of evidence, consider whether they need to find fault to justify their own questionable actions. When someone appears more interested in establishing guilt than in understanding truth, recognize that their agenda may have nothing to do with you and everything to do with their own psychological needs.

Stay focused on your legitimate objectives. Don't allow others' guilt to become your burden. Don't let their need for justification distract you from your commitment to excellence. Don't permit their problems to become your problems unless those problems genuinely affect shared interests.

The unfocused Buffoon will always search for trouble because they are trouble. They'll always look for problems in others because they can't face problems in themselves. They'll always need company in their guilt because isolation in wrongdoing becomes unbearable.

The focused Alley Cat remains committed to legitimate purposes pursued through ethical means. They don't create unnecessary problems because problems interfere with progress. They don't search for trouble because trouble distracts from meaningful objectives. They maintain clear conscience because clear conscience enables clear thinking.

When you encounter those who seem determined to find fault in your behavior despite evidence of your integrity, remember: their need to find problems says everything about them and nothing about you. Stay focused on what matters. Let your results speak louder than their accusations. Allow your consistency to prove what their criticisms cannot disprove.

Focus is power. Those who maintain it will always outperform those who dissipate it through unnecessary conflict, manufactured drama, and constant searching for problems that don't exist.

Which will you choose? The focused path of the Alley Cat, or the scattered approach of the Buffoon?

Your results will reflect your choice.

CHAPTER 31: TURNING SETBACKS INTO SETUPS

Every major setback in my life has eventually revealed itself as a setup for something better than what I originally thought I wanted. What initially appeared to be devastating losses, crushing defeats, or insurmountable obstacles later proved to be essential redirections that led to opportunities, capabilities, and insights that never would have developed through smooth, uninterrupted progress.

This isn't positive thinking or motivational rhetoric designed to make failure feel better. This is practical recognition of a pattern that becomes obvious once you learn to identify it: setbacks often contain the seeds of setups that produce outcomes superior to what would have been possible if the setback hadn't occurred.

The key distinction lies in how you respond to setbacks. The same challenging circumstances that destroy some people become launching platforms for others. The difference isn't the circumstances themselves, it's the internal response to those circumstances and the strategic use of forced change as opportunity for voluntary improvement.

The Buffoon treats setbacks as endings rather than as beginnings. When businesses fail, relationships end, health challenges arise, or financial difficulties emerge, they focus on what they've lost rather than on what they might gain. They become consumed by the gap between their expectations and their reality rather than exploring possibilities that the new reality might create.

The Alley Cat treats setbacks as redirections rather than as destinations. They understand that forced change often creates opportunities for voluntary change that wouldn't have been pursued during comfortable circumstances. They use external pressure as catalyst for internal transformation that generates capabilities exceeding what existed before the setback occurred.

This perspective shift requires overcoming natural human tendencies to resist change, mourn losses, and seek to restore previous conditions rather than to explore new possibilities. It demands viewing disruption as potential rather than just as problem, seeing obstacles as information rather than just as barriers, treating challenges as development opportunities rather than just as inconveniences.

When my business collapsed and I found myself homeless in Seattle, sleeping in a truck yard and delivering food on foot, every external indicator suggested complete failure. I had lost financial resources, professional status, and reliable transportation. By conventional measures, this represented devastating setback that had eliminated years of progress and left me worse off than when I'd started.

This apparent ending became the beginning of capabilities I never would have developed during comfortable circumstances. The extreme resource constraints forced innovation that abundance had never required. The social isolation created space for strategic thinking that constant networking had prevented. The urgent need for immediate income led to exploring opportunities that previous success had made unnecessary.

Most importantly, the complete elimination of external support systems forced reliance on internal resources I hadn't fully accessed during easier times. When you can't depend on anyone else, you discover capabilities within yourself that remain dormant when external assistance is readily available.

The $200 loan from Rance became possible only because my circumstances had stripped away everything that might have prevented that connection with the professional pretenses, the geographic limitations, and the social barriers that had existed during more comfortable periods. The extreme need created openness to relationships and opportunities that previous stability had made unnecessary to pursue.

The setback had created the setup for a transformation that comfortable circumstances never could have generated. The apparent loss had eliminated obstacles to growth that success had been maintaining. The forced change had created voluntary development that stability had been preventing.

This pattern repeats across different types of setbacks:

Business Failures: Often force recognition of weaknesses, development of new skills, and exploration of different approaches that lead to stronger subsequent ventures. The failure provides education that success couldn't deliver and motivation that comfort couldn't generate.

Relationship Endings: Frequently create opportunities for personal growth, improved partner selection criteria, and deeper self-understanding that enhance future relationships beyond what would have been possible if the original relationship had continued.

Health Challenges: Often motivate lifestyle changes, priority clarifications, and personal development that improve overall life quality beyond previous levels. The challenge forces attention to areas that had been neglected during healthy periods.

Financial Difficulties: Typically develop resourcefulness, creativity, and financial discipline that generate greater long-term wealth than would have been possible without the period of constraint. The limitation teaches capabilities that abundance doesn't require.

Career Setbacks: Usually lead to skill development, industry exploration, or entrepreneurial ventures that provide greater satisfaction and success than the original career path would have offered. The displacement creates exploration that employment had prevented.

The key to transforming setbacks into setups lies in asking different questions during challenging periods:

Instead of "Why is this happening to me?" ask "What is this teaching me?"

Instead of "How can I get back to where I was?" ask "Where might this lead that's better than where I was?"

Instead of "What have I lost?" ask "What capabilities might I develop?"

Instead of "How can I restore previous conditions?" ask "What new possibilities do current conditions create?"

Instead of "Why did this fail?" ask "What can I build from this experience?"

This reframing doesn't eliminate the genuine difficulty or emotional impact of setbacks. It redirects attention from lamenting what's gone toward exploring what's possible. It shifts energy from resistance toward adaptation, from restoration toward innovation, from looking backward toward moving forward.

The transformation process requires several key elements:

Acceptance: Acknowledging current reality rather than fighting against it or denying its implications. You cannot move forward effectively while simultaneously trying to undo what has already occurred.

Learning: Extracting maximum education from the experience rather than simply enduring it. Every setback contains information about what works, what doesn't, and what might work better in future situations.

Opportunity Recognition: Looking for possibilities that exist specifically because of the setback rather than in spite of it. Often the best opportunities emerge directly from challenging circumstances rather than from comfortable ones.

Capability Development: Using constraints and pressures to develop capabilities that abundance and comfort never require. Setbacks often force growth that success doesn't motivate.

Strategic Repositioning: Using forced change as opportunity for voluntary change in directions that align better with long-term objectives than previous paths did.

Resource Optimization: Learning to accomplish more with less, developing efficiency and creativity that provide permanent advantages even when resources later become abundant.

The timing of this transformation often creates initial confusion. The setup benefits typically don't become apparent immediately after the setback occurs. There's usually a period where the loss feels real and the gain isn't yet visible. This interim period tests commitment to the reframing process and determination to move forward despite uncertainty about outcomes.

During my truck yard period in Seattle, the eventual benefits weren't obvious. The education I was receiving through extreme constraint, the relationships I was building through vulnerability, the capabilities I was developing through necessity and none of these were immediately recognizable as advantages. They became apparent only as time revealed how these experiences contributed to subsequent opportunities and achievements.

This delayed gratification aspect of setback-to-setup transformation requires faith in the process rather than evidence of immediate benefits. It demands continued forward movement despite uncertainty about destination, continued growth despite unclear outcomes, continued optimism despite present difficulties.

The most important recognition is that setbacks often redirect you toward paths that align better with your authentic capabilities and genuine interests than the paths you were following before the setback occurred. What felt like failure in one direction becomes success in a different direction that proves more suitable for who you actually are rather than who you thought you should be. Sometimes setbacks remove you from situations that were gradually undermining your potential, relationships that were slowly limiting your growth, or circumstances that were preventing development of capabilities you needed but didn't know you lacked.

The business failure forced me to develop entrepreneurial skills rather than remaining an employee. The relationship betrayals taught me better judgment about character and partnership. The financial constraints developed resourcefulness and efficiency that abundance had never required. The social displacement created independence and self-reliance that comfort had never motivated.

Each apparent loss became actual gain once sufficient time revealed how the setback had created the setup for capabilities, opportunities, and outcomes that exceeded what would have been possible through uninterrupted progress along previous trajectories. This doesn't mean seeking setbacks or becoming grateful for genuine hardship. It means recognizing that when setbacks occur and they when will occur you will have the choice about how to respond to them. You can treat them as endings that limit future possibilities, or you can treat them as beginnings that create future possibilities.

The setback is often beyond your control. The setup is always within your influence.

Choose to turn your setbacks into setups. The results will exceed what comfort ever could have provided.

CHAPTER 32: THE ALLEY CAT'S NINE LIVES

The legend of cats having nine lives exists because cats possess an extraordinary ability to survive situations that would permanently disable or destroy other creatures. They land on their feet when others would crash. They find pathways out of circumstances that would trap others indefinitely. They recover from setbacks that would end most careers, relationships, or life trajectories.

True Alley Cats demonstrate this same regenerative capability, but through psychological and strategic resilience rather than physical agility. They possess an internal operating system that automatically converts defeats into education, failures into foundations, and endings into beginnings. They don't just survive setbacks, they use setbacks as launching platforms for comebacks that exceed their previous levels of achievement.

This isn't about magical thinking or pretending that failures don't hurt. It's about developing specific mental frameworks and strategic approaches that transform inevitable setbacks into voluntary setups for improvement. It's about building psychological infrastructure that remains intact when external circumstances collapse.

The Buffoon treats each setback as potentially fatal. When businesses fail, they conclude they're not entrepreneurial material. When relationships end, they decide love isn't worth the risk. When investments lose money, they determine wealth building is too dangerous. Each failure reinforces limiting beliefs about their capabilities rather than expanding understanding about what's possible.

This approach creates psychological fragility where single setbacks can end entire life directions. The Buffoon's identity becomes attached to specific outcomes rather than to ongoing processes, to particular achievements rather than to general capabilities, to external circumstances rather than to internal resources.

The Alley Cat treats each setback as educational rather than final. Business failures become market research for better ventures. Relationship endings become partner selection training for stronger connections. Investment losses become risk management education for superior strategies. Each failure expands understanding about what works rather than confirming beliefs about what's impossible.

This approach creates psychological antifragility where setbacks actually strengthen rather than weaken overall capabilities. The Alley Cat's identity attaches to learning processes rather than to specific outcomes, to developing capabilities rather than to particular achievements, to internal resources rather than to external circumstances.

I've experienced this nine lives phenomenon repeatedly throughout my journey. Each time circumstances appeared to have ended my progress permanently, I discovered capabilities, opportunities, or insights that enabled not just recovery but advancement beyond previous levels.

When drug dealing led to legal consequences that could have derailed everything, the experience taught strategic thinking and risk management that later proved invaluable in legitimate business. The apparent ending became beginning of capabilities that straight paths never would have developed.

When business partnerships collapsed through betrayal and poor decisions, the experience taught partner selection criteria and contract management that prevented similar problems in future ventures. The immediate loss became long-term protection that success never would have provided.

When corporate mismanagement closed the manufacturing plant despite my transformation of its operations, the experience taught me never to create value within systems I don't control. The apparent waste became foundational insight that guided all subsequent business development.

When legal challenges stemming from business dealings created years of supervision and constraint, the experience taught patience, systematic thinking, and long-term planning that produced better outcomes than unconstrained activity might have generated. The apparent limitation became strategic advantage that freedom alone couldn't create.

Each "death" of one life trajectory became "birth" of another life trajectory that incorporated lessons from previous experiences while avoiding their limitations. The setbacks didn't just teach what to avoid but they revealed what to pursue that hadn't been obvious during easier circumstances.

This regenerative capability depends on several key elements:

Identity Flexibility: Maintaining identity based on processes rather than outcomes, capabilities rather than achievements, internal resources rather than external circumstances. When your sense of self depends on learning and growing rather than on specific successes, setbacks become educational rather than existential threats.

Strategic Detachment: Avoiding emotional attachment to particular strategies, relationships, or opportunities that prevents adaptation when circumstances change. When you're committed to objectives rather than to specific pathways toward those objectives, obstacles redirect rather than stop progress.

Learning Orientation: Treating every experience as information rather than as judgment about your worth or capabilities. When failures provide education rather than evidence of inadequacy, they contribute to rather than detract from long-term success.

Resource Recognition: Understanding that capabilities, relationships, knowledge, and experience represent portable assets that survive external setbacks. When you recognize what can't be taken away, you maintain confidence despite temporary losses of what can be taken away.

Momentum Thinking: Viewing setbacks as temporary pauses rather than permanent stops, as redirections rather than endings. When you maintain forward orientation despite backward movement, recovery becomes acceleration rather than just restoration.

Pattern Recognition: Identifying how apparent failures contribute to eventual successes rather than just cataloging what went wrong. When you see setbacks as part of larger success patterns, they become stepping stones rather than roadblocks.

The nine lives capability also requires developing what I call "failure immunity". This is the ability to experience setbacks without allowing them to create lasting psychological damage that prevents future risk-taking and opportunity pursuit.

Many people experience single significant failures that create permanent risk aversion, limiting their willingness to pursue ambitious objectives that might also fail. They develop psychological scar tissue that prevents full engagement with opportunities that require vulnerability to potential setbacks.

The Alley Cat develops immunity through repeated exposure to setbacks combined with systematic recovery from them. Each successful comeback reduces fear of future setbacks while building confidence in recovery capabilities. Instead of avoiding risk to prevent failure, they engage with calculated risks knowing they can recover from potential failures.

This immunity doesn't come from avoiding failures or minimizing their impact. It comes from experiencing failures fully, learning from them completely, and recovering from them successfully enough times to prove that setbacks are temporary rather than permanent, educational rather than destructive, redirective rather than ending.

The process requires honestly acknowledging the genuine difficulty and emotional impact of setbacks rather than pretending they don't hurt or don't matter. Failure immunity comes from moving through the full experience rather than from avoiding or minimizing it.

It also requires maintaining perspective about the relationship between immediate circumstances and long-term trajectory. Setbacks affect current conditions without determining future possibilities unless you allow them to create permanent limitations through psychological damage or strategic abandonment.

The nine lives metaphor captures this perfectly: each "life" represents a different phase or trajectory that begins when the previous one ends. The ending of one phase creates space for the beginning of another phase that often proves superior to what was lost.

This only works if you actually use the additional "lives" rather than assuming the first major setback represents permanent ending. Many people allow single failures to end their willingness to pursue ambitious objectives, effectively wasting the additional lives that recovery would make available.

The Alley Cat uses all nine lives and sometimes discovers they have more than nine. Each comeback reveals additional resilience that wasn't obvious until tested. Each recovery builds confidence in the regenerative process that makes future setbacks less threatening and future comebacks more certain.

My own experience suggests that the regenerative capability actually strengthens through use rather than depleting through application. Each successful comeback from setback builds psychological infrastructure that makes subsequent recoveries faster and more complete.

The most important insight is that the nine lives aren't given, they're developed through consistent practice of the mental frameworks and strategic approaches that transform setbacks into setups. They represent capabilities you build rather than gifts you receive.

Start developing your nine lives capability now, before you need it. Practice the mental frameworks during smaller setbacks so they're available during larger ones. Build psychological antifragility through voluntary challenges that strengthen recovery capabilities.

Most importantly, understand that having nine lives doesn't mean you should be reckless with any of them. It means you can pursue ambitious objectives without paralyzing fear of setbacks, take calculated risks without terror of failures, and engage fully with opportunities without devastation from potential losses.

The Alley Cat's nine lives represent freedom to live boldly rather than license to live carelessly. They provide security for ambitious pursuit rather than excuse for reckless behavior.

Use them wisely, and you'll discover you have far more than nine.

CHAPTER 33: BUILDING IN HOSTILE ENVIRONMENTS

Some of the strongest structures in the world are built in the most challenging environments. Skyscrapers that withstand hurricanes are engineered to handle extreme forces. Bridges that span treacherous waters are designed to endure conditions that would destroy ordinary construction. Ships that navigate stormy seas are built with reinforcements that calm-water vessels never require.

The same principle applies to personal development, business building, and life construction. Some of the most resilient capabilities, innovative strategies, and powerful mindsets are developed specifically in response to hostile environments that would defeat those operating under easier conditions.

This isn't about romanticizing difficulty or suggesting that challenging circumstances are preferable to comfortable ones. It's about recognizing that when you find yourself in hostile environments (everyone does at various points) you have the option to use those environments as construction sites for capabilities that favorable conditions could never develop.

The Buffoon allows hostile environments to defeat them before they begin building. They wait for conditions to improve before taking action, seek to escape challenges rather than using them strategically, and blame external circumstances for internal limitations. They treat hostile environments as reasons why building is impossible rather than as opportunities to build something extraordinary.

The Alley Cat recognizes hostile environments as ideal conditions for developing extraordinary capabilities. They understand that the same forces that make building difficult also make builders stronger, more creative, and more resilient. They use environmental hostility as motivation for innovation rather than as excuse for limitation.

I learned this principle during my childhood in North Tulsa, where the environment seemed designed to prevent rather than enable success. Schools that barely provided education. Neighborhoods where violence was routine. Economic conditions that offered minimal legitimate opportunities. Social pressures that rewarded conformity to limiting patterns. These hostile conditions forced development of capabilities that favorable environments never would have required: strategic thinking under pressure, resource maximization under constraint, relationship building without institutional support, and goal pursuit despite systematic discouragement.

The hostility wasn't beneficial in itself, it created genuine hardships that easier conditions would have prevented. But responding to that hostility with determination to build despite it developed problem-solving capabilities, adaptive strategies, and psychological resilience that favorable conditions alone could never have generated.

140

The pattern repeated throughout my life. Each hostile environment became a construction site for capabilities that the previous environment hadn't required:

The drug dealing environment taught market analysis, risk assessment, customer psychology, and financial management under extreme pressure. The hostility of legal consequences and violent competition forced development of strategic thinking that legitimate business education might not have provided as intensively.

The manufacturing plant environment was initially hostile to excellence. Most workers resisted productivity, management provided minimal support, and the system rewarded mediocrity over achievement. This hostility created opportunities to demonstrate exceptional value that supportive environments might not have made possible.

The business collapse and homelessness in Seattle represented one of the hostile environments that I have faced with no stable housing, minimal resources, unknown city, no local connections, and urgent need for immediate income generation. This extreme hostility forced innovation, resourcefulness, and relationship building that comfortable circumstances never would have required.

Each hostile environment demanded construction of capabilities specifically designed to handle that environment's particular challenges. But those capabilities proved valuable far beyond their original context, providing competitive advantages in subsequent environments that others who hadn't faced similar hostility couldn't match.

Building in hostile environments requires several key strategies:

Environmental Assessment: Understanding the specific hostilities you're facing rather than just reacting emotionally to general difficulty. Different hostile environments require different construction approaches, just as different weather conditions require different engineering solutions.

Advantage Identification: Finding aspects of hostile environments that can be used strategically rather than just endured passively. Often the same conditions that create challenges also create opportunities for those who can identify and exploit them.

Resource Maximization: Making optimal use of whatever resources exist within hostile environments rather than waiting for better resource availability. Hostile environments typically offer fewer resources but also less competition for those resources.

Innovation Motivation: Using environmental pressure as catalyst for creative problem-solving rather than as excuse for conventional thinking. Hostile environments often require innovative approaches that favorable environments don't motivate.

Resilience Development: Building psychological and strategic capabilities that handle environmental stress rather than avoiding stress entirely. Just as physical exercise builds strength through controlled stress, environmental challenges build capabilities through managed difficulty.

Selective Engagement: Choosing which aspects of hostile environments to engage with directly versus which to avoid when possible. Not every challenge needs to be confronted head-on, but some challenges provide development opportunities worth pursuing.

Long-term Perspective: Understanding that capabilities developed in hostile environments often provide advantages in subsequent favorable environments. The construction period might be difficult, but the resulting capabilities prove valuable across many contexts.

The key insight is that hostile environments often contain resources and opportunities invisible to those who only know favorable conditions. When everyone else is avoiding or complaining about difficult circumstances, there's often less competition for the opportunities that do exist within those circumstances.

During the manufacturing plant period, the hostile night shift environment meant that anyone willing to work seriously had enormous opportunity to demonstrate exceptional value. The hostility of widespread dysfunction created space for individual excellence to stand out dramatically. A supportive, well-functioning environment might not have provided such clear opportunities for advancement.

During the Seattle homelessness period, the hostile circumstances eliminated social barriers and conventional expectations that might have prevented certain connections and opportunities. The vulnerability created by extreme circumstances enabled relationships and insights that comfort might have made unnecessary to pursue.

This doesn't mean seeking hostile environments or remaining in them longer than necessary. It means recognizing that when you find yourself in challenging circumstances (through choice or through circumstance) you can use those conditions as construction sites for capabilities that will serve you long after the hostile environment ends.

The capabilities developed in hostile environments often prove more valuable and durable than those developed in favorable conditions because they're tested under stress rather than just practiced during comfort. They're proven under pressure rather than just theorized during ease.

Consider how this applies to current challenges you might be facing:

Financial Constraints: Can force innovation, efficiency, and resourcefulness that abundance doesn't require. The limitations might teach value maximization and strategic thinking that wealth alone couldn't provide.

Professional Obstacles: Often develop problem-solving capabilities, political skills, and resilience that smooth career paths don't demand. The resistance might build capabilities that advancement alone couldn't create.

Relationship Difficulties: Frequently teach communication skills, boundary setting, and emotional intelligence that harmonious relationships don't exercise. The challenges might develop interpersonal capabilities that easy relationships don't require.

Health Challenges: Usually motivate lifestyle optimization, priority clarification, and personal development that good health doesn't inspire. The difficulties might create wellness strategies that feeling fine doesn't generate.

Social Hostility: Can develop independence, authentic self-expression, and strong personal values that social acceptance doesn't strengthen. The resistance might build character that approval doesn't create.

The most important recognition is that you cannot wait for favorable environments to begin building the life you want. If you only build during favorable conditions, you'll have very few opportunities to build anything substantial. Most of life involves mixed conditions where some elements are favorable and others are hostile.

The Alley Cat learns to build regardless of environmental conditions, using favorable elements strategically while neutralizing or converting hostile elements when possible. They don't require perfect conditions to begin construction. They use whatever conditions exist as raw materials for building something valuable.

This approach requires mental toughness that comfortable circumstances don't develop. It demands strategic thinking that easy conditions don't require. It necessitates problem-solving capabilities that supportive environments don't exercise.

It also provides freedom from environmental dependence that those requiring favorable conditions never achieve. When you can build in hostile environments, you can build anywhere. When you can create value despite opposition, you can create value under any circumstances.

The hostile environment becomes your construction site rather than your limitation. The resistance becomes your weight training rather than your barrier. The difficulty becomes your competitive advantage rather than your excuse.

Build where you are, with what you have, under whatever conditions exist. Use environmental hostility as motivation for innovation rather than as justification for limitation. Some of the strongest structures are built in the most challenging environments. Make sure yours is one of them.

CHAPTER 34: QUIT WHEN YOU DIE

There's no reason to ever quit. Ever.

I've seen too many people abandon their objectives seconds before breakthrough, give up on their dreams just before they manifest, walk away from their goals when they're literally at the finish line. They quit when they're exhausted, discouraged, or facing temporary setbacks that feel permanent but aren't.

The lesson I've learned from observing countless examples of premature abandonment is simple: you can change the plan, but you never change the goal. You can adjust strategies, modify approaches, and adapt tactics but you never surrender the ultimate objective that drives everything else.

The difference between those who achieve extraordinary results and those who remain stuck in mediocrity isn't talent, resources, or opportunity. It's the simple refusal to quit regardless of circumstances, setbacks, or temporary defeats. It's understanding that the only real failure is stopping before you succeed.

The Buffoon quits when things get difficult. They abandon objectives when progress slows, change goals when obstacles appear, and convince themselves that "being realistic" means accepting limitations rather than overcoming them. They treat temporary circumstances as permanent conditions and allow current difficulties to determine future possibilities.

The Alley Cat understands that quitting guarantees the very failure that persistence might prevent. They recognize that most objectives worth achieving require pushing through periods of discouragement, uncertainty, and apparent futility. They know that the darkest moments often occur just before breakthrough arrives.

This isn't about blind stubbornness or refusing to adapt when circumstances clearly indicate better approaches. It's about maintaining unwavering commitment to core objectives while remaining flexible about the methods for achieving them. It's about distinguishing between strategic adjustments and goal abandonment.

I've experienced this principle repeatedly throughout my journey. Multiple times, I've been on the verge of quitting when persistence for just a little longer produced breakthrough results that quitting would have prevented entirely.

During the manufacturing plant period, there were moments when the effort required to transform that dysfunctional environment seemed futile. The resistance from other workers, the lack of initial recognition from management, the exhaustion of working 12-hour shifts while living in a hotel. All of these factors created pressure to accept mediocrity and stop pushing for excellence.

Maintaining commitment to the goal of creating stability for my family, while adjusting strategies for achieving that goal, eventually produced the breakthrough that changed everything. The promotion, pay increase, and expanded responsibilities came only after pushing through periods when quitting would have seemed reasonable.

During the business collapse and homelessness in Seattle, there were countless moments when giving up would have seemed logical. Sleeping in truck yards, delivering food on foot, surviving on minimal resources while trying to rebuild. These circumstances created constant pressure to abandon entrepreneurial objectives and settle for conventional employment that provided immediate stability without long-term potential.

Maintaining commitment to the goal of business ownership while adapting strategies for achieving it eventually led to the opportunities and relationships that enabled rebuilding. The transformation from homelessness to business development happened only because quitting was never considered an option.

The pattern is consistent: the breakthrough often comes just after the point where most people would quit. Not immediately after, but close enough that persistence for slightly longer makes the difference between failure and success, between dreams abandoned and objectives achieved.

This proximity of breakthrough to potential quitting points isn't coincidental. It's structural. The same forces that create pressure to quit also indicate that you're approaching breakthrough territory. The difficulty you're experiencing often signals that you're close to achieving something significant rather than far from it.

Consider the analogy of physical exercise. The greatest strength gains occur during the final repetitions when your muscles are most fatigued and continuing feels most difficult. Quitting when exercise becomes challenging prevents the very adaptation that exercise is designed to create. The discomfort indicates progress rather than the need to stop.

The same principle applies to achieving ambitious objectives. The greatest progress often occurs during periods when continuing feels most difficult and quitting seems most reasonable. The pressure to quit indicates you're in the zone where transformation happens rather than in the zone where it's impossible.

This only works if you maintain clear distinction between goals and plans. Goals represent ultimate objectives that justify significant effort and sacrifice. Plans represent current strategies for achieving those goals. Goals should remain constant until achieved; plans should adapt constantly based on results and changing circumstances. Many people confuse these categories, treating specific plans as if they were ultimate goals and abandoning objectives when particular strategies don't work. This confusion causes them to quit on goals when they should be adjusting plans, to abandon dreams when they should be modifying approaches.

The commitment to never quit applies to goals, not to plans. You should quit ineffective plans quickly and frequently while never quitting the underlying goals those plans were designed to achieve. You should abandon strategies that aren't working while maintaining objectives that are worth achieving.

This requires developing what I call "strategic persistence" the ability to maintain unwavering commitment to objectives while remaining completely flexible about methods. It means being absolutely stubborn about destinations while being completely adaptable about routes.

Strategic persistence involves several key elements:

Goal Clarity: Maintaining crystal clear understanding of what you're ultimately trying to achieve rather than getting lost in the details of how you're trying to achieve it. When goals are clear, plan adjustments become navigation corrections rather than destination changes.

Plan Flexibility: Remaining completely open to changing strategies, tactics, and approaches when current methods aren't producing desired results. Flexibility about plans enables persistence toward goals by preventing attachment to ineffective methods.

Progress Measurement: Tracking advancement toward goals rather than just execution of plans. Sometimes progress toward objectives occurs through completely different paths than originally anticipated.

Learning Integration: Using setbacks and failures as information for improving approaches rather than as evidence that goals are impossible. Every failure teaches something valuable about what doesn't work and often suggests what might work better.

Resource Optimization: Continuously looking for better ways to apply available resources toward goal achievement rather than assuming current resource allocation represents optimal usage.

Timeline Flexibility: Understanding that significant objectives often take longer than initially anticipated without this extended timeline meaning the goals are impossible. Many people quit because achievements take longer than expected rather than because they're genuinely impossible.

Support System Development: Building relationships and resources that provide encouragement during difficult periods when quitting feels tempting. Isolation makes quitting easier while connection makes persistence more sustainable.

The most important insight is recognizing that quitting becomes permanent immediately while persistence always maintains possibility of eventual success. When you quit, the probability of achieving your objective drops to zero and remains there permanently. When you persist, the probability might fluctuate but never reaches zero as long as you continue trying.

This mathematical reality alone justifies never quitting on objectives that genuinely matter to you. Even if success probability feels low, maintaining any probability exceeds accepting zero probability through abandonment.

Beyond mathematical logic, there's practical wisdom in the never-quit principle. I've discovered that the capability to persist through difficulty is itself valuable regardless of specific objective achievement. The psychological strength, problem-solving skills, and resilience developed through refusing to quit serve you across all areas of life. People who develop the habit of persistence on important objectives also develop confidence in their ability to overcome challenges generally. They know from experience that temporary setbacks don't predict permanent failure, that difficult periods don't last forever, that breakthrough often follows breakdown.

This confidence creates willingness to pursue ambitious objectives that others avoid due to fear of failure. When you know you won't quit regardless of difficulties, you can pursue goals that require persistence beyond what most people can sustain.

The never-quit principle also attracts support from others who recognize and respect determination. People prefer to invest time, energy, and resources in those who demonstrate commitment to their objectives rather than those who abandon goals when circumstances become challenging.

Persistence signals seriousness about objectives in ways that talent, intelligence, or initial enthusiasm cannot match. When others see that you won't quit regardless of setbacks, they develop confidence in your eventual success that encourages their support and partnership. Most importantly, the refusal to quit often outlasts the specific obstacles that created pressure to quit in the first place. Circumstances change, new opportunities emerge, better resources become available, and problems that seemed permanent prove temporary but only if you persist long enough for these improvements to occur.

Quitting guarantees that you won't benefit from positive changes that might happen after you stop trying. Persistence ensures that you'll be positioned to benefit from improvements whenever they occur. You can change the plan as many times as necessary. You can adjust strategies, modify approaches, and completely reinvent methods. You can pivot, adapt, and evolve your tactics based on results and changing circumstances. Never change the goal. Never quit on objectives that genuinely matter to you. Never abandon dreams that align with your authentic purpose and values.

The only acceptable time to quit is when you die. Until then, keep going.

Your breakthrough might be one more day, one more attempt, one more adjustment away from arriving. Don't quit before you find out.

CHAPTER 35: FOREVER A STUDENT

Learn from everything and everyone. Every person you encounter possesses a lesson worth understanding, regardless of their circumstances, background, or apparent limitations. Every situation contains information that can improve your judgment, enhance your strategies, or expand your perspective. If you maintain the curiosity and humility to extract that information.

This principle has guided me through every phase of my journey, from the most challenging circumstances to the most successful periods. I've learned valuable lessons from drug addicts and billionaires, from homeless individuals and corporate executives, from failure and success, from supporters and enemies. The wisdom has come from unexpected sources at unexpected times, often when I least expected it but most needed it.

The Buffoon believes learning comes only from credentialed experts, prestigious institutions, or officially recognized authorities. They dismiss insights from unconventional sources, ignore lessons from difficult circumstances, and assume that valuable knowledge only emerges from approved channels. This limitation prevents them from accessing the full spectrum of human experience and wisdom.

The Alley Cat understands that the universe provides education through every experience and every encounter if you maintain openness to receiving it. They extract lessons from success and failure, from friends and enemies, from planned learning and unexpected teaching moments. They recognize that some of the most valuable insights come from sources that conventional thinking would overlook or dismiss.

One of the most profound learning experiences of my life occurred on a subway train in Philadelphia at 11:43 PM Eastern time. I was there to conduct business that had been postponed at the last minute, leaving me stranded overnight without money for a hotel or rental car. I was riding the subway for hours, trying to find places to sleep in five or six-hour stretches.

During my second trip back onto the train, I encountered a man who was clearly high on some type of opioid or heroin or something similar. He was basically drooling and rambling, but as I listened more carefully, I realized he was talking directly to me. "I'm talking to you, young brother," he kept saying.

Most people would have ignored someone in his condition, dismissed his words as drug-induced nonsense, or moved away to avoid interaction. But something made me pay attention to what he was actually saying rather than just how he was saying it.

He was talking about horses and land. "If you want to really control something in this America," he said, "control horses and land." As I listened more carefully, I realized he was talking about vehicles and real estate. His altered state hadn't prevented him from understanding fundamental principles of wealth building and control.

This insight hit me powerfully because I was already in the fleet business at the time, working with vehicles, and his words connected with my existing experience in ways that crystallized my thinking about real estate investment. When I later ended up in Seattle and met Rance, who introduced me to wholesale real estate investing, I recognized this as another piece of the puzzle that homeless man had helped me identify.

Here was someone whom society would completely dismiss as a drug addict on a subway train at midnight. He was providing insights about wealth building that many formally educated business professionals never grasp. His condition didn't invalidate the wisdom of his observation. His circumstances didn't eliminate the value of his perspective.

That man dropped jewels right into my lap. At the exact moment I needed to hear them in the exact circumstances where I was open to receiving them. If I had been comfortable and successful at the time, I might not have been on that train. If I had been closed-minded about learning sources, I might not have listened carefully enough to understand what he was telling me.

This experience taught me that education happens everywhere, at any time of day or night, through any type of person, in any kind of circumstances. You must be willing to learn from everything and everyone if you want to access the full spectrum of available wisdom.

The principle applies across all categories of experience:

Learn from Success: When things go well, extract maximum understanding about what worked, why it worked, and how it can be replicated or improved. Success contains lessons about effective strategies, optimal timing, and beneficial approaches that shouldn't be taken for granted.

Learn from Failure: When things go wrong, analyze what didn't work, why it failed, and how similar problems can be prevented or handled better in the future. Failure often teaches more valuable lessons than success because it reveals weaknesses and limitations that success might hide.

Learn from Supporters: People who help you succeed provide insights about valuable relationships, effective collaboration, and beneficial partnerships. Don't just appreciate their support, study how they operate, what motivates them, and how they create value in their own lives.

Learn from Opponents: People who oppose or compete with you reveal information about different strategies, alternative approaches, and potential weaknesses in your own methods. Their resistance can highlight areas for improvement or blind spots you hadn't recognized.

Learn from Peers: People at similar levels provide insights about parallel challenges, comparable strategies, and shared opportunities. They offer perspective about what's working for others facing similar circumstances and what obstacles are common to your situation.

Learn from Mentors: People ahead of you provide roadmaps for advancement, warnings about potential pitfalls, and encouragement about what's possible. Remember that their paths might not be identical to yours but extract principles rather than copying specifics.

Learn from Observers: People outside your situation often see patterns, opportunities, or problems that aren't visible from within your circumstances. Their external perspective can provide valuable insights about your approaches and their effectiveness.

The key is maintaining what I call "learning posture" a mental orientation that actively seeks valuable information from every experience rather than passively hoping that good information will somehow appear when needed.

Learning posture involves several specific practices:

Active Listening: Paying attention to what people actually say rather than just waiting for your turn to speak. Many valuable insights are missed because we're formulating responses rather than absorbing information.

Question Asking: Inquiring about people's experiences, strategies, and perspectives rather than just sharing your own. The right questions can unlock insights that wouldn't emerge through casual conversation.

Pattern Recognition: Looking for connections between different experiences, common themes across various encounters, and recurring principles that appear in multiple contexts.

Judgment Suspension: Avoiding immediate evaluation of sources based on their appearance, credentials, or circumstances. Valuable information can come from unexpected sources if you remain open to receiving it.

Application Focus: Considering how insights might apply to your circumstances rather than just appreciating them intellectually. The goal is practical application rather than academic understanding.

Documentation: Recording valuable insights when they occur rather than trusting memory to retain them. Important lessons can be lost if not captured systematically.

Integration: Connecting new information with existing knowledge to develop comprehensive understanding rather than treating each insight as isolated information.

This learning orientation becomes particularly valuable during challenging periods when conventional sources of education might not be accessible. When you're struggling financially, you might not be able to afford expensive courses or coaching. When you're geographically isolated, you might not have access to networking events or professional development opportunities.

If you maintain learning posture, education continues regardless of circumstances. Every person you encounter, every situation you experience, every challenge you face becomes a potential source of valuable information that can improve your understanding and enhance your capabilities.

The homeless man on that Philadelphia subway couldn't provide formal education about real estate investing, but his insight about the fundamental relationship between control and wealth was more valuable than many expensive seminars I could have attended. His lesson was perfectly timed, completely relevant, and immediately applicable to my circumstances.

This doesn't mean accepting everything you hear without evaluation or assuming that all sources provide equally valuable information. It means maintaining openness to learning while applying judgment about which insights are worth integrating and how they might apply to your specific circumstances.

Some people will provide insights about what to pursue. Others will demonstrate what to avoid. Some will offer strategies worth implementing. Others will reveal approaches worth rejecting. All of this information has value if you maintain learning posture that extracts maximum education from every encounter.

The forever student mentality also prevents the intellectual arrogance that often develops with success or expertise. When you assume you already know everything important, you stop learning new information that could improve your results or prevent future problems.

When you maintain student mentality regardless of your achievements, you continue discovering insights that enhance your capabilities and expand your possibilities. You remain curious rather than complacent, open rather than closed, growing rather than static.

This approach has served me consistently throughout every phase of my journey. During difficult periods, it provided education that formal sources couldn't offer. During successful periods, it prevented complacency that might have led to stagnation or decline.

Most importantly, it's enabled me to extract maximum value from every experience rather than just enduring some experiences while only learning from others. Every encounter becomes educational. Every situation provides information. Every person offers insights.

You are surrounded by teachers if you maintain the wisdom to recognize them and the humility to learn from them. Your next crucial insight might come from the most unexpected source at the most unlikely time.

Stay curious. Stay humble. Stay learning. Forever a student means forever growing, forever improving, forever expanding your understanding of what's possible and how to achieve it. The education never ends unless you decide to stop learning. Don't stop learning.

CHAPTER 36: ALLEY CATS UNDERSTAND THAT IF THEY CAN'T GUARD THEIR MIND, THEY CAN'T GUARD THEIR BODY

Your mind is the control center for everything. It's the gateway to your body, your decisions, your relationships, and your future. If you can't protect your mind from harmful influences, negative thinking, and destructive impulses, you cannot protect your body from the consequences of poor decisions that mental weakness inevitably produces.

This principle extends far beyond individual self-protection. You can't depend on people to protect themselves or you if they can't control their own mental processes. You can't rely on people to keep themselves safe, healthy, or free from dangerous situations if their minds are compromised by substances, toxic relationships, or inability to resist harmful temptations.

The connection between mental control and physical safety isn't philosophical, it's practical and immediate. Every poor physical decision begins with a mental weakness that allowed harmful thinking to override good judgment. Every dangerous situation someone enters started with mental processes that couldn't properly evaluate risks or resist temptations.

The Buffoon doesn't understand this connection. They think they can maintain physical safety while allowing mental compromise. They believe they can engage in substance abuse, toxic relationships, or dangerous thinking patterns without these mental weaknesses eventually creating physical consequences. They don't recognize that mental vulnerability inevitably becomes physical vulnerability.

The Alley Cat understands that mental protection is the foundation of all other protection. They guard their thinking as carefully as they guard their possessions because they recognize that compromised thinking leads to compromised everything else. They know that mental strength enables physical safety while mental weakness guarantees physical danger.

This understanding shapes how they evaluate relationships, assess potential partners, and determine who can be trusted with important responsibilities. They look for evidence of mental discipline and self-control because these qualities predict reliability in all other areas.

You can't depend on people to keep themselves safe and sanitary if they can't protect their minds. You can't rely on them to avoid STDs, dangerous situations, or harmful behaviors if their mental defenses are compromised. When someone's mind is not protected, their body becomes vulnerable to everything their compromised judgment exposes them to.

The signs of mental vulnerability are usually obvious if you know what to look for:

Substance Dependency: People who cannot function without alcohol, drugs, or other chemical alterations demonstrate fundamental inability to handle reality with clear thinking. If they need substances to cope with normal life circumstances, they lack the mental resilience required for handling genuine challenges.

Toxic Relationship Patterns: People who consistently maintain relationships with individuals who harm them demonstrate inability to protect themselves from obviously damaging influences. If they can't guard against people who are clearly bad for them, they can't guard against subtler threats.

Impulse Control Issues: People who cannot resist immediate gratification when it conflicts with long-term wellbeing demonstrate compromised decision-making capability. If they can't control minor impulses, they certainly can't control major ones when stakes are higher.

Emotional Instability: People whose moods, decisions, and behaviors fluctuate dramatically based on temporary feelings demonstrate unreliable mental processes. If their thinking changes based on emotions rather than logic, they can't be trusted with important responsibilities.

Reality Distortion: People who consistently blame external circumstances for problems clearly caused by their own choices demonstrate inability to process information accurately. If they can't see reality clearly, they can't make decisions based on actual conditions.

Boundary Weakness: People who allow others to violate their standards, manipulate their decisions, or control their actions demonstrate inability to maintain personal sovereignty. If they can't protect their own boundaries, they can't protect anything else.

These warning signs indicate fundamental problems with mental defense systems that make such individuals unreliable for any important purpose. They cannot protect themselves effectively, which means they certainly cannot protect others or shared objectives.

The Alley Cat identifies these patterns quickly and adjusts their level of trust and dependency accordingly. They don't try to fix people who demonstrate mental weakness. They protect themselves from the consequences of that weakness while maintaining appropriate compassion for the individuals struggling with these issues.

This doesn't mean abandoning people who face mental health challenges or judging those dealing with difficult circumstances. It means recognizing that certain types of relationships and responsibilities require mental strength and reliability that not everyone possesses at every point in their lives.

154

You can care about someone while recognizing that they're not currently capable of protecting themselves adequately. You can wish them well while understanding that their mental vulnerability makes them unsuitable for roles requiring strong judgment, reliable decision-making, or consistent self-protection.

The principle applies equally to evaluating your own mental defenses. Are you maintaining the thinking patterns, relationships, and habits that strengthen your mental control, or are you engaging in activities that weaken your ability to think clearly and make good decisions?

Mental Strengthening Activities: Regular exercise, adequate sleep, healthy nutrition, challenging learning, meaningful relationships, spiritual practices, and activities that require discipline and focus. These strengthen your mental resilience and decision-making capability.

Mental Weakening Activities: Substance abuse, toxic relationships, excessive entertainment consumption, avoidance of challenges, isolation from positive influences, and activities that provide immediate gratification while undermining long-term wellbeing.

The quality of your mental defenses determines the quality of everything else in your life. Strong mental defenses enable good decisions that create positive outcomes across all areas. Weak mental defenses lead to poor decisions that create negative consequences that compound over time.

This becomes particularly important when dealing with temptations that promise immediate pleasure while creating long-term problems. The strength of your mental defenses determines whether you can resist these temptations or whether you'll succumb to them despite knowing better.

People with strong mental defenses can evaluate long-term consequences and make decisions based on overall benefit rather than immediate gratification. People with weak mental defenses consistently choose immediate pleasure despite knowing it will create future problems.

The same principle applies to relationships and partnerships. If you're building something important that requires reliable collaboration, you need partners whose mental defenses are strong enough to maintain good judgment even when circumstances become challenging.

You can't build a business with someone who can't control their impulses. You can't maintain a healthy relationship with someone who can't resist toxic influences. You can't achieve long-term objectives with people who can't think beyond immediate gratification.

This doesn't mean requiring perfection from yourself or others. Everyone faces mental challenges and occasionally makes poor decisions. The key distinction is between people who generally maintain strong mental defenses while occasionally struggling versus people who consistently demonstrate mental weakness across multiple areas.

People with generally strong mental defenses recover from poor decisions, learn from mistakes, and implement improvements that prevent similar problems in the future. People with consistently weak mental defenses repeat the same poor decisions, blame external circumstances for predictable consequences, and continue patterns they know are harmful.

The Alley Cat builds relationships with those who demonstrate mental strength while maintaining appropriate distance from those who consistently demonstrate mental weakness. This isn't about being judgmental, it's about being strategic about who you trust with important aspects of your life.

Your mental defenses are your first and most important line of protection against everything that could harm you. Strengthen them through deliberate practice, protect them from harmful influences, and use them to evaluate the mental strength of others who want access to your time, energy, and resources.

If you can't guard your mind, you can't guard anything else. If others can't guard their minds, they can't guard themselves or contribute reliably to shared objectives. Guard your mental defenses carefully. Choose relationships with those who guard theirs effectively. Everything else depends on this foundation.

Your mind is your control tower. Keep it secure, keep it strong, and keep it focused on decisions that serve your long-term wellbeing rather than just your immediate desires. Everything else in your life depends on the strength of this foundation.

CHAPTER 37: MAKE SURE THE REASON IS A GOOD REASON

Before you pursue anything significant from relationships, business ventures, investments, career changes, major purchases. Make absolutely certain you understand why you want it and whether that reason serves your long-term wellbeing rather than just satisfying immediate impulses or filling psychological voids.

Too many people end up in situations they don't need to be in, with people who don't benefit their lives, pursuing objectives that don't align with their authentic values, simply because they never took time to examine their motivations clearly and honestly.

When we do things without purpose, we end up with unnecessary people, unnecessary problems, and unnecessary complications that drain energy from meaningful objectives while providing minimal genuine satisfaction. We mistake motion for progress, activity for achievement, and busyness for purpose.

The Buffoon pursues things for reasons they haven't examined like social pressure, immediate gratification, ego satisfaction, or unconscious attempts to fill emotional needs through external achievements. They chase relationships because they're lonely rather than because they've found compatible partners. They start businesses because entrepreneurship sounds glamorous rather than because they have valuable solutions to offer. They make purchases to project status rather than to serve genuine needs.

The Alley Cat examines their motivations carefully before making significant commitments. They pursue relationships because they've identified genuine compatibility and mutual benefit potential. They start businesses because they have valuable solutions that serve real market needs. They make decisions based on authentic purpose rather than superficial appeal.

This distinction becomes particularly important in romantic relationships, where poor motivation leads to partnerships that create more problems than they solve. If a man pursues a woman, he should know exactly why he wants that woman in his life beyond surface attraction or temporary loneliness.

Of course he should love her, but love alone isn't sufficient foundation for building a life together. He needs to see a whole world he can build with this woman. Seeking values like shared objectives, complementary capabilities, mutual growth potential, compatible values, and collaborative possibilities that extend far beyond emotional satisfaction.

Can they build businesses together? Can they create financial security together? Can they develop a family structure that serves everyone involved? Can they handle life's challenges as an effective team rather than just as two individuals who happen to live in the same space?

The same applies to women evaluating potential partners. They should look at men as potential teammates rather than just as sources of emotional validation or financial security. What can we build together? How does his presence enhance my ability to achieve my objectives? How do our capabilities complement each other to create possibilities neither could achieve alone?

This is about what each person can add to the other rather than what each can take from the other. It's about mutual value creation rather than mutual dependency. It's about building something larger together rather than just enjoying each other's company.

Without this emphasis on teamwork, it becomes very difficult to see relationships from a strategic perspective that serves long-term success rather than just short-term satisfaction. When the focus remains on immediate emotional gratification rather than collaborative potential, people end up in relationships that feel good temporarily but don't contribute to meaningful progress.

This principle of examining reasons applies equally to business decisions. Why are you starting this particular business? Is it because you have genuine passion for solving specific problems, or because you want to escape traditional employment? Is it because you've identified real market needs you can serve effectively, or because entrepreneurship seems more exciting than your current situation?

Starting businesses to escape something usually produces different results than starting businesses to create something. Escape motivation focuses on getting away from current circumstances rather than building toward specific objectives. Creation motivation focuses on bringing valuable solutions into existence that serve genuine needs.

The same examination applies to financial decisions. Why are you making this investment? Is it because you understand the fundamentals and believe in long-term value creation, or because you're hoping for quick profits? Is it because the opportunity aligns with your strategic objectives, or because you're trying to impress others with sophisticated investments?

Investment decisions based on genuine understanding tend to produce better results than those based on speculation, social pressure, or get-rich-quick fantasies. When you understand why you're investing and how the investment serves your larger financial strategy, you make better decisions about when to hold, when to sell, and when to avoid particular opportunities entirely.

This principle becomes even more important when evaluating people and relationships. Why do you want to associate with particular individuals? Is it because they possess qualities that inspire your growth and support your objectives, or because their association makes you feel important? Is it because you can create mutual value together, or because their success makes you look good by association?

158

Relationships built on mutual value creation tend to be more satisfying and durable than those built on status enhancement or ego gratification. When both parties understand what they're contributing and receiving, the relationship serves authentic needs rather than psychological insecurities.

The process of examining reasons requires honest self-assessment that many people find uncomfortable. It means acknowledging when your motivations are shallow, selfish, or based on insecurity rather than genuine purpose. It means admitting when you're pursuing things for reasons that don't serve your long-term wellbeing.

This discomfort is temporary, while the consequences of poor motivation are often permanent. Better to face uncomfortable truths about your reasons before making commitments than to deal with the problems that inevitably result from decisions based on unexamined impulses.

Consider this framework for evaluating your reasons:

Purpose Alignment: Does this decision align with your authentic values and long-term objectives, or does it serve temporary impulses that might conflict with what you genuinely want to achieve?

Value Creation: Will this pursuit create genuine value for yourself and others, or does it primarily serve ego gratification, status enhancement, or escape from current circumstances?

Mutual Benefit: In relationships and partnerships, are you offering value that serves others' authentic needs while receiving value that serves your genuine requirements?

Strategic Contribution: Does this decision contribute to your larger strategy for creating the life you want, or is it a distraction from more important objectives?

Sustainability: Can you maintain this pursuit over time while honoring your other commitments and responsibilities, or does it require sacrificing things that matter more?

Growth Potential: Will this engagement help you develop capabilities, expand opportunities, and become more effective, or will it primarily consume resources without generating corresponding development?

Authenticity: Are you pursuing this because it genuinely appeals to you, or because you think you should want it based on social expectations or comparison with others?

This examination process isn't meant to eliminate all spontaneity or emotional decision-making. Some of life's best experiences come from decisions that feel right even when they don't seem logical. But it's meant to prevent major life decisions from being driven primarily by unexamined impulses that don't serve your authentic interests.

The goal is ensuring that your significant investments of time, energy, and resources align with purposes that actually matter to you rather than just satisfying temporary desires or social pressures that don't contribute to genuine fulfillment.

In my own experience, the decisions that created the most positive long-term impact were those based on clear understanding of purpose and genuine assessment of value creation potential. The decisions that created the most problems were those driven by unclear motivations, social pressure, or attempts to fill emotional needs through external achievements.

When I met people who became important partners or mentors, the relationships succeeded because both parties understood what we were building together and why that collaboration served our authentic objectives. When relationships failed, it was usually because one or both parties had unclear motivations that led to misaligned expectations and mutual disappointment.

The same pattern applies to business ventures, investment decisions, and major life changes. Clear reasons based on authentic purpose tend to produce satisfying outcomes. Unclear reasons based on temporary impulses tend to create problems that require significant energy to resolve.

This world is like a big chess board, and you definitely need to build up your pieces strategically rather than moving them randomly. Every significant decision should serve your larger strategy rather than just responding to immediate circumstances or momentary desires.

Make sure the reason is a good reason before you commit significant resources to pursuing anything. Take time to understand your motivations clearly and honestly. Examine whether your purposes align with authentic values rather than just temporary impulses.

This investment in self-awareness and purpose clarity will save you enormous amounts of time, energy, and emotional difficulty while directing your resources toward objectives that actually serve your long-term wellbeing and genuine satisfaction.

Good reasons lead to good outcomes. Poor reasons lead to problems you could have avoided with better initial evaluation.

Choose your reasons as carefully as you choose your objectives. Everything else flows from this foundation.

CHAPTER 38: WEAK PEOPLE SEEK PEOPLE, STRONG PEOPLE

SEEK SUCCESS

One of the most profound distinctions between those who achieve lasting success and those who remain perpetually disappointed lies in what they seek first: external validation or internal achievement. Weak people prioritize being liked, accepted, and validated by others. Strong people prioritize accomplishing objectives that align with their authentic values and long-term vision.

This difference in primary focus creates entirely different life trajectories. Those who seek people first often sacrifice their authentic goals to maintain relationships that may not serve their growth. Those who seek success first attract people who respect their achievements and share their commitment to meaningful objectives.

The Buffoon measures their worth by how many people approve of them, accept them, and validate their choices. They modify their behavior, compromise their values, and abandon their objectives to maintain social acceptance. They fear rejection so intensely that they never fully commit to anything that might create disapproval, even when that commitment would serve their long-term interests.

The Alley Cat measures their worth by how effectively they achieve objectives that align with their authentic purpose. They build their identity around capability, contribution, and consistent progress toward meaningful goals. They attract relationships based on mutual respect for achievement rather than seeking relationships based on mutual need for validation.

This distinction explains why successful people often seem to have abundant, high-quality relationships while unsuccessful people struggle to maintain satisfying connections despite investing enormous energy in people-pleasing behaviors. The causation flows in the opposite direction than most people assume.

Success attracts quality relationships. Weakness repels them.

When you focus primarily on achieving worthwhile objectives, several things happen that naturally enhance your relationship potential:

Confidence Development: Accomplishing challenging goals builds genuine self-confidence that makes you more attractive to others. People are naturally drawn to those who demonstrate competence and self-assurance rather than neediness and insecurity.

Value Creation: Success typically involves creating value for others, which makes you valuable to know and associate with. People want relationships with those who contribute positively rather than drain energy through constant validation needs.

Standards Elevation: Achieving meaningful objectives requires developing and maintaining high standards, which attracts others who share those standards while repelling those who don't.

Purpose Clarity: Success requires clear understanding of your objectives and values, which enables authentic self-expression that resonates with compatible people while filtering out incompatible ones.

Magnetic Positioning: Achievement creates natural magnetism that draws people toward you rather than requiring you to chase after their approval or acceptance.

Conversely, when you focus primarily on seeking people's approval, you often undermine the very qualities that would make you genuinely attractive:

Validation Dependency: Needing others' approval to feel worthy creates needy energy that repels rather than attracts quality relationships.

Authenticity Compromise: Modifying yourself to please others prevents authentic self-expression that would attract compatible people.

Standards Lowering: Prioritizing acceptance over achievement often leads to accepting substandard behavior from others while compromising your own standards.

Purpose Confusion: Focusing on what others want rather than what you authentically value creates internal confusion that others can sense and find unappealing.

Chase Energy: Pursuing people's approval creates desperate energy that makes you less attractive rather than more appealing.

I've observed this pattern repeatedly throughout my life. During periods when I focused intensely on achieving specific objectives like transforming the manufacturing plant, building businesses, developing capabilities. I naturally attracted relationships with people who respected competence and shared commitment to meaningful goals.

During periods when I was more concerned with social acceptance or worried about others' opinions of my choices, I attracted relationships with people who were similarly focused on external validation rather than internal development. These relationships typically proved less satisfying and durable because they were based on mutual weakness rather than mutual strength.

The principle extends beyond romantic relationships to professional partnerships, friendships, and all forms of human connection. People respect and want to associate with those who demonstrate capability, achievement, and commitment to meaningful objectives. They avoid or exploit those who prioritize social acceptance over personal development.

This doesn't mean ignoring relationships or treating people poorly in pursuit of success. It means understanding that the most satisfying relationships emerge naturally when you become someone worth knowing rather than desperately seeking to be known by anyone who will accept you.

The practical application involves several key shifts:

Identity Foundation: Build your sense of self around your capabilities, achievements, and progress toward meaningful objectives rather than around others' opinions of you.

Relationship Selection: Choose relationships based on mutual respect and shared values rather than just on availability and acceptance. Quality over quantity in all human connections.

Boundary Maintenance: Maintain standards for how others treat you rather than accepting poor behavior to avoid rejection. Respect flows toward those who respect themselves.

Value Contribution: Focus on what you can offer others rather than what you can extract from them. Relationships based on mutual value creation prove more satisfying than those based on mutual need.

Authentic Expression: Present your genuine self rather than a carefully crafted version designed to please others. Authenticity attracts compatible people while filtering out incompatible ones.

Achievement Priority: Pursue objectives that align with your authentic values rather than goals you think will impress others. Genuine accomplishment creates lasting satisfaction while status-seeking creates temporary highs followed by deeper emptiness.

The "you never lose people chasing money, but you do lose money chasing people" principle captures this perfectly. When you prioritize achievement and value creation, relationships typically follow naturally. When you prioritize relationships over achievement, you often sacrifice the very qualities that would make you valuable in relationships.

This doesn't mean money should be your primary objective, it means that pursuing meaningful goals (which might include financial success) tends to attract quality relationships while pursuing relationships first often leads to compromising the goals that would create genuine satisfaction.

The psychological mechanism behind this pattern involves the difference between attractive and needy energy. When you're focused on creating value and achieving meaningful objectives, you project confidence, purpose, and capability that others find attractive. When you're focused on being liked and accepted, you project neediness, insecurity, and dependency that others find draining.

People want to be around energy that enhances their own lives rather than energy that depletes them. Success-focused individuals typically enhance others' lives through their example, capabilities, and positive energy. People-focused individuals often drain others' energy through their validation needs and emotional dependency.

This principle becomes particularly important during challenging periods when you might be tempted to compromise your standards or abandon your objectives to maintain social support. These are precisely the moments when staying focused on your authentic goals serves you best, even if it temporarily creates social discomfort.

During my most difficult periods like sleeping in truck yards, rebuilding after business failures, and facing legal challenges. Maintaining focus on my long-term objectives rather than seeking sympathy or validation from others proved essential for eventual recovery and growth. The relationships that provided genuine support were with people who respected determination and shared commitment to overcoming obstacles rather than people who offered comfort that might have undermined my motivation to change circumstances.

Strong people seek success because they understand that genuine success creates the foundation for all other forms of satisfaction, including satisfying relationships. Weak people seek people because they hope external validation will substitute for internal development that they're unwilling to pursue.

The irony is that weak people who seek people often end up lonely despite their social focus, while strong people who seek success often end up surrounded by quality relationships despite their achievement focus. Choose strength. Choose success. Choose internal development over external validation.

The people worth knowing will notice and respect your choice. The people not worth knowing will be filtered out by your standards. Both outcomes serve your long-term interests better than compromising your authentic objectives to maintain relationships that don't support your growth. Seek success first. Quality relationships will follow naturally.

That's not just strategy, it's the natural order of human attraction and respect.

CHAPTER 39: THE 200 DOLLAR LOAN THAT BUILT AN EMPIRE

Sometimes the smallest seeds produce the largest trees. Sometimes the most minimal resources create the most substantial results. Sometimes what appears to be insignificant assistance becomes the foundation for extraordinary transformation.

The $200 loan I received from Rance in Seattle represents one of the most important financial transactions of my life. Not because of the amount, but because of how I leveraged that minimal capital into the foundation for rebuilding everything I had lost and more.

This story isn't about the money itself. It's about the principles of resource maximization, strategic thinking, and compound growth that can transform any small advantage into substantial progress when applied with discipline and vision.

When my business collapsed and I found myself stranded in Seattle for almost 3 and a half months, sleeping in truck yards and delivering food on foot, I had reached what appeared to be rock bottom. No immediate housing, no reliable transportation, minimal resources, and no obvious pathway forward. Most people in similar circumstances would focus on immediate survival rather than long-term strategy.

I understood something crucial: how you handle minimal resources determines whether you eventually gain access to substantial resources. The principles that govern small amounts of money are identical to those that govern large amounts, efficiency, strategic allocation, return on investment, and compound growth.

Rance, a real estate investor I met through delivering food orders via Postmates, recognized potential in my situation that I was still developing confidence about. He saw work ethic, strategic thinking, and determination to rebuild rather than just survive. Most importantly, he recognized that small investments in people with the right mindset often produce returns that exceed large investments in people with the wrong approach.

When he offered the $200 loan, I didn't treat it as charity or temporary assistance. I approached it as seed capital for systematic rebuilding that would eventually generate returns far exceeding the initial investment. I understood that this wasn't just about the money, it was about proving that I could transform minimal resources into meaningful progress.

The specific uses of that $200 were less important than the principles I applied to maximize its impact:

Strategic Prioritization: Every dollar was allocated based on which expenditures would generate the highest return rather than which would provide the most immediate comfort. I prioritized investments that would improve my income-generating capability over expenses that would only improve my circumstances temporarily.

Compound Thinking: I focused on uses that would create ongoing benefits rather than one-time improvements. Instead of spending money on immediate needs that would be consumed, I invested in capabilities that would continue generating value over time.

Efficiency Maximization: I squeezed maximum utility from every expenditure, often finding ways to serve multiple purposes with single investments. Every purchase had to justify itself through multiple forms of value creation.

Risk Management: I avoided any use that could result in total loss of the capital while pursuing opportunities that offered potential for significant return. The goal was preservation and growth rather than speculation or consumption.

Timeline Optimization: I balanced immediate needs with future potential, ensuring that short-term uses didn't compromise long-term possibilities while addressing urgent requirements that could undermine progress if ignored.

The key insight was understanding that $200 deployed strategically could generate more value than $2,000 used carelessly. The amount matters less than the principles applied to that amount. Discipline, efficiency, and strategic thinking multiply the impact of whatever resources you possess.

This loan became the foundation not just for immediate improvement but for long-term transformation. The principles I refined while maximizing this minimal amount prepared me to handle substantially larger resources when they became available. The mental frameworks I developed while operating under extreme constraint proved valuable when operating under abundance.

More importantly, successfully leveraging this small opportunity created confidence in my ability to transform any resource level into progress toward larger objectives. It proved that external circumstances don't determine outcomes, internal responses to those circumstances create results.

The relationship with Rance that made this loan possible also illustrates important principles about building connections that transcend immediate circumstances. He didn't help me because he felt sorry for my situation, he invested in me because he recognized potential that temporary setbacks hadn't eliminated.

This distinction matters enormously. Charity creates dependency while investment creates partnership. When someone views assistance as investment in your potential rather than rescue from your circumstances, both parties approach the interaction differently. The giver expects returns rather than just expressing sympathy. The receiver commits to generating returns rather than just accepting help.

The $200 loan carried implicit expectations about performance, repayment, and continued relationship that charity wouldn't have included. These expectations created accountability that charity might have undermined. The structure encouraged strategic thinking rather than just grateful consumption.

Rance also provided something more valuable than money: education about real estate investing, business strategy, and wealth building that expanded my understanding of what was possible and how to achieve it. The financial assistance opened the door to knowledge that proved more valuable than the capital itself.

This education came naturally through our relationship rather than through formal instruction. By observing his approach to business, his strategic thinking about investments, and his methods for building wealth, I learned principles that no amount of money could have purchased directly.

The loan enabled immediate progress while the education enabled long-term transformation. Both were necessary, but the education proved more valuable because it created lasting capability rather than temporary improvement.

Years later, I'm still living off the foundation that $200 loan provided. Not because I haven't earned substantially more since then, but because the principles I learned while maximizing that minimal resource continue generating returns. The strategic thinking, resource optimization, and compound growth approaches I refined during that period remain central to how I approach all financial decisions.

This experience taught me that the amount of capital matters far less than the principles applied to that capital. I've seen people waste millions through poor strategic thinking while others transform hundreds into thousands through disciplined application of sound principles.

The same frameworks that maximize $200 also maximize $200,000. They are efficiency, strategic allocation, compound thinking, risk management, and timeline optimization. The amounts change, but the principles remain constant. Learning these principles with small amounts prepares you to apply them effectively with large amounts.

The loan also reinforced my understanding that opportunities often come from unexpected sources at unexpected times. I couldn't have predicted that delivering food to a stranger would lead to the relationship and assistance that enabled rebuilding everything I had lost. But I was positioned to recognize and leverage the opportunity when it appeared.

This positioning came from maintaining forward focus despite backward circumstances. Instead of dwelling on what I had lost, I concentrated on what I could build. Instead of accepting circumstances as permanent, I treated them as temporary conditions requiring strategic response.

167

The $200 loan succeeded because I was ready to succeed with whatever resources became available. The preparation for success created the opportunity to succeed when minimal resources appeared. The mindset enabled the money to have maximum impact.

The broader principle is this: prepare to maximize whatever resources become available rather than waiting for adequate resources before beginning preparation. Develop the strategic thinking, discipline, and efficiency that will enable you to transform small opportunities into substantial progress.

When resources do become available, whether $200, $2,000, or $200,000. You'll be ready to apply principles that generate maximum return rather than learning those principles while trying to apply them simultaneously.

The empire isn't built by the loan, it's built by the mindset that knows how to leverage the loan. The money provides opportunity, but capability determines outcome. Build the capability first. The money will follow.

When it does, you'll know exactly how to transform it into something substantial, regardless of how small it initially appears.

The $200 empire proves that size of seed matters less than quality of soil, strategic planting, and consistent cultivation. Plant strategically.

Cultivate consistently. Harvest exponentially. That's how $200 becomes everything.

CHAPTER 40: TO PROACT IS GREAT, TO REACT IS LATE

The difference between extraordinary success and chronic struggle often comes down to timing. Not the timing of when opportunities appear, but the timing of when you respond to patterns, trends, and emerging situations. Those who proact get ahead of circumstances. Those who only react get dragged behind them.

Proactive thinking means identifying and addressing situations before they become problems, recognizing opportunities before they become obvious to everyone else, and positioning yourself advantageously before advantageous positioning becomes necessary for survival. Reactive thinking means responding to problems after they've already created damage, pursuing opportunities after they've become competitive, and scrambling to improve positions after those positions have already become disadvantageous.

The Buffoon operates in constant reactive mode. They wait until problems become crises before addressing them. They pursue opportunities only after reading about others' success in those areas. They develop skills only after their lack of those skills has already created professional or personal damage. They're always playing catch-up rather than getting ahead.

The Alley Cat operates proactively whenever possible. They identify potential problems while solutions are still easy to implement. They recognize emerging opportunities while they're still accessible to early adopters. They develop capabilities before those capabilities become essential rather than after their absence has created limitations.

This distinction explains why some people consistently seem to be in the right place at the right time while others consistently seem to miss opportunities that were "obvious" in retrospect. The difference isn't luck or intuition, it's the habit of looking ahead rather than just responding to immediate circumstances.

Proactive thinking operates across multiple time horizons and application areas:

Problem Prevention: Identifying potential issues while they're still manageable rather than waiting until they become crises. This includes financial problems, health issues, relationship conflicts, and business challenges that typically develop gradually before becoming acute.

Opportunity Recognition: Spotting emerging trends, market shifts, or technological developments before they become mainstream knowledge. This enables positioning that provides advantages when trends fully develop rather than scrambling to participate after they're already saturated.

Skill Development: Building capabilities that will become valuable rather than just acquiring skills that are currently in demand. This creates competitive advantages for future opportunities rather than just qualifying for current positions.

Relationship Building: Developing connections and partnerships before you need them rather than networking only when you're seeking something specific. This creates resource availability when opportunities arise rather than having to build relationships under pressure.

Resource Accumulation: Building financial reserves, knowledge assets, and strategic positioning during favorable periods rather than trying to develop these resources during challenging circumstances when options are limited and pressure is high.

Strategic Positioning: Establishing favorable circumstances before you need them rather than trying to improve your position after it's already become disadvantageous. This includes geographic positioning, industry positioning, and competitive positioning.

The proactive approach requires developing what I call "anticipatory thinking". This is the ability to project current patterns forward and identify where they're likely to lead. This isn't about predicting the future perfectly but about recognizing directional trends and positioning yourself to benefit from probable developments rather than being damaged by them.

During my time at the manufacturing plant, I practiced anticipatory thinking by identifying problems with inventory management before they created production delays. Instead of waiting for shortages to occur and then scrambling to address them, I developed systems that predicted requirements and prevented disruptions before they could affect operations.

This proactive approach didn't just solve immediate problems, it created competitive advantages that reactive approaches couldn't match. While other facilities were constantly firefighting inventory crises, our operation ran smoothly because potential problems were addressed before they became actual problems.

The same principle applied when I began rebuilding after business setbacks. Instead of waiting until I had lost everything to start thinking about alternatives, I had been observing market trends and developing contingency plans that enabled faster recovery when setbacks occurred.

I had noticed the emergence of delivery apps and gig economy opportunities before they became mainstream survival strategies. When circumstances forced me to need immediate income, I was already positioned to leverage these emerging platforms rather than having to learn about them under pressure.

This positioning wasn't accidental, it came from maintaining awareness of developing trends even when I didn't immediately need alternative income sources. The proactive observation during stable periods enabled reactive capability during unstable periods.

The key distinction is between preparing for specific outcomes versus building general adaptive capability. Specific outcome preparation becomes obsolete when circumstances change in unexpected ways. General adaptive capability remains valuable regardless of how circumstances evolve.

Proactive thinking focuses on building adaptive capability rather than just preparing for particular scenarios. This means developing skills that transfer across industries, building relationships that provide opportunities in multiple directions, and creating resources that serve various purposes rather than just single objectives.

The anticipatory approach also requires accepting that not all proactive investments will prove immediately useful. Some skills you develop won't be needed for years. Some relationships you build won't provide immediate benefits. Some positioning you establish won't pay off until circumstances change in ways that make that positioning valuable.

This delayed gratification aspect of proactive thinking challenges people who prefer immediate returns on their investments. But the compound benefits of proactive positioning typically exceed the opportunity costs of resources invested in preparation that doesn't provide immediate utility.

The mathematical reality is simple: reactive approaches guarantee that you'll always be behind optimal timing, while proactive approaches create possibilities for optimal timing even if specific predictions prove incorrect. Being early is better than being late, even when being early requires patience before benefits manifest.

Consider how this applies to technological adoption. Those who learn new technologies while they're still emerging gain advantages when those technologies become essential. Those who wait until technologies are fully established face steeper learning curves and more competition from others who adopted earlier.

The same principle applies to geographic positioning, career development, investment strategies, and relationship building. Early positioning creates advantages that late positioning cannot match, even when early positioning requires patience and speculation about future developments.

The proactive mindset also enables better reactive capability when unexpected circumstances do require rapid response. People who think ahead generally develop problem-solving skills, resource networks, and adaptive capabilities that serve them well even when facing completely unexpected challenges.

During my homelessness period in Seattle, the proactive skills I had developed in previous environments like strategic thinking, resource optimization, and relationship building enabled more effective reactive responses to immediate survival challenges. The proactive capability didn't prevent the crisis but provided tools for handling it more effectively than purely reactive approaches would have allowed.

This demonstrates the interconnection between proactive and reactive approaches. You can't always prevent the need for reactive responses, but proactive preparation can dramatically improve the quality of those reactive responses when they become necessary.

The practical application involves developing habits that maintain awareness of emerging patterns while building capabilities that will serve future needs even when those specific needs aren't yet apparent:

Trend Monitoring: Regularly observing developments in technology, markets, social patterns, and other areas that might affect your objectives. This doesn't require extensive research, just consistent attention to directional changes.

Skill Anticipation: Learning capabilities that complement your existing strengths and might become valuable even if they're not immediately needed. This includes both technical skills and general capabilities like communication, analysis, and strategic thinking.

Relationship Investment: Building connections with people whose capabilities complement yours and who might become valuable collaborators even if immediate partnership opportunities don't exist.

Resource Building: Accumulating financial reserves, knowledge assets, and strategic positioning during favorable periods rather than waiting until you need these resources to begin developing them.

Option Creation: Establishing multiple potential pathways for achieving objectives rather than depending on single strategies that might not work or might become unavailable.

The goal isn't perfect prediction but positioning that provides advantages regardless of how specific circumstances develop. It's about creating readiness for opportunity rather than just preparation for known challenges. To proact is great because it positions you ahead of circumstances rather than behind them. To react is late because it forces you to respond to situations after optimal timing has already passed. Choose proaction when possible. Build reactive capability for when proaction isn't sufficient. Always remember, those who act first get first choice of opportunities. Those who act last get last choice, if any choice remains at all.

Be early. Be ready. Be proactive. The future belongs to those who position themselves for it before it arrives.

172

CHAPTER 41: SUBSTANCE OVER APPEARANCE

I'd rather have a reliable vehicle and wear simple clothes than walk everywhere in designer outfits. I'd rather drive a dependable car in basic clothing than catch public transportation dressed like I'm attending a fashion show. I'd rather have functional transportation and modest appearance than impressive appearance and no transportation.

This preference reflects a fundamental principle that separates those who build lasting success from those who create impressive illusions: substance always outperforms appearance when measured over time, even though appearance might create better impressions initially.

The distinction between substance and appearance manifests across every area of life from finances, relationships, career development, and personal presentation. Those who prioritize substance focus on building capabilities, assets, and systems that create lasting value. Those who prioritize appearance focus on creating impressions that may or may not correspond to underlying reality.

The Buffoon approaches life as a performance designed to create specific impressions rather than as a construction project designed to create lasting value. They spend money they don't have to appear wealthy, pursue relationships that look good rather than feel good, and make career choices based on status rather than satisfaction or growth potential.

This appearance-focused approach creates what I call "hollow success". These are outcomes that look impressive from the outside but provide minimal genuine satisfaction or security for those experiencing them. The external presentation exceeds the internal reality, creating ongoing pressure to maintain performances that become increasingly difficult to sustain.

The Alley Cat approaches life as a construction project where each decision either builds or undermines long-term capability and satisfaction. They make choices based on actual utility and genuine value rather than on how those choices might be perceived by others. They prioritize function over form, effectiveness over impression, and lasting value over temporary status.

This substance-focused approach creates what I call "authentic success". These are outcomes that might not always look impressive initially but provide genuine satisfaction and sustainable security. The internal reality meets or exceeds the external presentation, creating alignment that makes life easier rather than more complicated.

Consider how this principle applies to transportation and clothing choices. The person with designer clothes and no reliable vehicle might look successful while waiting for buses or depending on others for transportation. The person with dependable transportation and modest clothes might look ordinary while maintaining complete independence and mobility.

Over time, which position provides more opportunities? Which creates more freedom? Which enables better positioning for taking advantage of unexpected possibilities?

The reliable vehicle enables employment opportunities that aren't accessible via public transportation. It provides flexibility for pursuing multiple income sources, handling emergencies, and maintaining consistent schedules regardless of external circumstances. It represents genuine capability that serves practical objectives.

The designer clothes provide temporary impression management that might enhance some social interactions but doesn't create lasting capabilities or solve practical problems. They represent appearance investment that consumes resources without generating ongoing utility.

This doesn't mean appearance is irrelevant or that presentation never matters. It means ensuring that appearance investments serve substance rather than substituting for it. It means building genuine capability first, then enhancing presentation as resources and circumstances allow.

The principle extends to financial management, where the substance versus appearance distinction often determines long-term wealth building success. Many people with impressive incomes remain financially unstable because they direct most resources toward lifestyle inflation that creates the appearance of prosperity while undermining actual wealth accumulation.

Meanwhile, others with modest incomes build substantial wealth by prioritizing asset accumulation over lifestyle enhancement, value creation over status signaling, and financial independence over financial appearance. Their external presentation might seem ordinary while their financial reality becomes extraordinary.

I've observed this pattern repeatedly among people I've encountered throughout my journey. Those focused on appearing successful often struggle financially despite impressive incomes, expensive possessions, and high-status lifestyles. They're trapped in cycles where maintaining appearances consumes most resources, preventing accumulation of assets that would create genuine security.

Those focused on building substance often achieve genuine prosperity while maintaining modest presentations. They direct resources toward investments, business development, and capability building rather than toward consumption that provides temporary satisfaction without lasting benefit.

The substance-focused approach requires patience because building genuine capability takes longer than creating impressive appearances. You can purchase status symbols immediately with credit, but you must develop valuable skills through sustained effort over time. You can project success quickly through careful image management, but you must build actual success through consistent value creation.

This patience requirement eliminates many people who prefer immediate gratification over delayed achievement. They choose appearance because it provides instant satisfaction, not recognizing that this choice often prevents the substance development that would create lasting satisfaction.

The Alley Cat accepts this timeline because they understand that genuine accomplishment provides more durable satisfaction than impressive performances. They're willing to appear ordinary while building extraordinary capabilities, knowing that substance eventually creates its own impressive presentation without requiring ongoing maintenance or performance pressure.

This approach also provides psychological benefits that appearance-focused strategies cannot match. When your external presentation accurately reflects internal reality, you experience alignment that reduces stress and increases confidence. You don't worry about being "found out" or exposed as fraudulent because there's no gap between reality and presentation to maintain.

When external presentation exceeds internal reality, you experience ongoing anxiety about maintaining performances that become increasingly difficult to sustain. The gap between reality and appearance creates psychological pressure that undermines the very confidence the appearance was designed to create.

The substance-first approach eliminates this performance pressure by ensuring that presentation grows naturally from capability rather than being artificially constructed independently of underlying reality. Your confidence becomes genuine rather than performed because it's based on actual competence rather than carefully managed impressions.

Consider how this applies to career development. The appearance-focused professional emphasizes titles, credentials, networking events, and industry recognition while potentially neglecting skill development, value creation, and actual performance excellence. They look successful while remaining vulnerable to economic downturns, industry changes, or performance evaluations.

The substance-focused professional emphasizes capability development, problem-solving expertise, and value creation while allowing recognition to follow naturally from demonstrated competence. They might seem ordinary initially but become indispensable through genuine contribution, creating security that appearances alone cannot provide.

The same principle applies to relationship building. Appearance-focused relationship strategies emphasize creating impressive profiles, attending high-status events, and associating with people who enhance your image rather than your life. These approaches might generate initial attraction but often fail to create lasting satisfaction because they're based on mutual performance rather than genuine compatibility.

Substance-focused relationship strategies emphasize developing genuine attractiveness through personal growth, authentic self-expression, and valuable contribution to others' lives. This approach might take longer to generate results but typically creates more satisfying and durable connections because they're based on mutual reality rather than mutual illusion.

The transition from appearance-focused to substance-focused thinking often requires temporarily accepting lower external status while building higher internal capability. This temporary status reduction challenges people who measure their worth through others' perceptions rather than through their own development and contribution.

But this temporary appearance sacrifice enables permanent substance gains that eventually produce better appearances naturally, without ongoing maintenance requirements or performance pressure. The substance creates its own attractive presentation without needing artificial enhancement or careful image management.

In my own experience, the periods when I focused on building substance rather than managing appearances consistently produced better long-term outcomes, even when initial appearances suggested otherwise. The discipline, capability development, and value creation that characterize substance-focused approaches create compound benefits that appearance-focused approaches cannot match.

The reliable vehicle might not impress anyone initially, but it enables opportunities, provides independence, and serves practical objectives that designer clothes cannot accomplish. Over time, the capability advantage compounds while the appearance advantage diminishes.

Choose substance over appearance. Build capability over impression. Create value over status. The appearances will follow naturally from genuine substance, but substance rarely follows from artificial appearances. Function first. Form follows. That's not just design philosophy, it's life philosophy that creates lasting success rather than temporary impression.

CHAPTER 42: FULLY PROCESS INFORMATION BEFORE

MISINTERPRETATION

Before you judge anyone for their decisions, circumstances, or behaviors, take time to understand the environment that shaped those choices. Before you condemn someone for actions that seem wrong or incomprehensible, consider the context that made those actions seem necessary or logical from their perspective.

Just as a fish needs water to survive, a plant needs soil and sunlight to grow, a lizard needs bugs to eat and cool environments to regulate body temperature, and a snake must remain cold-blooded to function properly. Every person's choices are shaped by the environmental conditions they navigate to survive and thrive.

You cannot judge a fish for needing water just because you breathe air. You cannot condemn a plant for requiring sunlight just because you derive energy from food. You cannot criticize a snake for being cold-blooded just because you are warm-blooded.

Similarly, you cannot judge people for making survival decisions within environments you have never experienced. You cannot condemn choices that enabled them to navigate circumstances you have never faced. You cannot criticize adaptations that were necessary for their survival in conditions you cannot fully comprehend.

This principle doesn't excuse harmful behavior or suggest that all choices are equally valid regardless of their consequences. It requires understanding the difference between explaining behavior and justifying it, between comprehending context and condoning outcomes, between recognizing environmental pressures and absolving personal responsibility.

When I made decisions as a child that led me into drug dealing, those choices weren't made in a vacuum of pure free will. They were made within specific environmental constraints that severely limited my perceived options. I was a straight-A student who loved learning and wanted to make everyone happy, but I was also small, frail, and frequently targeted by larger children who saw violence as entertainment.

The environment I was trying to survive in (underfunded schools in high-crime neighborhoods, constant violence, extreme poverty, and minimal legitimate opportunities) created pressures that made illegal activity seem like the only pathway to basic safety and dignity. This context doesn't justify my choices, but it explains them in ways that simple moral judgment cannot.

Just because you had the luxury of safe neighborhoods, quality schools, and abundant legitimate opportunities doesn't mean everyone else enjoyed those same advantages.

Just because you could succeed through conventional paths doesn't mean those paths were accessible to everyone facing different circumstances.

Some children are born into war zones where they must learn to handle weapons to protect themselves and their families after witnessing unthinkable violence. Some grow up in economic environments where illegal activity provides the only visible pathway out of generational poverty. Some develop in social contexts where violence is so routine that peaceful alternatives seem naive or impossible.

These environmental realities don't make harmful choices acceptable, but they make those choices understandable when viewed from the perspective of someone trying to survive rather than someone judging from the comfort of safer circumstances.

The same principle applies to adults making decisions under extreme pressure, financial desperation, social isolation, or other circumstances that create constraints most people never experience. The mother who shoplifts food for her children isn't choosing theft over honesty in an abstract moral sense, she's choosing feeding her family over following rules that seem irrelevant when children are hungry.

The father who works multiple jobs while neglecting family time isn't choosing money over relationships, he's choosing immediate financial survival over long-term relationship building when both seem impossible to achieve simultaneously.

The entrepreneur who cuts ethical corners isn't choosing dishonesty over integrity, they're choosing business survival over moral purity when their understanding of available options seems limited to success through compromise or failure through righteousness.

None of these choices are optimal, and all create consequences that affect both the decision-makers and those around them. But understanding the environmental pressures that shaped these decisions enables more productive responses than simple condemnation.

Instead of judging people for choices you cannot fully understand, focus on changing the environmental conditions that make harmful choices seem necessary. Instead of condemning individuals for surviving in systems designed for their failure, work to improve those systems so better choices become accessible.

This shift from judgment to understanding enables more effective problem-solving while maintaining accountability for outcomes. You can acknowledge that someone's choices were shaped by difficult circumstances while still requiring them to take responsibility for improving future decisions and outcomes.

The key insight is recognizing that environments shape behavior more powerfully than most people realize. When you place people in environments designed for failure, some will fail regardless of their character, intelligence, or initial intentions.

When you place people in environments designed for success, most will succeed even if they lack exceptional capabilities.

This environmental influence explains why changing circumstances often produces more reliable behavior change than trying to change character or mindset while leaving circumstances unchanged. Moving someone from an environment that rewards harmful behavior to one that rewards beneficial behavior typically produces better results than lecturing them about making better choices while leaving them in the same harmful environment.

I learned this principle directly through my own transformation. The same strategic thinking and determination that enabled success in illegal environments eventually enabled success in legitimate environments once those opportunities became accessible. The capabilities transferred across contexts even though the specific applications changed dramatically.

The difference wasn't fundamental character change, it was environmental change that allowed existing capabilities to be applied toward beneficial rather than harmful objectives. The strategic thinking remained constant; the contexts for applying it evolved to align with legal and ethical goals.

This experience taught me to evaluate people based on their capabilities and potential rather than just their current circumstances or past decisions. Someone making poor choices within limited environments might demonstrate exceptional capabilities when provided access to better environments with expanded opportunities.

The practical application involves several key shifts in how you process information about people and their choices:

Context Consideration: Before judging decisions, attempt to understand the constraints and pressures that influenced those choices. What alternatives were actually available versus what alternatives you think should have been available?

Environmental Awareness: Recognize how circumstances shape behavior by influencing what seems possible, necessary, or rational from the perspective of someone operating within those circumstances.

Capability Recognition: Look for evidence of intelligence, determination, and strategic thinking that might be applied toward beneficial objectives when environmental conditions change to support those applications.

System Focus: Direct attention toward changing the systems and environments that produce harmful choices rather than just condemning individuals who make those choices within existing systems.

Future Orientation: Evaluate people based on their potential for growth and positive contribution rather than just their current circumstances or past mistakes.

Proportional Response: Ensure that your reactions to people's choices reflect understanding of the circumstances that influenced those choices, while still maintaining appropriate boundaries and accountability.

This approach doesn't require accepting harmful behavior or ignoring legitimate concerns about others' choices. It requires processing complete information about context and constraints before forming judgments that might be based on incomplete understanding.

The goal is wisdom rather than quick judgment, understanding rather than immediate condemnation, productive response rather than reactive criticism. This processing approach leads to better relationships, more effective problem-solving, and increased ability to help people transition from harmful to beneficial behavior patterns.

Remember that your own good choices might have been easier to make because of advantages you possessed rather than purely because of superior character. Your ability to succeed through conventional means might have resulted from access to those means rather than from inherent moral superiority.

This recognition creates humility that improves your ability to understand others and help them find pathways to better outcomes. It prevents the arrogance that destroys relationships and eliminates opportunities for positive influence.

Process information fully. Consider context completely. Judge wisely rather than quickly.

That's not about lowering standards or excusing harmful behavior. It's about understanding reality completely enough to respond effectively rather than just emotionally.

Understanding doesn't require agreement, but it enables wisdom that judgment alone cannot provide.

CHAPTER 43: GEOGRAPHICAL EXPANSION AS MENTAL

EXPANSION

When you move your body through different environments, you simultaneously move your mind through different possibilities. Travel isn't just about seeing new places, it's about expanding your understanding of what's possible, how people live, how business operates, and how success can be achieved through methods you never would have discovered staying in familiar territory.

My experience traveling through 44 states by vehicle while building and rebuilding businesses taught me that geographical expansion and mental expansion are inseparably connected. Each new location exposed me to different ways of thinking, different approaches to common problems, and different perspectives on opportunity that fundamentally changed how I understood my own potential.

The Buffoon approaches travel as consumption. Visiting places to check them off lists, taking photos to prove they were there, collecting experiences to impress others with their worldliness. They see different locations as entertainment rather than education, as diversions from their regular life rather than as expansions of what their regular life could become.

The Alley Cat approaches travel as research. Thus studying how different environments create different opportunities, observing how people succeed in various contexts, learning strategies and perspectives that can be applied regardless of location. They see different places as laboratories for understanding human potential and possibility rather than just as destinations for temporary enjoyment.

This distinction creates entirely different outcomes from the same travel experiences. The Buffoon returns home unchanged except for having new stories to tell and photos to share. The Alley Cat returns home transformed by insights, connections, and perspectives that permanently expand their understanding of what's achievable.

During my business development travels, I wasn't just visiting different states, I was studying different economic ecosystems, regulatory environments, cultural approaches to business, and regional variations in customer psychology. Each location provided education that no classroom or textbook could have delivered as effectively.

I discovered that business practices considered normal in one region might be innovative in another region, creating arbitrage opportunities for those willing to transport ideas across geographical boundaries. I learned that customer service standards varied dramatically between locations, revealing opportunities to exceed expectations in areas where standards were lower.

Most importantly, I observed that success strategies that seemed universal actually worked differently in different contexts, requiring adaptation rather than simple replication. This geographic perspective prevented me from assuming that what worked in one location would automatically work in another without modification.

The psychological impact of geographical expansion extends beyond business education to fundamental changes in how you perceive limitations. When you experience firsthand how differently people live, work, and succeed in various locations, you realize that many constraints you assumed were universal are actually just local conditions that can be changed through relocation or adaptation.

Consider how this applies to income potential. In some areas, certain salary levels represent exceptional achievement that few people ever reach. In other areas, those same salary levels represent entry-level compensation that anyone with basic skills can achieve. Geographical movement exposes these variations and expands your understanding of what's financially possible.

The same principle applies to business opportunities. Industries that are saturated in one location might be underserved in another location. Customer needs that are met by abundant competition in some markets might represent untapped opportunities in other markets. Services considered standard in urban areas might be revolutionary in rural areas.

This geographical arbitrage extends beyond just economic opportunities to lifestyle possibilities, relationship dynamics, and personal development opportunities. Different locations provide different resources, different communities, and different environmental factors that can dramatically affect quality of life and personal growth potential.

The Alley Cat recognizes these variations and uses geographical movement strategically rather than just recreationally. They don't just visit places, they evaluate places as potential platforms for building the lives they want to create. They assess locations based on opportunity density, resource availability, competitive landscapes, and alignment with their objectives.

This strategic approach to geographical expansion requires developing what I call "location intelligence" This is the ability to quickly assess the opportunities, challenges, and possibilities that different environments provide. This involves understanding economic conditions, regulatory environments, cultural factors, and competitive situations that affect success potential in various locations.

Location intelligence also includes recognizing which of your capabilities are location-dependent versus location-independent. Some skills and strategies work anywhere, while others are optimized for specific types of environments. Understanding these distinctions enables better decisions about where to apply different capabilities for maximum impact.

During my travels, I developed systematic approaches for rapidly assessing new locations. I would observe business districts to understand local commercial activity, study housing markets to understand economic conditions, engage with local people to understand cultural factors, and research regulatory environments to understand operational requirements.

This assessment process enabled me to identify locations that offered advantages for specific types of business development while avoiding locations where environmental factors would make success more difficult or less profitable.

The geographical expansion also provided psychological benefits that staying in familiar environments could never have generated. Experiencing success in multiple different contexts built confidence that transcended local limitations. Proving that I could navigate unfamiliar environments and create opportunities wherever I went eliminated fear of change and uncertainty about relocation.

This mobility confidence becomes a form of psychological freedom that opens up possibilities unavailable to those who feel constrained to specific locations. When you know you can succeed anywhere, you gain leverage in negotiations, flexibility in decision-making, and options for life design that location-dependent thinking cannot provide.

The networking benefits of geographical expansion also prove substantial. Building relationships across multiple locations creates distributed networks that provide opportunities, resources, and perspectives that local networks cannot match. These distributed relationships often become valuable when pursuing opportunities that require multi-location coordination or market expansion.

But geographical expansion provides maximum benefit only when combined with intellectual openness that enables learning from different environments rather than just passing through them. This requires suspending judgment about unfamiliar approaches long enough to understand their logic and potential applications.

Many people travel extensively while remaining mentally provincial. They observe differences without learning from them, experience variety without gaining insights, and visit new places while maintaining old thinking patterns. They protect themselves from being changed by their travels rather than allowing those travels to expand their possibilities.

The Alley Cat approaches geographical expansion as intentional education rather than just recreational activity. They maintain curiosity about why things work differently in different places, how local conditions shape opportunities, and what insights from one location might apply to opportunities in other locations.

This learning orientation transforms travel from entertainment into investment, investment in perspectives, relationships, and understanding that provides returns long after the trips have ended. The insights gained through geographical expansion compound over time, enabling better decisions about where to live, where to build businesses, and where to pursue opportunities.

The practical application involves approaching geographical movement with specific learning objectives rather than just entertainment goals. Instead of simply visiting places, study them. Instead of just passing through environments, analyze them. Instead of merely collecting experiences, extract insights that expand your understanding of possibility.

Ask questions that reveal how success works in different contexts: What opportunities exist here that don't exist elsewhere? What challenges do people face here that I haven't encountered before? What strategies work here that might not work in my familiar environments? What approaches used here might work better in my familiar environments?

This systematic approach to geographical expansion creates education that formal schooling rarely provides. You develop practical understanding of economic diversity, cultural variation, and opportunity distribution that textbooks cannot convey as effectively as direct experience.

Most importantly, you develop confidence in your ability to adapt and succeed regardless of environmental changes. This adaptability confidence eliminates fear-based decision-making while enabling strategic positioning that takes advantage of geographical opportunities rather than just local possibilities.

The world is too diverse to understand from a single location. The opportunities are too varied to access from a single environment. The perspectives are too valuable to acquire from a single culture.

Expand geographically. Expand mentally. Expand possibilities.

The movement of your body through space enables the movement of your mind through potential that staying in place could never reveal.

Travel strategically. Learn systematically. Expand continuously.

That's how geographical movement becomes mental expansion that creates opportunities unavailable to stationary thinking.

CHAPTER 44: THE SLOT MACHINE ANALOGY

Life operates like a massive slot machine where you will occasionally get lucky and win, but you'd better take heed and invest those winnings wisely because the machine is fundamentally designed to take in far more than it pays out.

This isn't pessimism or cynicism, it's mathematical reality. Whether we're talking about business opportunities, investment markets, career advancement, or any other domain where success is possible but not guaranteed, the odds are typically stacked against consistent winning. Most attempts fail. Most opportunities don't materialize. Most investments lose money. Most new ventures collapse.

Understanding this reality doesn't mean avoiding risk or abandoning ambition. It means recognizing that when you do win, when opportunities do materialize, when investments do pay off, when ventures do succeed. You must treat those wins strategically rather than as evidence that continued winning is guaranteed.

The Buffoon treats wins as proof of their superior abilities rather than as fortunate outcomes that should be leveraged carefully. When they experience business success, they assume they've mastered business and make increasingly risky bets. When investments pay off, they conclude they understand markets and increase their exposure. When opportunities materialize, they believe opportunity will always be available and spend winnings on consumption rather than positioning for future opportunities.

This approach virtually guarantees that temporary wins become permanent losses. The slot machine eventually takes back everything it paid out, plus more, because the Buffoon mistakes luck for skill and treats exceptional outcomes as normal expectations.

The Alley Cat understands that wins are statistical anomalies that should be converted into sustainable advantages as quickly as possible. When business succeeds, they use profits to build systems that increase future success probability rather than just enjoying higher lifestyle levels. When investments pay off, they diversify holdings and reduce risk rather than increasing exposure. When opportunities materialize, they use resources gained to create more opportunities rather than consuming winnings.

This approach transforms temporary luck into permanent positioning. The slot machine might eventually try to take back what it paid out, but strategic investment of winnings creates assets and capabilities that exist independent of continued gambling success.

The key insight is understanding the difference between outcomes you can control and outcomes that depend significantly on factors beyond your influence. You can

185

control effort, strategy, skill development, and resource allocation. You cannot control market conditions, timing, competitive responses, or the numerous other variables that affect whether specific efforts produce desired results.

This distinction explains why focusing on process rather than outcomes typically produces better long-term results than focusing on outcomes while neglecting process. Good processes occasionally produce poor outcomes due to factors beyond your control, but they increase the probability of positive outcomes over time. Poor processes occasionally produce good outcomes due to lucky circumstances, but they decrease the probability of sustained success.

The slot machine pays out just often enough to keep people playing, but not often enough to make playing profitable for most participants. Similarly, economic systems provide just enough success stories to maintain belief in opportunity while ensuring that most participants contribute more value than they extract.

Recognizing this dynamic enables strategic positioning that maximizes benefit from wins while minimizing damage from losses. Instead of assuming that success represents a new normal that will continue indefinitely, you treat success as fortunate outcome that should be converted into sustainable advantage before circumstances change.

Consider how this applies to business development. When a business becomes profitable, the slot machine has paid out. The smart response is using those profits to build systems, capabilities, and resources that increase future profitability rather than just increasing consumption or lifestyle. The profits should be invested in assets that continue generating value even if the original business faces challenges.

Many entrepreneurs experience initial success and immediately upgrade their lifestyles to match their new income levels, assuming that current profits represent minimum future earnings. When market conditions change, competition increases, or other factors reduce profitability, they're left with expensive lifestyles that require continued high earnings but fewer resources for adapting to changed circumstances.

The Alley Cat approach involves using business profits to build multiple income streams, develop transferable capabilities, and create financial reserves that provide security during challenging periods. Instead of consuming winnings, they invest winnings in assets that reduce dependence on continued winning.

The same principle applies to investment success. When investments perform well, the wise response is taking profits and diversifying holdings rather than increasing exposure to the same strategies that produced initial success. Markets that reward specific approaches for periods of time eventually change in ways that make those approaches less effective or counterproductive.

Investors who mistake temporary market success for permanent skill often increase their risk exposure precisely when their previous strategies are becoming less effective. They treat wins as evidence of their superior abilities rather than as fortunate timing that should be preserved through strategic position adjustment.

The slot machine analogy also applies to career development. When professional opportunities materialize (promotions, salary increases, industry recognition) the strategic response involves using those advances to build capabilities and relationships that provide security rather than just enjoying higher status and compensation.

Professionals who treat career success as guaranteed often fail to continue developing skills, building networks, or creating options that would serve them if circumstances change. They become dependent on continued organizational success rather than building personal capabilities that transcend specific positions or companies.

The mathematical reality underlying the slot machine analogy is "mean reversion". The tendency for extreme outcomes to be followed by more typical outcomes. Exceptional wins are usually followed by more ordinary results, just as exceptional losses are usually followed by recovery toward normal performance levels.

Understanding mean reversion enables better timing for strategic decisions. During winning periods, focus on consolidating gains and building sustainable advantages. During losing periods, focus on maintaining perspective and positioning for eventual recovery rather than making desperate attempts to immediately restore previous performance levels.

The practical application involves developing what I call "win discipline". This is the ability to treat successes strategically rather than emotionally. This means:

Profit Taking: Converting wins into assets rather than consuming them as lifestyle improvements that create ongoing expenses without generating corresponding income.

Risk Management: Reducing exposure after wins rather than increasing it based on confidence from recent success.

Capability Building: Using resources gained through wins to develop skills and systems that increase future success probability rather than just celebrating current achievement.

Option Creation: Directing winnings toward creating multiple pathways for future success rather than just reinforcing the single approach that produced current wins.

Reserve Building: Maintaining resources that provide security during inevitable future challenges rather than spending everything based on assumption that current success will continue indefinitely.

The discipline required for this approach challenges natural human tendencies toward overconfidence after success and lifestyle inflation after income increases. It requires maintaining long-term perspective during periods when short-term results suggest that caution is unnecessary.

But this discipline creates the sustainable success that consumption-focused approaches cannot match. It enables compound growth of resources and capabilities rather than cyclical patterns of winning and losing that leave people no better off despite occasional successes.

My own experience has repeatedly validated this approach. The periods when I treated wins strategically by investing them in capabilities and assets created foundations for sustained progress. The periods when I treated wins as evidence of guaranteed future success and increased consumption accordingly created vulnerabilities that later setbacks exposed.

The slot machine will occasionally pay out. When it does, remember that it's designed to take back more than it gives. Use your winnings to build something the machine can't reclaim.

Invest your luck. Don't just enjoy it.

The machine might eventually want its money back, but it can't reclaim capabilities, relationships, and assets you've built with strategic deployment of temporary wins.

Play the game, but play it strategically. When you win, win permanently by converting temporary advantages into lasting capabilities.

Also this is a quote of my own that I want to soak in with you.

"Those who cannot accept to break even have already accepted to lose it all."

That's how you beat a game that's designed to beat you.

CHAPTER 45: FROM SURVIVAL TO THRIVING

There's a fundamental difference between surviving and thriving that most people never recognize, much less deliberately transition between. Survival mode keeps you alive but limits your growth. Thriving mode enables exponential development that transforms not just your circumstances but your entire understanding of what's possible.

The transition from survival to thriving isn't automatic, it requires deliberate shift in mindset, strategy, and resource allocation that many people resist even when their circumstances improve enough to make thriving possible. They remain locked in survival thinking long after survival itself is no longer in question.

Understanding this distinction and learning to navigate the transition becomes crucial for anyone serious about creating extraordinary rather than merely adequate outcomes. It's the difference between getting by and getting ahead, between maintaining status quo and creating transformation, between reacting to circumstances and proactively designing circumstances.

Survival mode operates from scarcity, limited resources, immediate threats, and focus on preventing losses rather than creating gains. In survival mode, success means avoiding failure, security means eliminating risk, and progress means maintaining current position rather than advancing to better positions.

Thriving mode operates from abundance, expanding resources, emerging opportunities, and focus on creating gains rather than just preventing losses. In thriving mode, success means achieving objectives, security means building capabilities, and progress means continuous advancement toward increasingly ambitious goals.

The Buffoon remains stuck in survival mode even when circumstances no longer require it. They continue making decisions based on fear of loss rather than potential for gain, focusing on protection rather than on expansion, measuring success by what they avoid rather than by what they achieve.

The Alley Cat recognizes when circumstances have shifted enough to enable transition from survival to thriving mode and deliberately makes the mental, strategic, and resource allocation adjustments that this transition requires. They use periods of stability to build toward periods of growth rather than just maintaining survival-level existence indefinitely.

189

I experienced this transition multiple times throughout my journey, each time requiring conscious recognition that circumstances had changed enough to warrant different approaches. The most significant transition occurred during my time at the manufacturing plant, when I moved from immediate survival concerns to strategic capability building.

During the hotel period with my family, every decision was driven by immediate survival needs. Generating enough income to maintain basic shelter, food, and transportation. Success meant making it through each day without falling further behind. Planning extended no further than the next week because longer-term thinking seemed irrelevant when short-term survival remained uncertain.

But as my performance at the manufacturing plant created opportunities for advancement and income increases, circumstances gradually shifted from survival-level scarcity to stability that enabled longer-term thinking. Instead of focusing exclusively on immediate income, I could begin investing time and energy in capability development that would pay off over months rather than days.

This transition required consciously shifting from survival strategies to growth strategies:

Time Horizon Extension: Moving from day-to-day thinking to month-to-month and eventually year-to-year planning as stability increased and longer-term investments became viable.

Risk Tolerance Adjustment: Gradually accepting calculated risks that offered growth potential rather than just pursuing guaranteed but limited returns that survival mode demanded.

Resource Allocation Modification: Directing increasing portions of time, energy, and money toward investments that would create future capabilities rather than just meet immediate needs.

Learning Prioritization: Focusing on skills and knowledge that would enable advancement rather than just competencies required for current position maintenance.

Relationship Evolution: Building connections that could provide future opportunities rather than just maintaining relationships that served immediate support needs.

Goal Recalibration: Expanding objectives beyond survival to include growth, development, and increasingly ambitious achievement targets.

The challenge lies in recognizing when circumstances have improved enough to warrant this transition. Many people continue operating in survival mode long after it's necessary because survival thinking becomes habitual rather than situational. They mistake familiar patterns for required approaches and resist change even when change would serve their interests.

Others attempt the transition prematurely, before they've established sufficient stability to support growth-oriented strategies. They abandon survival approaches while still facing survival-level challenges, creating vulnerability that forces them back into reactive mode under worse circumstances.

The key is accurate assessment of your actual circumstances versus your emotional relationship with those circumstances. Emotions often lag behind reality. You might continue feeling survival pressure even after achieving stability, or you might feel overconfident about stability that hasn't been thoroughly established.

This assessment requires examining objective indicators rather than just emotional states:

Financial Stability: Do you have reserves that could handle typical emergencies, or are you still living paycheck to paycheck? Can you absorb temporary income reductions, or would any disruption create immediate crisis?

Capability Foundation: Have you developed skills and knowledge that provide security independent of specific positions, or are you dependent on circumstances remaining unchanged?

Relationship Network: Have you built connections that could provide opportunities and support during challenges, or are you isolated in ways that increase vulnerability?

Health and Energy: Do you have physical and mental resources that enable sustained effort toward ambitious goals, or are you depleted by ongoing survival demands?

Environmental Stability: Are the external factors affecting your life relatively predictable and manageable, or are you still subject to constant disruption and uncertainty?

When these indicators suggest genuine stability rather than just temporary improvement, the transition from survival to thriving becomes not just possible but necessary for continued progress. Remaining in survival mode when circumstances support thriving mode limits your potential and wastes opportunities that stability creates.

The practical implementation involves systematic changes across multiple domains:

Strategic Thinking: Shifting from reactive problem-solving to proactive opportunity creation. Instead of just responding to immediate challenges, you begin identifying and pursuing possibilities for improvement and advancement.

Investment Behavior: Allocating resources toward future capability rather than just current maintenance. This includes financial investments, time investments in learning, and energy investments in relationship building.

Risk Management: Transitioning from risk avoidance to risk optimization. Instead of avoiding all uncertainty, you begin taking calculated risks that offer substantial upside potential while maintaining adequate downside protection.

Goal Setting: Expanding objectives beyond survival to include growth, contribution, and achievement. Instead of just trying to maintain current position, you begin pursuing advancement toward better positions.

Time Allocation: Directing increasing portions of time toward activities that create future value rather than just meeting immediate requirements. This includes learning, planning, relationship building, and strategic positioning.

Mental Models: Updating fundamental assumptions about what's possible, necessary, and achievable. Survival mode creates mental models based on scarcity and limitation. Thriving mode requires mental models based on abundance and possibility.

The transition isn't always smooth or permanent. External circumstances can change in ways that require temporary return to survival mode, even after you've successfully operated in thriving mode for extended periods. The key is maintaining flexibility that enables appropriate responses to changing conditions while building capabilities that make survival periods shorter and less damaging when they do occur.

My own experience included multiple cycles between survival and thriving modes as circumstances evolved. Each transition taught me more about recognizing when shifts were appropriate and how to implement them effectively. The capabilities developed during thriving periods consistently enabled better performance during subsequent survival periods, creating overall upward trajectory despite temporary setbacks.

The most important insight is understanding that thriving is a choice you make rather than something that happens to you. Circumstances create the possibility for thriving, but actualizing that possibility requires deliberate decisions about how to think, how to allocate resources, and how to engage with available opportunities.

Many people wait for external circumstances to force them into thriving mode, not realizing that thriving requires internal decisions that external circumstances alone cannot create. They expect better results without making the mental and strategic adjustments that better results require.

192

Make the transition deliberately when circumstances support it. Recognize survival mode as necessary but temporary rather than as permanent limitation. Use stability as foundation for growth rather than just as improved survival.

The distance between surviving and thriving is shorter than most people imagine, but crossing it requires conscious decision to change approaches rather than just hoping for improved outcomes from unchanged strategies.

Choose thriving when circumstances allow it. Build capabilities that make thriving more sustainable and survival periods less damaging.

That's how you progress from just getting by to actually getting ahead, from maintaining position to advancing position, from reacting to circumstances to creating circumstances.

The transition is available when you're ready to make it.

CHAPTER 46: CREATING GENERATIONAL PROSPERITY

Breaking generational cycles of limitation isn't just about improving your own circumstances, it's about establishing foundations that enable future generations to start from advantages rather than disadvantages, to build upon progress rather than recovering from setbacks, to pursue opportunities rather than just surviving challenges.

This mission requires thinking beyond individual achievement to systemic transformation that affects not just your lifetime but the lifetimes of those who come after you. It demands building assets, capabilities, and knowledge that transcend your personal existence while creating platforms that others can use to reach heights that would be impossible starting from ground zero.

The Buffoon focuses exclusively on their own immediate circumstances and temporary satisfaction. They consume resources rather than building assets, pursue lifestyle improvements rather than capability development, and measure success by what they acquire for themselves rather than by what they create for others.

This approach ensures that each generation starts over from similar disadvantaged positions, facing the same obstacles and limitations that previous generations faced. Progress remains individual and temporary rather than collective and cumulative. Each person must build everything from scratch rather than building upon foundations that others have established.

The Alley Cat understands that true success involves creating systems and resources that enable others to achieve more than would be possible through individual effort alone. They build businesses that can operate without them, accumulate assets that generate ongoing value, develop knowledge that can be transferred, and establish relationships that provide opportunities for multiple generations.

My commitment to breaking generational curses stems from observing how limitation patterns repeat across families when no one takes responsibility for creating transformation that extends beyond their own lifetime. I watched previous generations in my family struggle with similar challenges, make similar mistakes, and achieve similar limited outcomes because no one had established different patterns or built foundations for different possibilities.

The generational curse I was determined to break included patterns of:

Financial Instability: Generations of working hard but never building wealth, surviving paycheck to paycheck, lacking resources for emergencies or opportunities, and remaining vulnerable to economic changes beyond their control.

Limited Opportunities: Restricted access to quality education, professional development, business ownership, and investment opportunities that would enable advancement beyond basic survival.

Reactive Thinking: Responding to circumstances rather than creating them, accepting limitations rather than challenging them, and maintaining scarcity mindsets that prevent recognition of abundance possibilities.

Knowledge Gaps: Lacking practical education about wealth building, business development, strategic thinking, and opportunity creation that would enable different outcomes.

Network Limitations: Operating within circles that provided emotional support but limited professional or business opportunities, without access to mentors, partners, or collaborators who could accelerate progress.

Mindset Constraints: Accepting that struggle was normal, that extraordinary success was for "other people," and that working hard within existing systems represented the only viable path forward.

Breaking these patterns required more than individual success, it required building systems that would enable others to achieve success more easily and sustainably than I had been able to achieve it starting from disadvantaged circumstances.

The foundation-building process involves several key components:

Asset Accumulation: Building wealth in forms that generate ongoing income and appreciate over time rather than just increasing personal consumption. This includes real estate, business equity, investment portfolios, and intellectual property that continue creating value beyond my direct involvement.

Knowledge Documentation: Recording insights, strategies, and lessons learned so others can benefit from experience without having to repeat all the same learning curves and mistakes. This includes both formal education and practical wisdom about navigating challenges and creating opportunities.

System Development: Creating businesses, processes, and structures that can operate independently while providing opportunities and resources for others. This enables multiple people to benefit from systematic value creation rather than just individual achievement.

Relationship Networks: Building connections that provide opportunities not just for me but for family members and others who can leverage these relationships for their own advancement. Quality networks multiply opportunities rather than limiting them to single individuals.

Educational Investment: Ensuring that future generations have access to quality education, skill development, and learning opportunities that enable them to pursue objectives based on interests and abilities rather than just economic necessity.

Mindset Transformation: Modeling approaches to challenges and opportunities that demonstrate possibility thinking rather than limitation thinking, strategic planning rather than reactive responses, and abundance mindsets rather than scarcity perspectives.

The practical implementation requires balancing immediate needs with long-term foundation building. You cannot sacrifice current survival for future generations, but you also cannot consume everything for current comfort while leaving nothing for those who follow.

This balance involves strategic allocation of resources toward:

Immediate Stability: Ensuring current basic needs are met and immediate family members have security and opportunity for their own development and advancement.

Medium-term Growth: Building capabilities, assets, and systems that provide increasing returns over time while remaining accessible and beneficial during your lifetime.

Long-term Legacy: Creating resources and structures that will continue generating value and opportunity long after your direct involvement ends, enabling others to build upon rather than restart the wealth and capability building process.

The generational wealth building process also requires education and involvement of those who will eventually inherit or benefit from these foundations. Simply accumulating assets isn't sufficient if those assets are consumed rather than maintained and expanded by subsequent generations.

This education involves teaching principles rather than just providing resources:

Financial Literacy: Understanding how wealth is created, preserved, and expanded rather than just consumed. This includes investment principles, business fundamentals, and strategic thinking about money and opportunity.

Work Ethic: Maintaining commitment to value creation and contribution rather than just consumption and extraction. Generational wealth requires generational contribution rather than generational entitlement.

Strategic Thinking: Developing capability to identify opportunities, solve problems, and create value rather than just managing existing resources. Each generation should add value rather than just preserving what previous generations created.

Character Development: Building integrity, reliability, and judgment that enable others to trust them with responsibility and opportunity. Reputation and relationships often prove more valuable than financial assets alone.

Adaptability: Learning to navigate changing circumstances rather than just operating within established patterns. Economic, technological, and social changes require ongoing adaptation that rigid thinking cannot handle.

The most important insight is understanding that generational prosperity isn't just about money, it's about creating expanding possibilities that enable each generation to achieve more than previous generations while building foundations for even greater achievements by subsequent generations.

This expanding possibility requires that each generation focus not just on their own advancement but on creating platforms, systems, and resources that the next generation can use to reach higher levels. It's about building stairs rather than just climbing them.

My businesses are designed to operate without my constant involvement while providing opportunities for others. My investments are structured to generate ongoing returns while building capital for reinvestment and expansion. My knowledge and experience are being documented and shared so others can benefit from lessons learned without repeating all the same learning processes.

Most importantly, I'm modeling approaches to challenges and opportunities that demonstrate what's possible when someone refuses to accept limitation as permanent condition. I'm proving that background doesn't determine destiny, that circumstances don't dictate outcomes, and that extraordinary results are possible through strategic thinking and persistent effort regardless of starting position.

The generational transformation I'm creating won't be complete in my lifetime. It's designed to unfold across multiple generations as capabilities, assets, and opportunities compound over time. But the foundation is being established now through decisions and investments that prioritize long-term impact over short-term gratification.

Breaking generational curses requires someone to accept responsibility for transformation that extends beyond their own lifetime. It requires building something larger than yourself for people beyond yourself. It requires patience for results that you might not fully see but that others will definitely experience.

That responsibility is both burden and privilege. The burden comes from maintaining long-term perspective during periods when short-term consumption would be more immediately satisfying. The privilege comes from knowing that your efforts will enable others to achieve possibilities that your efforts make available.

Choose to build foundations rather than just enjoying current success. Create systems that serve others rather than just accumulating resources for yourself. Think generationally rather than just individually.

The wealth you build, the systems you create, and the knowledge you share can transform multiple lifetimes rather than just your own.

That's how you break generational limitations while building generational possibilities.

That's how you ensure that your success becomes a beginning rather than an ending.

CHAPTER 47: TRANSFORMING SYSTEMS RATHER THAN

PARTICIPATING

The highest level of success isn't excelling within existing systems, it's creating new systems that make the old systems obsolete. It's not about becoming the best player in someone else's game; it's about designing better games that serve more people more effectively.

Most people spend their entire lives trying to succeed within systems that were designed by others, for others, to benefit others. They accept the rules, structures, and limitations of existing frameworks without questioning whether those frameworks actually serve their interests or whether better alternatives might be possible.

This approach limits their potential to whatever the existing systems allow, which is typically far less than what they could achieve if they focused on creating new systems rather than just participating in established ones.

The Buffoon seeks to climb hierarchies within existing systems. They want better positions, higher ranks, and increased status within frameworks that others control. They measure success by how high they rise within established structures rather than by their ability to create structures that better serve their objectives.

The Alley Cat recognizes that the most powerful position isn't at the top of someone else's system, it's at the center of a system you create yourself. They focus on building platforms, frameworks, and networks that enable them to serve others while serving their own objectives, creating value for many people rather than just extracting value from existing arrangements.

This distinction explains why some entrepreneurs create businesses that make existing businesses obsolete while others create businesses that simply compete within existing industries. The former group transforms how entire sectors operate while the latter group fights for market share within static frameworks.

My experience at the manufacturing plant illustrates this principle perfectly. I could have focused on advancing within the existing organizational structure, working toward management positions, seeking recognition within established systems, and accepting the limitations of how that company operated.

Instead, I transformed how operations functioned by creating new systems for inventory management, production scheduling, and quality control that made the previous approaches obsolete. I didn't just succeed within the existing framework, I replaced that framework with something more effective.

The transformation generated benefits for everyone involved: workers had more consistent employment because production flowed smoothly, management achieved better results with less stress, customers received higher quality products delivered on schedule, and I gained experience building systems rather than just working within them.

This system-building approach proved more valuable than position advancement within existing structures. Even when the company eventually closed due to corporate mismanagement, the capabilities I had developed through system creation transferred to other contexts in ways that position-based advancement never could have matched.

The same principle applies across domains. In technology, the most successful companies don't just build better products within existing categories, they create new categories that make previous products seem primitive. In business, the most successful entrepreneurs don't just compete more effectively within existing markets, they create new markets that didn't exist before.

In personal development, the most successful people don't just get better at playing existing games, they create new games where their unique combinations of strengths provide natural advantages that traditional approaches cannot match.

This system-transformation approach requires several key shifts in thinking:

Problem Identification: Instead of accepting limitations as permanent features of existing systems, you begin identifying which aspects of those systems create unnecessary restrictions, inefficiencies, or poor outcomes.

Solution Design: Rather than working around systemic problems, you focus on designing alternative approaches that eliminate those problems entirely through better fundamental structures.

Value Creation: Instead of competing for limited opportunities within existing frameworks, you create new opportunities that expand possibilities for everyone involved rather than just redistributing existing resources.

Platform Building: Rather than seeking positions within other people's organizations, you focus on building platforms that enable multiple people to succeed while achieving your own objectives through their success.

Network Effects: Instead of individual advancement, you create systems that become more valuable as more people participate, generating compound benefits that individual achievement cannot match.

The transition from participation to transformation requires overcoming natural tendencies toward seeking security within established systems rather than accepting uncertainty that comes with creating new ones. Most people prefer competing for known opportunities rather than creating unknown possibilities.

But this preference for security within existing systems often provides less actual security than creating new systems that you control. Positions within other people's systems can be eliminated through decisions beyond your influence. Systems you create provide security that depends on your capability rather than on others' choices.

The system-building process typically involves several phases:

Observation: Studying how existing systems operate, identifying their strengths and weaknesses, understanding which aspects serve users well and which create unnecessary limitations or inefficiencies.

Innovation: Developing alternative approaches that preserve beneficial aspects of existing systems while eliminating problematic elements through fundamentally different structural designs.

Testing: Implementing new approaches on small scales to prove effectiveness before investing resources in large-scale system development.

Scaling: Expanding successful system designs to serve larger numbers of people while maintaining effectiveness and improving based on user feedback and operational experience.

Optimization: Continuously improving system performance based on results, user needs, and changing circumstances rather than assuming initial designs represent final solutions.

Replication: Sharing successful system designs so others can implement similar approaches in different contexts, amplifying positive impact beyond what single implementations could achieve.

The most important recognition is that system transformation provides exponentially greater impact than individual excellence within existing systems. When you excel within someone else's framework, you might improve your own circumstances substantially. When you create better frameworks, you can improve circumstances for many people while building assets and capabilities that provide long-term value.

This exponential impact potential justifies the additional effort and risk that system building requires compared to system participation. The learning curve is steeper, the uncertainty is greater, and the initial results might be less impressive than achieving success within established frameworks.

But the long-term benefits include freedom from dependence on others' decisions, capability to create opportunities rather than just seeking them, and potential to generate value at scales that participation alone cannot achieve.

The system transformation approach also provides more sustainable competitive advantages than individual excellence within existing systems. When you're exceptionally good at playing someone else's game, others can eventually match your performance level. When you create new games, you maintain natural advantages through superior understanding of how those games work.

This sustainable advantage becomes particularly important as markets, technologies, and social structures continue evolving rapidly. Excellence within static systems becomes obsolete when those systems change. Capability to create new systems remains valuable regardless of how external circumstances evolve.

My current business development focuses on creating platforms that serve multiple participants rather than just competing within existing industries. Instead of trying to become the best provider of traditional services, I'm building systems that enable others to provide better services while generating value through platform ownership rather than just service delivery.

This approach takes longer to develop than competing within existing frameworks, but it creates more durable advantages and broader impact than individual service excellence could provide. The platforms become valuable independent of my direct involvement while enabling others to achieve results they couldn't accomplish without systematic support.

The ultimate goal isn't just personal success, it's creating systems that make success more accessible and sustainable for others while achieving success yourself through the value creation process. This alignment between personal objectives and broader impact ensures that your success contributes to rather than detracts from others' success.

Think systematically rather than just individually. Build platforms rather than just seeking positions. Create frameworks rather than just excelling within existing structures.

The most powerful success comes not from being the best at what already exists but from creating what doesn't yet exist in ways that serve needs existing systems cannot adequately address.

Transform systems rather than just participating in them. The impact will exceed anything participation alone could provide, and the satisfaction will come from creation rather than just consumption.

That's how you move from being successful within limitations to creating possibilities that transcend those limitations entirely.

CHAPTER 48: THE BUFFOON'S REVELATION

In this world, the Buffoon will never put the suit down. They will always be a Buffoon, committed to their ways even on their deathbed. This isn't pessimism, it's practical recognition that fundamental mindset patterns become so deeply ingrained they resist change even when change would obviously serve their interests.

You must learn to recognize the signs of Buffoon mentality early and remove yourself from these individuals because not even death will change their approaches to life, relationships, and opportunity. They will remain trapped in limitation thinking, extraction mentality, and superficial approaches regardless of evidence that these patterns consistently produce disappointing results.

This chapter isn't about judgment or condemnation, it's about protection and strategic positioning. Understanding that some people will never embrace the growth, authenticity, and value creation that characterize the Alley Cat mentality enables you to allocate your time, energy, and resources toward relationships and collaborations that actually serve your development rather than drain it.

The Buffoon's revelation is that they prefer familiar limitation to unfamiliar possibility. They choose known patterns of mediocrity over unknown potential for extraordinary achievement. They select comfortable conformity over challenging authenticity. They maintain these preferences even when those preferences consistently prevent them from achieving what they claim to want.

This preference for familiar limitation manifests in several predictable patterns:

Resistance to Growth: When presented with opportunities for development, learning, or advancement, the Buffoon finds reasons why these opportunities won't work for them, are too risky, or require changes they're unwilling to make. They prefer complaining about their circumstances to changing their approaches.

Blame Externalization: Rather than examining how their choices contribute to their outcomes, the Buffoon consistently attributes disappointing results to external factors beyond their control. They become victims of circumstances that their own patterns help create and maintain.

Surface-Level Solutions: When problems persist despite superficial attempts to address them, the Buffoon seeks new surface-level solutions rather than examining whether fundamental approaches might need revision. They change tactics without changing strategy, methods without changing mindset.

Validation Seeking: Instead of building confidence through achievement and capability development, the Buffoon pursues external validation that makes them feel better temporarily without creating lasting improvement in their circumstances or capabilities.

Pattern Repetition: Despite repeatedly experiencing similar disappointing outcomes from similar approaches, the Buffoon continues the same patterns while expecting different results. They mistake hope for strategy and intention for action.

Change Avoidance: Even when current approaches clearly aren't serving their stated objectives, the Buffoon resists modifications that would require stepping outside familiar comfort zones or challenging established beliefs about what's possible or necessary.

The persistence of these patterns isn't accidental, it serves psychological functions that the Buffoon finds more valuable than the achievement they claim to desire. Maintaining limitation patterns provides:

Predictability: Known limitations feel safer than unknown possibilities because they eliminate uncertainty about outcomes, even when those outcomes are consistently disappointing.

Excuse Availability: Established limitation patterns provide ready explanations for disappointing results that don't require acknowledging personal responsibility for change.

Effort Minimization: Familiar approaches require less energy than learning new methods, even when familiar approaches consistently produce inferior results.

Identity Protection: Changing fundamental patterns would require admitting that current identity and approaches have been suboptimal, which challenges self-concept in ways many people find intolerable.

Social Conformity: Limitation patterns often align with social norms that make the Buffoon feel accepted within groups that share similar approaches, even when those groups consistently fail to achieve their stated objectives.

Understanding these psychological benefits of limitation patterns explains why evidence, opportunity, and even obvious self-interest often fail to motivate Buffoon transformation. They're not choosing limitation because they don't see alternatives.

They're choosing limitation because alternatives feel more threatening than continued mediocrity.

This insight should inform how you approach relationships with people who demonstrate persistent Buffoon patterns. Traditional approaches to helping such individuals are providing information, offering opportunities, sharing insights, or modeling better approaches. Buffoons rarely produce lasting change because they address symptoms rather than underlying preference for familiar limitation.

The Alley Cat recognizes these patterns quickly and adjusts their relationship approach accordingly:

Limited Investment: Rather than exhausting energy trying to convince Buffoons to embrace growth approaches, the Alley Cat limits their investment in these relationships to levels that match demonstrated commitment to change.

Boundary Maintenance: Instead of allowing Buffoon energy drain to affect their own progress, the Alley Cat maintains clear boundaries that protect their time, energy, and resources from extraction without reciprocal value creation.

Expectation Adjustment: Rather than expecting Buffoons to change fundamental patterns, the Alley Cat adjusts expectations to match demonstrated capabilities and commitment levels, reducing disappointment and frustration.

Opportunity Protection: Instead of sharing valuable opportunities with those unlikely to maximize them, the Alley Cat directs opportunities toward people who demonstrate capability and commitment to value creation.

Distance Creation: Rather than maintaining close relationships with people whose patterns consistently undermine growth and achievement, the Alley Cat creates appropriate distance while maintaining basic courtesy and respect.

This approach isn't about abandoning people who struggle or giving up on those facing challenges. It's about recognizing the difference between people who are struggling while working to improve their circumstances versus people who prefer struggling to changing their approaches.

The former group deserves support, encouragement, and opportunity because they're committed to growth despite temporary setbacks. The latter group drains resources from those who could benefit more substantially from support while contributing less to collective success.

You cannot save people from themselves, and attempting to do so often prevents you from maximizing your own potential while failing to create lasting change in those you're trying to help. The most loving approach sometimes involves allowing people to experience the full consequences of their choices rather than enabling continued patterns that prevent growth.

The Buffoon's revelation ultimately serves as warning and motivation for your own development. Observing how limitation patterns persist despite obvious alternatives provides insight into the importance of constantly challenging your own approaches, examining your own patterns, and maintaining commitment to growth even when growth requires discomfort.

The same psychological forces that trap Buffoons in limitation patterns can affect anyone who stops questioning their approaches, becomes comfortable with current results, or prioritizes familiarity over effectiveness. The difference lies in maintaining awareness of these tendencies and consciously choosing growth despite natural preferences for comfort.

The Alley Cat mentality isn't a permanent achievement, it's an ongoing choice to prioritize effectiveness over comfort, growth over stagnation, authenticity over performance, and value creation over value extraction. This choice must be renewed continuously because the natural tendency toward comfort and familiarity affects everyone.

But understanding the Buffoon's revelation provides clarity about the stakes involved in these choices. You can see where limitation thinking leads over time, how it compounds into increasingly restricted possibilities, and why temporary discomfort of growth proves preferable to permanent limitations of stagnation.

Use this understanding to fuel your commitment to continued development. When growth requires challenging yourself, remember the alternative of becoming trapped in patterns that prevent progress. When change feels uncomfortable, remember that avoiding change often leads to circumstances far more uncomfortable than temporary growth discomfort.

Most importantly, use this understanding to select relationships and collaborations that support rather than undermine your development. Surround yourself with people who share commitment to growth, value creation, and authentic achievement rather than those who prefer familiar limitation to unfamiliar possibility.

The Buffoon will remain a Buffoon. That's their choice and their revelation.

Your choice is whether you'll allow their patterns to influence your own or whether you'll use their example as motivation to maintain your commitment to growth, authenticity, and value creation.

Choose wisely. The difference between these approaches compounds over time into entirely different life trajectories.

The Buffoon's suit will never come off. Make sure you never put it on.

GLOSSARY

A

Action Currency - The principle that momentum can only be created through movement, not through preparation, planning, or thinking about action.

Adaptation Capability - The ability to recognize emerging trends, assess their implications, master new tools, and integrate innovations effectively.

Alley Cat - An individual who thinks unconventionally, operates with authenticity, creates value through resourcefulness, and refuses to be limited by conventional expectations or systems.

Alley Cat Circle - A deliberately small, carefully curated inner circle of trusted allies who demonstrate loyalty, capability, and alignment with shared objectives.

Alley Cat Energy - The unmistakable authenticity and strategic purpose that radiates from someone regardless of their environment, clothing, or external circumstances.

Alley Cat Mentality - A mindset characterized by resourcefulness, strategic thinking, authenticity, value creation, and refusal to accept conventional limitations.

Anticipatory Thinking - The ability to project current patterns forward and identify where they're likely to lead, enabling proactive positioning.

B

Boundary Weakness - The inability to maintain personal standards, allowing others to violate boundaries, manipulate decisions, or control actions.

Buffoon in the Suit - An individual who prioritizes appearance over substance, seeks validation over achievement, and conforms to conventional expectations while achieving mediocre results.

Buffoon Mentality - A mindset characterized by seeking external validation, prioritizing appearance over substance, following conventional paths, and accepting limitations as permanent.

Buffoon's Revelation - The understanding that some people prefer familiar limitation to unfamiliar possibility and will resist growth even when it serves their interests.

C

Charity Case - Someone who consistently receives value from relationships without providing equivalent contribution, creating dependency rather than mutual benefit.

Comfort as Terminal Illness - The principle that excessive comfort prevents growth and becomes a form of slow death to potential and achievement.

Conductor Approach - A leadership style that arranges people strategically based on their natural capabilities rather than trying to change their fundamental characteristics.

Credit Nuclear Power Supply - Excellent credit that provides access to substantial capital at favorable terms, functioning like a power source for wealth creation and business development.

D

Diamond Cutter Pressure - The extreme circumstances that forge Alley Cats through enormous pressure, creating strength and capabilities that comfortable conditions cannot develop.

Discipline as Currency - The principle that self-discipline represents the most valuable asset that can be exchanged for opportunities money alone cannot buy.

Disassociation and Disbanding - Strategic separation from individuals or groups whose behavior threatens your objectives or compromises your mission.

E

External Validation Dependency - The psychological need for others' approval to feel worthy, creating weakness that undermines authentic achievement and decision-making.

F

Failure Immunity - The ability to experience setbacks without allowing them to create lasting psychological damage that prevents future risk-taking and opportunity pursuit.

False Confidence - Artificial self-assurance that depends on external validation and performance rather than genuine capability and achievement.

Forever Student Mentality - The commitment to learning from every experience and every person, regardless of their apparent status or circumstances.

Focused Energy - The laser-focused approach of Alley Cats who make every move with specific purpose and don't waste energy on random activity or unnecessary conflict.

G

Generational Curse Breaking - The deliberate effort to transform limitation patterns that have persisted across multiple generations, creating new possibilities for future generations.

Geographical Arbitrage - Leveraging opportunities that exist in one location but not another, or applying successful strategies from one environment to different environments.

H

Hamster Wheel Theory - The concept that most people work frantically while remaining in the same position, generating energy for others' benefit while making minimal progress themselves.

Hollow Success - Outcomes that appear impressive externally but provide minimal genuine satisfaction or security, requiring ongoing performance to maintain.

I

Implementation Advantage - The exponential benefits that accrue to those who consistently translate knowledge into action without delay.

Implementation Without Hesitation - The ability to act immediately on valuable insights rather than waiting for perfect conditions or complete information.

Inner Circle - The small group of trusted individuals who have access to your plans, resources, and vulnerabilities, requiring the highest standards of loyalty and capability.

L

Learning Posture - A mental orientation that actively seeks valuable information from every experience rather than passively hoping good information will appear when needed.

Location Intelligence - The ability to quickly assess opportunities, challenges, and possibilities that different environments provide for achieving specific objectives.

M

Mental Vulnerability - Compromised thinking patterns that make individuals unreliable for protection themselves or contributing to shared objectives.

Merchant Mindset - A strategic approach focused on value creation and opportunity development rather than dependency and consumption.

Momentum Thinking - Viewing setbacks as temporary pauses rather than permanent stops, maintaining forward orientation despite backward movement.

N

Never Quit Principle - The commitment to change plans as needed while never changing core goals, persisting until objectives are achieved regardless of obstacles.

Nine Lives Capability - The regenerative ability to recover from setbacks stronger than before, using failures as education rather than evidence of limitation.

Nuclear Power Supply Credit - See Credit Nuclear Power Supply.

P

Proactive Positioning - Taking action before circumstances require it, positioning advantageously before advantageous positioning becomes necessary for survival.

Process Over Outcomes - Focusing on controllable actions and strategies rather than on results that depend significantly on factors beyond your influence.

R

Reactive Limitation - Operating in constant response mode, always playing catch-up rather than getting ahead of circumstances.

Respect as Axis - The principle that respect forms the center around which all meaningful relationships and collaborations revolve.

Resource Maximization - Making optimal use of whatever resources exist rather than waiting for better resource availability.

S

Setback to Setup Transformation - The process of converting apparent failures into foundations for opportunities that exceed what would have been possible without the setback.

Slot Machine Analogy - The understanding that life occasionally provides wins, but systems are designed to take more than they give, requiring strategic investment of winnings.

Sobriety as Superpower - The competitive advantage gained through maintaining consistent mental clarity without chemical interference.

Strategic Detachment - Avoiding emotional attachment to particular strategies or relationships that prevents adaptation when circumstances change.

Strategic Persistence - Maintaining unwavering commitment to objectives while remaining completely flexible about methods for achieving them.

Substance Over Appearance - Prioritizing genuine capability and actual value over impressive presentations and status symbols.

Survival to Thriving Transition - The deliberate shift from scarcity-based thinking focused on preventing losses to abundance-based thinking focused on creating gains.

T

Teammates Manning the Tower - Genuine collaborators who solve problems proactively rather than leaving them for others to handle.

True Confidence - Genuine self-assurance based on actual capabilities and achievements rather than on external validation or performance.

V

Value Creation Focus - Prioritizing contribution and benefit to others rather than extraction and personal advantage.

Victim Mentality - The mindset that attributes outcomes primarily to external circumstances rather than to personal choices and responses.

W

Weak People Seek People - The principle that those lacking internal strength prioritize external validation over authentic achievement.

Win Discipline - The ability to treat successes strategically rather than emotionally, converting wins into sustainable advantages.

Key Principles and Frameworks

The 200 Dollar Principle - Small resources deployed strategically can generate more value than large resources used carelessly.

The Conductor's Rule - You can tune instruments and improve their performance, but you cannot change their fundamental nature.

The Fish Needs Water Principle - Everyone's choices are shaped by environmental conditions necessary for their survival and success.

The Grass Cut Low Rule - Maintaining small, visible circles allows you to see threats and opportunities more clearly.

The Hamster Wheel Equation - Working harder within limiting systems often generates energy for others' benefit while producing minimal personal progress.

The Implementation Gap - The difference between knowing what to do and actually doing it consistently.

The Nuclear Power Supply Concept - Excellent credit provides massive capability that can be deployed strategically when opportunities arise.

The Slot Machine Reality - Life provides occasional wins, but systems are designed to extract more value than they provide.

The Substance Equation - Function first, form follows naturally from genuine capability and value creation.

The Teammate Test - True collaborators solve problems before bringing them to your attention rather than just identifying issues for you to handle.

This glossary provides definitions for key terms, concepts, and principles referenced throughout "The Alley Cat and the Buffoon in the Suit." These concepts form the foundation of the Alley Cat philosophy and approach to creating unconventional success through authentic value creation and strategic thinking.

www.ingramcontent.com/pod-product-compliance
Lightning Source LLC
Chambersburg PA
CBHW080132270326
41926CB00021B/4454